PREACHER'S KIDS

By Grace Nies Fletcher

IN MY FATHER'S HOUSE
PREACHER'S KIDS

Preacher's Kids

BY

GRACE NIES FLETCHER

E. P. Dutton & Company, Inc.

New York 1959

Copyright, ©, 1958, *by* GRACE NIES FLETCHER
All rights reserved. Printed in the U.S.A.

First Printing September 1958
Second Printing October 1958
Third Printing November 1958
Fourth Printing March 1959

¶ *No part of this book may be reproduced
in any form without permission in writing
from the publisher, except by a reviewer
who wishes to quote brief passages in connection with a review written for inclusion
in a magazine, newspaper or broadcast.*

LIBRARY OF CONGRESS CATALOG CARD NUMBER: 58-9596

To

RICK

With Love

TABLE OF CONTENTS

PREACHER'S KIDS

Chapter One

THE WATERS OF SHILOAH
THAT GO SOFTLY

I WAS six but my brother Ike was only three when the Nies family moved into the square white colonial parsonage in Dorchester in the early 1900's. All we owned of value was a battered upright piano, Dad's books, a fifthhand typewriter with the letter *a* missing, and our clothes. But it never occurred to us we were poor. Our wealth was in the coin of the spirit, in music, laughter, and the reality of the unseen, treasure which can neither be stolen nor taxed away. Heaven was as much a place to me as Chicago, which I'd never seen either, so it didn't surprise me at all that bright June morning when I discovered angels on Boston Common.

Because she couldn't afford a baby-sitter, Mother took us children to town with her, promised that if we didn't fuss while she shopped, we could feed the pigeons on the Common. We loved the pigeons almost as much as the peanuts which came hot in a striped paper bag, and every now and then you could snitch one for yourself. On tiptoe with excitement, we walked up that chameleon street where one block called Summer leads into the next block named frigidly Winter which in turn disappears entirely into grass and tall elms, a garden in the heart of a great city. Just above from its little hill, the glittering gilt dome of the statehouse gleams down through the trees. We bought peanuts for a nickel from the man with his little whistling cart and the pigeons descended in a blue-gray cloud; but just as I dug happily into my paper bag, I happened to look up. . . .

"Look!" I gasped. "The golden street where the angels walk . . . shining up there through those leaves!"

"It's only the statehouse dome," my mother might have smiled, but instead she put her arm around me. Who was she to snatch glory from a child? "Heaven is inside you too, Susie," she said. "Never forget that." She was right; when I closed my eyes, I distinctly heard the shy whisper of angel wings.

On the way home Mother had quite a fright; she couldn't find her streetcar fare! Ike was on her lap and I was leaning against her knee, while the conductor stood there waiting as, red-faced and embarrassed, she searched her handbag, her coat pockets but couldn't dig up a frantic penny. Could she possibly have spent her fare for the peanuts? Then she gave a great sigh of relief, remembering she'd tucked the nickel for safekeeping into the thumb of her glove.

We were always short of cash by the end of the month, not only because a preacher's salary was so small but because Dad gave so much of his away. Fortunately Mother knew more ways to cook "chewed-up meat" than any chef. (In those days hamburger cost twenty cents a pound, was not "chopped sirloin steak" for millionaires.) She served it broiled with parsley, pan-fried with onions, wrapped in bacon, seasoned with fruit juices left over in the bottoms of tin cans; and, when it neared the last desperate days before Dad got paid, a few brown specks floating in a sea of white sauce were moored to large pieces of toast. Lacking meat, we ate cereal sprinkled with brown sugar till pay day.

The Waters of Shiloah That Go Softly

Yet the Puritan parsonage of our childhood was a pleasant place, full of flavor and spiced with good companionship. We were not only blood kin; we liked each other. It is true that the stern creed by which Ike and I were brought up would give a modern child psychologist the jitters, with his array of urges you mustn't suppress lest a complex pop up like a rabbit out of the conjurer's hat. We neither danced, played cards, nor went to the theater, and to us a woman smoking a cigarette was merely giving indication of her future fiery destination. Every Sunday, unless we were flat on our backs in bed, we were expected to attend four services—morning and evening worship, Sunday school at noon, Junior League in the afternoon. By all the rules we should have grown up soured for life on the church, in jail or a mental hospital!

But there were so many more Do's than there were Don't's in our house. Whatever the table menu, our hearts and minds were always richly fed. Ike and I learned to read from the King James Version, standing between Dad's big knees and picking out the large print with a small finger in the family Bible; the thunder and glory of that mighty primer will echo in my ears until I die. Laughter was another highly-seasoned parsonage fare. Dad could even chuckle that hot August evening when His Honor, the Governor of Massachusetts, was coming to dinner before he spoke at our church, and Mother, in her excitement, had cut off the tail of Dad's only good white shirt to use as a dust cloth; so though the temperature soared above eighty, Dad had to keep his long-tailed wool preacher's coat tightly buttoned.

Music to us was another form of laughter, unplanned and uninhibited; we were apt to burst into song at any instant. Dad was a big man with such rough-hewn features in his red jolly face that his smooth golden tenor voice was a surprise; Mother was small with soft, short brown curls all over her head, a come-hither look in her violet eyes, and her soprano was as high and clear as a wood thrush calling. Since both of them sang as naturally as they breathed, Ike and I could carry a tune almost before we could talk, and by the time we went to school we began nearly every day with a hilarious quartet.

" 'My Lord, what a mornin'!' " Dad would wake us up, shouting from the bathroom where he was shaving. "Susie, have you been cutting out paper dolls with my razor again? Ike, if you don't stir your stumps, you'll be late to school. 'My Lord. . . .' "

" 'What a mornin'!' " Mother's clear soprano would join Dad's tenor from the kitchen. "Cornbread and honey for breakfast, children!" Then Ike and I would chime in, all singing together lustily, " 'When the stars begin to fall!' "

When the quartet had finished dressing, Mother would be taking out of the gas oven the golden-brown Texas hotbread, baked ranch-fashion in the big black skillet and set on an iron trivet on the breakfast table to keep it piping hot. The smell of hot bread and honey in the blue pot was so heavenly delicious, it was hard not to grab a golden triangle while the rest had their eyes shut, inviting the Lord to join us at breakfast. We said grace in either German or English (Grandfather Nies had fled from Germany to be an American) but the ending was the same:

> " 'Come, dear Lord, our guest to be;
>   Bless this food bestowed by Thee.'
>   Please pass the honey!"

The Dorchester parsonage, where we were to stay for eleven years, was comfortably furnished; but Mrs. Newte, the committee chairman, made it very plain when she showed us around the first day that our home was chiefly an annex to

The Waters of Shiloah That Go Softly

the church. The front and back parlors could be shut off from each other by folding doors in case two committees wanted to meet there at once she pointed out; the dining room was large enough to hold all the church ladies at tea if they didn't sit down; and stored under the sink in the big sunny kitchen was a gallon coffee pot. But upstairs was wonderfully ours. Dad's study (The Slough of Despond, we kids called it because so many people dropped their troubles there) was next to the bathroom with its huge tin tub, excellent to slide down, and there were three bedrooms, enough—oh happy day!—so that I could graduate from the nursery I had shared with Ike.

A room of your own is doubly precious when you live in a house where you're apt to bump into a wedding party or a baptism complete with howling baby and godparents in your front hall. My dear private place boasted a white-painted iron bed with shining brass knobs and a snowy coverlet crocheted by Mother. Dad built me a hanging shelf to hold my treasures: a wooden duck with no tail (Ike had bitten it off when he was teething); my red glass christening mug which the afternoon sun shining through my window turned to rubies; my Japanese doll with its fringe of real hair that could be combed although its silken robe was too delicate to play with; my Bible and *Lullaby Land*, Eugene Field's poems, whose red and gold binding was broken from much loving handling.

I used to paint word pictures too, lying there in my bed while the autumn wind wailed, "Whooooo?" and blew leaves from the golden maple on the lawn against my window:

> The lost leaves whisper against the pane,
> "Let me in!"
> Go away, little leaves,
> Until spring. . . .

There is nothing so delicious as a poem in the head, the wind calling outside, and you safe in a room of your own with the door shut.

But being a preacher's kid was not all song, cornbread, and honey. Ike and I early discovered that where most children had only two parents to please, we had two hundred; it seemed to us that the entire congregation was heaven-bent on bringing us up in the way we should go.

"Your daughter, Susan, just ruined Mrs. Brainerd's petunia bed!" Dad's phone was sure to clamor when I wabbled off the sidewalk, learning to ride my new (to me) bike. Or, "Did you know, Mrs. Nies, that Isaac was sent out of kindergarten today for scaring the little girls nearly into fits?" Ike had taken Mr. and Mrs. Abou Ben Adam, his two white rats, to school in his middy blouse.

Ike at five was no sissy, even if he did wear his brown hair in a long Dutch clip, had wide blue eyes, and white braid around the collar of his dark-blue Sunday sailor suit. He once kicked a fellow choirboy in the shins as they paced down the aisle together, for chanting an insulting doggerel when he should have been singing "Onward, Christian Soldiers":

> Preacher's kids and cackling hens.
> Seldom come to any good ends!

Naturally "that little Nies brat" was sent home for Dad to punish.

"But it's worth a switching not to be allowed to sing for a month," Ike boasted later, while I pretended not to notice the smears on his cheek where he'd wiped away the tears. "With that wide white collar you have to wash your neck every single Sunday!"

The Waters of Shiloah That Go Softly

"Sure," I agreed. "What do you care?"

My sailor suit was exactly like Ike's except that I wore a pleated skirt instead of short pants and I was such a tomboy that Mother, sighing, bought me the same sturdy boots she did Ike, with the shining brass eyelets to hook the laces over. We PK's reacted to all this parish spotlight as might have been expected, by becoming exactly the brats they thought us. For months, to our parents' despair, we were two against the devil, the choir, and the congregation.

The climax came one spring afternoon when four parishioners had reported to Dad as fast as they could get the busy parsonage phone that his small son's baseball had crashed through the glass roof of a neighbor's greenhouse. Ike, accused, went completely berserk. He rushed down to the corner grocery store, grabbed up two cartons of eggs without paying, ran back up our street to hurl all twenty-four eggs at the pristine front doors of the tattletale parishioners! Then, purged of his wrath, Ike marched back home to face Dad and the music.

"I spent three months earning that baseball!" small Ike glared up at his tall Dad who stood six feet two in his black cotton stocking feet. Right now Dad was dressed in his long-tailed preacher's coat and striped pants to go calling, with his high white collar, black tie, pince-nez glasses, and his shining gold hair parted smoothly down the middle. Ike told him, his blue eyes flashing, "I don't mind paying for the glass but—you know what that ole meanie did? She built a bonfire on her front walk and dropped my baseball into the fire *right while I was looking!*"

Ike, stared anxiously up at his Dad's face growing redder and redder till even the part in his silken-blond hair was fiery; he must be awful mad. Young Ike braced himself for the explosion but when it came, it surprised him.

"A grown woman has no need to take out her spleen on a child," Dad decided. "But you'll have to be punished, young man, for not being more careful. Susie," he called to me, "get a basin of very hot water and some rags."

What was Dad going to do to Ike? Boil him? Shivering inside at whatever terrible penalty Ike might have to pay, I didn't dare disobey. I got the hot water and rags. Together, Dad with his long-tailed preacher's coat flapping and Ike following reluctantly in his short pants and middy blouse, walked back down the street, and washed the egg off all the irate parishioners' front doors. Acutely conscious of the watching eyes behind the stiffly-starched curtains at the windows, Ike stammered, "You don't have to help, Dad. It was me who was bad."

" 'No man liveth unto himself and no man dieth unto himself,' " Dad said, scrubbing away, then leaning back to admire his handiwork. "I bet this door was never so clean before! Let's go home, Son."

Thus Dad proved to us that our family stood together even in sin, so it didn't seem worth while to be "smart alecks" any longer. This family solidarity was the rock upon which we stood; we were partners in the family business.

"A preacher's family sees the seamy side of the patchwork quilt people make of their lives; how they pick up the pieces after their mistakes, sew them together again into a brave pattern," Dad explained to the wide-eyed Ike and me. "Only the Great Designer knows what the final pattern will be, but it's our wonderful job to help a little in the mending."

What more could any child want than to grow tall in responsibility and to be firmly rooted in love? We knew that our parents loved the Lord, then each other, and then us, in that order. The Lord was as much a member of our household as Dad; the chief difference was that you couldn't hear Him speak except in your mind when you kept still and listened. But you could bring Him a broken heart or a broken doll. It was amazing how soon after I prayed aloud at family prayers about Amelia's head being cracked and wouldn't the Lord who'd raised Lazarus from the dead please do something about it, Amelia reappeared in my room, glued together as good as new.

Ike and I found that acting as doorkeepers in the house of the Lord was as exciting as any play on Broadway. What need had we of painted scenery or of actors mouthing printed words, when laughter and tears, comedy and tragedy in real life came daily to our own front door? In one afternoon we had ushered into the Slough of Despond for Dad to loosen their burdens a shoe manufacturer seeking the Christian way to treat his employees who were on strike, a widow so lonely she'd tried to take too many sleeping pills, an ex-thief needing a job, a college president, and two adolescents wanting to tell Dad first of all that they were engaged to be married because he had introduced them at Epworth League.

That life can be tragic as well as gay our parents never tried to hide from Ike and me; it would have been impossible, anyway, living in a parsonage dripping daily weal and woe. But it wasn't until Nan came to live with us when I was twelve and Ike was nine that it really came home to us that all children were not loved as we were, that we were the lucky ones.

I first heard Dad and Mother talking about Nan one night through the crack in my bedroom door next to theirs, when I was supposed to be asleep. They lay there murmuring together in their big bed covered with the red-and-white pieced quilt upon which a hundred parishioners had written their names in indelible ink at ten cents apiece for the missionary fund. I listened drowsily to Dad saying that the deaconess from our church had dropped by his study that afternoon to talk over the terribly pathetic case of poor little Nan. . . .

"Lee," my mother said, "I think we should keep her here at the parsonage, for the next month at least. Till she goes to the hospital."

"Here!" my Dad gasped. "But, Sugar, it's impossible!"

"She's 'one of those little ones,'" my mother said firmly. She meant, I knew, one of those strange infants whom you mustn't offend or it were better a millstone were hung around your neck. I'd always wondered why. "With no father or mother and that awful uncle—she's just scared to death, poor baby. Do you realize she's exactly the same age as our Susie, only twelve?"

"But . . . but . . ." my Dad stammered, "the parish would never stand for her being here and you know it!" But it was obvious he was weakening. My mother was a soft-voiced woman with wise gentle eyes that could look right through you to what you were thinking. She could charm the unwary into doing what she wanted without their even realizing it. While she considered Dad the unquestioned head of the family—"Your father says" was the law of the Medes and the Persians to Ike and me—she frequently maneuvered him into thinking as she did by the simplicity of her love. As a girl in Fort Worth, Texas, she had turned down the heir to a great cattle ranch to marry a penniless preacher, but she'd never been sorry, for her heart was where her treasure was, in my Dad. She was no scholar as he was, seldom read a book except her well-thumbed Bible, but Dad once told Ike and me, "Your mother lives in other peoples' lives, writes her own stories in their laughter and their tears. Sometimes I think she's the real minister, not me."

Perhaps Dad was thinking this now, for he wavered concerning Nan, "But, Sugar, what about our own children?"

The Waters of Shiloah That Go Softly

"Nan needs us more than they do," my mother insisted. "They are already 'rooted and founded in love.' What if our Susie was in 'a delicate condition,' and no one offered to take *her* in?"

As Dad exploded into shocked incoherence, I wondered what was 'a delicate condition'? I'd already had measles, whooping cough, and that very summer had lost my appendix to a bottle in the hospital. "All right," Dad finally gave in to Mother. "If you feel this is your duty, I'll back you up with the official board. But they're bound to be upset." There was a short silence in the bedroom next to mine and then a murmur. "Darling," my Dad asked tenderly, "did I ever remember to tell you that I love you?"

"Upset" was hardly the word for the parish reaction when the news seeped around that "That Nan" was coming to stay at their parsonage. Mother was away ahead of her day in her tolerance, and that is always dangerous. In Victorian New England, biology books with pictures were kept in locked cases in the library and a lady in a delicate condition was smothered in ruffles, kept out of public sight as much as possible. The whole parish was shocked, up in arms. For the parson's wife to take under her wing the neighborhood scandal, however young, was not only unheard of, it was downright dangerous to the church's reputation.

The president of the Ladies' Aid came to my mother to protest. "But Nan came only once to your Sunday school class," she pointed out. "She's got no claim on us. . . ."

"She's got every claim," my mother interrupted. "She has no one but us and the Lord. 'When thy father and mother forsake thee, then . . .'"

"But Susie and Ike are old enough to ask questions!" the president interrupted again, hotly. "What are you going to tell *them?*"

Two bright red spots were beginning to burn in my mother's cheeks. It wasn't wise to antagonize the Ladies' Aid from whom all blessings flowed—new parsonage curtains, dishes, rugs; but when a little girl's whole future happiness might be at stake. . . . "I'll tell them the truth," my mother promised. "At least as much as it's necessary for them to know." Fortunately that very afternoon "Aunt Laura," as Ike and I called my mother's dearest friend in the parish, came in to bring a little blue jacket she'd knitted for Nan's baby. She and Mother cried together over the tiny garment, had a cup of tea, and felt much better.

My mother merely explained to Ike and me that having a baby was the most wonderful thing that could happen to a girl, that the day she herself knew I was coming, her first child, was the happiest of her life. Nan, Mother announced calmly, was to stay with us till her dear little baby arrived and because we had no guest room, a cot for her would be put up in Susie's room.

"But I don't want anyone in my room!" I wailed. My private place where I could dream that some day I'd be beautiful instead of having the Nies nose (much as I loved Dad, I couldn't pretend that it was small), straight blonde hair, and silver-rimmed spectacles as my mirror showed.

"It won't be for long, Susie," my mother soothed.

I'll never forget how Nan looked when she came to our house that evening. She stood there in our front hall, wearing a shapeless brown coat much too large for her and her fair hair was caught back with a comb like Alice in Wonderland; but her gray eyes were black with fear. I stared, my own face blank and unwelcoming, while my mother took off the awful coat, knelt down to put her arms around the frightened little girl.

"Don't cry, dear," my mother urged. "You're home now."

The Waters of Shiloah That Go Softly

"This isn't my home! It's the parsonage," Nan said stonily. "You don't want me here."

"We do want you, don't we, Susie?" My mother smiled brightly but I couldn't smile back. There was something queer here I didn't understand. "A parsonage is the Lord's house. You and Susie are going to room together. Don't just stand there." My mother handed me Nan's cardboard suitcase, and her eyes begged, "I'm depending on you!" "I cleared out your bottom bureau drawer today; take Nan upstairs and help her unpack."

We went together but we didn't speak all the time we were emptying the suitcase. What had we to say? When we went down to supper, Nan couldn't eat her scrambled egg yolks, but Mother didn't urge her to clean up her plate as she did Ike and me; she just went on chattering to Dad how the Ladies' Aid was having a food sale next Saturday so she'd saved the twelve egg whites to make her angel cake. The tension was even worse when Nan and I went up to bed. As she eased her heavy body onto the cot across from where I lay, my throat was inexplicably dry and my heart beat so fast I could hear it thumping against my pillow, for I was sure now that something was terribly wrong. What I didn't know was that Nan's own uncle, supposed to be her guardian, was the father of her child.

"Have you two said your prayers?" Mother came quietly into my room to say good night as usual and when neither of us answered, she snapped off the light, pulled up a rocking chair between our two beds and put out a hand to each child.

"I'll sing you a going-to-sleep song," Mother said. Her voice was smiling even in the dark and she squeezed my hand comfortingly. Was she squeezing Nan's too? I sniffed jealously. Mother smelt of violet talcum powder, of the starch in her clean cotton dress as she rocked and sang in her high clear voice, but softly, about the Lord and his crown of stars.

> When He cometh, when He cometh
> To make up His jewels,
> All His jewels, precious jewels,
> Bright gems for His crown.
> > Like the stars of the morning,
> > His bright crown adorning,
> > They shall shine in their beauty
> > Bright gems for His crown.

Jewels of the King . . . that was Nan and I. Peace came, soft-footed, into my quiet room. Nan was no longer "queer," just another girl like me, precious to the Lord who loved little children. Mother bent down to kiss us both. "There's a line from Isaiah I often say when I find it hard to go to sleep," my mother told us. " 'The waters of Shiloah that go softly.' . . . Go softly to sleep, my dears."

Nan's baby was named Jonathan and both of them stayed with us several months after they came home from the hospital. Ike thought the new baby "a pain in the night" because he howled and couldn't hold a baseball bat; but I loved Jonathan dearly, learned to bathe and burp him, and wept bitterly when he was adopted by a family up in Maine. Nan went away, too, to boarding school, and my room was very empty. But Mother was radiant because Nan and her parsonage baby had been adopted by our parish, led by gentle Aunt Laura. Jonathan took with him a bountiful layette which members of the Ladies' Aid had sewed and knitted; there were tiny shirts, snowy diapers, gay sweaters and socks, baby dresses edged with hand-crocheted lace so that "their baby" would not go to his foster parents empty-handed but proudly, proving he had been loved.

"Keep your child from too early contact with injustice,

The Waters of Shiloah That Go Softly

cruelty, lest this injure his delicate ego," some of today's prophets advise. I find the ego as hard to picture as that mysterious sin against the Holy Ghost which I used to imagine, when I was small, as a damp unpleasant fog. How can a child pass without anguish from a safe pretty world to a roaring atom age? Is it not kinder to admit the evil, but to cushion the blow as my mother did by telling Ike and me, "Everyone has bad trouble but it can be met bravely as Nan did"?

Compassion was the gift my mother gave to Ike and me; she turned what might have been a whispered horror into what was essentially immaculate conception. By literally suffering through with another child in deep trouble, we learned that the peace that passes understanding is always shared, that it lies by the waters of Shiloah that go softly.

Chapter Two

ISAAC MEANS LAUGHTER

IKE was so proud of being named for his Grandpaw, Isaac Rouse, he almost burst the large white buttons off his sailor blouse boasting to the other neighborhood kids that he was a Texas cowboy. That he lived in a staid New England parsonage was a mere accident to be brushed aside:

"I was born in Texas," Ike would insist. "My Gramp wasn't afraid of anyone and I'm not either. *Bang!* Bang!" He'd crook his finger, shoot off his imaginary gun, and then leap astride our parsonage white picket fence and gallop so furiously he almost ruined himself.

When I'd point out, with sisterly smugness, that he'd merely been born in Fort Worth when Mother went home there on a visit, had come back to Boston at the age of six weeks, riding in a market basket in the train, Ike would yell, furious, "I am *not* a damyankee like you!"

It was true that I'd been born in Townsend, a quiet pine-scented Massachusetts town, while the first sound young Ike ever heard had been Grandpaw Rouse's rebel yell of triumph. What red-blooded boy could resist hero-worshiping a grandparent who could ride anything on four legs, rope a steer, or cut a thin rope with a bullet from his .45? "I hope you'll inherit a lot more than your name," Mother told Ike. "I hope you'll learn as your grandfather did that no battle is won with bullets. A man has first to conquer himself, get hate out of his heart."

And then Mother would tell us the story of how Grandpaw at twenty had met the biggest man in these United States, and of how this meeting had changed Isaac Rouse's whole thinking, his way of life.

We had enough blood and thunder right in our own family to run a whole TV series for children; and the story hour was for Ike and me the peak of our parsonage day, for then Dad and Mother belonged only to us.

No matter how many parishioners got a pain they had to tell the minister about or were worried about their immortal souls, every evening, right after our early supper, clean for once and rosy and warm from our baths, Ike and I would snuggle down in the big shabby chintz armchair in Ike's bedroom. There'd be room on each side of Mother for a child in a long white flannelette nightgown. I liked this arrangement because Ike couldn't pinch me when he got mad, with Mother in between. Not that I was any angel either but I used my tongue to pinch instead of fingers.

"You forgot to wash behind your ears!" I'd point out virtuously and Ike would counter, "Your crowning glory's got a rat's nest in it!"

"Hush, children!" Mother would warn automatically.

I never could understand why she called my fine golden hair that grew long enough to sit on (but who wanted to?) my "crowning glory." To me it was a horror to comb every day; I hated also my silver-rimmed glasses I had to wear or people looked like clouds, walking, for my spectacles were always slipping down my nose or getting broken when I climbed a tree or slugged a baseball. I seldom looked at myself in the mirror but when I did, I stuck my tongue out. Could this scrawny little owl-eyes be *me*? I longed to be as beautiful as my Mother sitting there in the smooth-to-touch blue silk kimono she wore because she was getting ready to go out later to a church supper with Dad. I rubbed my cheek against her softness and wondered if anyone would ever carry my picture in the back of his watch as my Dad did hers and show it proudly at the slightest provocation. But that picture had been taken years ago. Now as she smoothed back my hair, the strands caught in the cracks in her hands which had drowned in parsonage dishwater for so many years.

"Whose choice is it tonight?" Mother asked. "Mine!" shouted Ike. "Tell about Grandpaw and the bloody battle! How he marked the number seventeen in his shoes so he could say he was 'over seventeen' and get into the Army. When I grow up, I'm going to fight, too!"

"Your Grandpaw says the war between the states set us back as a nation a hundred years. Both sides would have come out better if we'd left the safety on our tempers and on our guns." Mother yanked at the tail of Ike's long cherub night-gown. "Sit still! How can I talk with you jumping up and down?"

"Young Isaac was on sentry duty that night after the bloody battle," my mother began the story. (I wish now I'd listened closer so I'd know which battle this was, but Grandpaw was at Bull Run, Antietam, Fredericksburg, and Gettysburg, and he saw Lee surrender "under the old apple tree," so it must have been one of these.) "Isaac was so flat-out-tired," she went on, "he thought he must be dreaming when he saw, picking its way between the camp fires, a very small donkey ridden by a man so tall that he had to hold up his long legs to keep them from dragging on the ground. But he didn't seem to notice or care how queer he looked. His shaggy head was bare but he wore a shawl around his shoulders against the night's chill and he rode bent over as if weighted down by his heavy thoughts. Isaac wondered, watching, if Our Lord had been too tall for his donkey, too, when He rode that Palm Sunday into Jerusalem. But a civilian had no business riding here, with the Johnny Rebs just back of that far stone wall.

Isaac Means Laughter

" 'Halt!' Isaac shifted his gun to ready. 'Who goes there?'

" 'It's all right, Son.' As the tall bearded man reined in his donkey obediently, sat there for a moment gazing out into the uneasy night, he and young Isaac could hear horses stamping, campfires crackling, the roughness of men's voices; but louder came the stifled cries as the stretcher bearers flitted here and there like dreadful fireflies, lighting in the wounded. Neither side shot at the endless procession of broken bodies in blue and gray, alike in their agony, as they were carried by. One boy in gray had a great hole in his chest and a bubble of blood around his mouth so he couldn't live very long; he looked only about thirteen, a drummer boy, maybe.

" 'They're taking 'em awful young these days,' Isaac said from the height of his own twenty years.

" 'Yes. Would God I could stop this bloody holocaust. . . .' "

Even in the dim light, the tall man on the little donkey looked strangely familiar. Those deep-set, sad eyes. Had he seen his picture perhaps in the newspaper? As young Isaac swung up his guard lantern, he saw the slow unashamed tears running down the deep lines beside the older man's bearded mouth. Isaac snapped to attention, frightened by what he knew. *This was Abraham Lincoln, President of what was left of these United States!*

" 'I felt like going down on my knees to him,' Isaac told his wife, Susan, later when what he'd seen that night had become a family heirloom to be packed away along with his bronze GAR medal. 'The Commander-in-Chief weeping over the killing he couldn't stop. He didn't hate the Johnny Rebs. And I didn't either.' "

This was when young Isaac decided that after the war he wanted to live in Texas, my mother explained to Ike and me sitting beside her, awed, for however often we heard this story it never failed to thrill us that a history book had come alive in our own family. After Isaac and Susan were married in Good Hope, Illinois, and had two children, they finally scraped together enough money to buy a Conestoga wagon to travel in. They moved to Texas, to find a place big enough to build themselves a future, for Isaac held stubbornly that even damyankees could be good neighbors to Johnny Rebs. It was a long hard journey from Illinois, seven hundred miles as the crow flies, in a slow covered wagon with all the Rouse family goods piled inside and a water barrel lashed to the side, a barrel which frequently went dry or was so full of loathsome maggots the little girls couldn't drink. Myrtie ("That was me," my mother said) was three but Gay was only six months old. The old-time residents of Fort Worth gave the newcomers small welcome. Who could blame the Johnny Rebs for thinking that Isaac was merely another carpetbagger come to grab what little they had left? But even when his little girls were frozen out of the Southern Methodist Sunday school because they were damyankees, Isaac wouldn't say a word against his new neighbors.

"They've been hurt bad," Isaac said. "You can't blame 'em. They're only human. We outlanders have to earn the right to belong to this big state of Texas!" He helped to start St. Paul's, the Northern Methodist Church where his little girls could go.

Isaac was a crack shot, rode a black stallion hard, and wasn't afraid of anything that walked, crawled, or flew, but he was also a deeply religious man, whose creed forbade him many things; he neither drank liquor nor smoked, though he'd learned to chew tobacco in the Army. In a frontier town like Fort Worth with a saloon on every corner, Isaac wasn't exactly a hail-fellow Westerner any more than he was a Southerner. Proving he was a real Texan wasn't easy.

"He had to be 'wise as a serpent and harmless as a dove,'"

Isaac Means Laughter

my mother explained to my brother Ike and me, sitting wide-eyed beside her in the big armchair in the Dorchester parsonage.

"Ugh, snakes!" I shuddered and Ike remarked he couldn't imagine anyone less like a dove than Grandpaw.

"It's in the Bible," Mother explained. "It means, don't tell lies but neither do you have to blurt out everything you know to the first person you meet. It means even a Christian can use common sense."

Isaac Rouse prospered in Fort Worth. At first he went into sheep ranching, ranged seven thousand head on the prairie with Mexican cowboys to help him; but when in one night a sudden norther, sweeping down, froze several thousand of the silly beasts huddled together into blocks of ice, Isaac, not daunted, took what carcasses he could save into town and opened a meat market. He bent over backward being friendly, giving anyone who needed it ample credit. All he wanted was to make a home place big enough under the vast blue arch of Texas sky so that his son, when he arrived, could carry on, could build up the name of Rouse till it meant something fine and proud.

More than anything else, Isaac Rouse wanted a son named for him. He himself had been adopted as a baby by the Rouses of Rouse's Point, New York, after his father and mother had both been killed in the same accident, but by the time Isaac was old enough to care, the record of his parents' name was lost. So Isaac Rouse, Junior, would mean far more than just a name; he would be the future for a man who had no past. Nobody likes to be left dangling in time; if he hasn't any ancestors, at least he wants sons. But for the first ten years after they married, Susan presented Isaac with only three daughters.

"I was the first, Myrtie Elvira, born in Good Hope," my

mother explained to my brother Ike and me. "Paw was so glad that Maw had come through all right, he couldn't worry about much else. 'The next one will be Isaac, Junior,' he told her. 'Myrtie can help care for him.' But when the next baby, Grace Viola, was a girl too, Paw began to fret. He told Maw that Gay was a right smart little tike if he did say so who'd fathered her, but a man needed a son, especially a man who was starting from scratch needed a boy to walk by his side, to swap man-talk, to be taught to fish, hunt, and ride.

" 'I'm sorry, Isaac,' Susan said, feeling she had failed him. 'We can try again.'

" 'Not till we get to Texas,' Isaac decided. Surely in this vast, vigorous country a son would be born.

"Paw had no idea he'd have to wait twenty-eight years for his second Isaac!" my mother sighed, as she held Ike a little closer in the crook of her arm, but I pushed jealously closer too. What made a boy so special?

Isaac's third daughter, Ethel, born in Fort Worth was the prettiest girl yet, but Grandpaw simply couldn't believe she wasn't a boy, his second Isaac he wanted so badly.

He even knew exactly how young Isaac would look, bouncing, big and happy as his name meant! He told his Susan, who grieved only because her husband did, for after all she had her three girls to help her around the house, "Remember Sarah, Abraham's wife? She was over ninety when her Isaac was born!"

"But you can't count on a miracle!" Susan gasped.

"The Lord isn't limited now any more than He was then," Isaac insisted, stubbornly. "Sarah waited so long for her son, too, that when he did come, there was great rejoicing and she called his name *Isaac*. You know what *Isaac* means? It means *laughter*. We'll celebrate my son's christening yet!"

Isaac Means Laughter

As his daughters grew up faster than a trumpet vine and as handsome, Isaac Rouse built a big brown-painted house on the outskirts of town, with a wide veranda where the girls entertained the gay young blades of Forth Worth. Isaac used to grumble that on Saturday nights he couldn't find a chair to sit down on in his own house, without dumping out some love-sick young buck. Actually he was proud of his beautiful daughters. It pleased him too that he was not only financially comfortable but his name meant something, for he'd helped start the public schools, as well as St. Paul's Church, and he was interested in town politics. When Isaac ran for the board of aldermen, no one was more surprised than he was when he got elected! Even some of the old-timers must have voted for him!

"He's a right white man, your Isaac," one of the native Texan admitted to Susan, his wife.

"You just finding that out?" she smiled in her gentle way.

"If every Yank was like you two, there wouldn't have been any war."

"It still takes two to make a fight," Susan pointed out. She might be soft-spoken, but she hadn't been Isaac's wife all these long years for nothing. Susan had gentled her hard-riding husband but Isaac had stiffened her own backbone. It was a pity they still had no son to combine the best qualities of them both, to be a real, native-born Texan.

On election night Isaac found himself in a dangerous spot. The saloons had been doing a brisk business all day and some of the whisky-happy cowboys had decided that for once the new alderman was going to celebrate their way. Fingering their six-shooters, the happy hombres herded Isaac into a hotel barroom, locked the door, bawling that any man too mean to set up drinks for those who'd elected him should be run out of town! He'd never be a *live* alderman here! Isaac looked at their flushed faces, saw they were in a state to be mighty handy with their guns.

"Set 'em up for everybody," he ordered the bartender. "But unlock the door for just a minute, won't you?" He grinned, explaining, "I have to walk down the hall a piece."

The boys, unrelenting, escorted Isaac as far as the bathroom door, which he locked behind him; but though the reception committee waited patiently for a long time, Isaac didn't come back out. He'd remembered a small window that gave on the back alley, had climbed out and headed for home, leaving the boys to pay for their own drinks. Isaac thought this a great joke, but Susan was frightened when he told her about his narrow escape, chuckling mightily.

"What if they come after you here?" she worried. "They're drunk enough to do anything and you know it!"

Even as she spoke, a terrific racket was roaring down their street, horses' feet going rat-ta-tat-tat, six-shooters plugging out street lamps, men shouting so loudly that, as they came nearer, they woke up the three girls, who huddled frightened in their nightclothes in the dark parlor, peering out at the mob. "Come on out here, Ike! We want you!" a voice bawled.

"Don't go!" Susan begged frantically, holding onto his arm. "Please, Isaac, don't go!"

But Grandpaw opened the door, walked out onto the wide veranda above the milling crowd, a fair target. Susan stood in the doorway, hardly able to breathe, wishing she'd never married a man who didn't know how to be afraid. She waited to be a widow but instead the men began to roar lustily:

> Our Ike's a mighty dry feller,
> But he's a jolly good feller. . . .

It wasn't a shooting after all; it was only a shivaree! Isaac Rouse belonged to his big beloved Texas at last.

Isaac Means Laughter

But what good was all this, Isaac ached bitterly, if he still had no son to carry on the good name he had built for himself? There must be a girl-jinx on the Rouse family! Even when Myrtie had married the young Dallas minister, Lee Nies, had gone with him to Boston to live, her first baby had been a girl. Then Ethel married and hers was a girl, too! Five girls so far. Isaac himself wasn't getting any younger. When he went back to New York to the GAR reunion, after the first five miles of parading in the sun, he'd felt dizzy. The next day he couldn't get out of the hotel bed; they'd sent for a doctor, but thank heaven Susan wasn't along so she didn't have to know what the doctor had said. Isaac sure wasn't going to begin to ride herd on himself at his age; better to die with his riding boots on, but the attack did make a man think. If only there was some way his name could go on in Forth Worth. . . .

When Grandpaw heard his daughter Myrtie was having her second baby, he knew it was his last chance. So he wrote her a wistful letter:

> If you could see your way clear to having my grandson, Isaac, here, I'd be glad to pay all your expenses, your fare here and back, the doctor, nurses, everything.

"But what if he doesn't turn out to be a boy?" Myrtie worried to her husband, torn between laughter and tears. Dear stubborn Paw. . . . "Besides, if he is, I want to name him for *you*, Lee! Seven months along is no time for me to go gallivanting three thousand miles!"

My Dad put his arm around her. "You do what you want to, Honey, and name him for anyone you like. If she's a girl, what about 'Myrtie'? I'm kind of partial to that."

"I like 'Cynthia' better," Myrtie sighed. "Paw's waited so long. Did you notice how short of breath he was when he visited us last winter? I'd better go home. If Maw could cross the country in a covered wagon when Gay was a baby, I reckon I can ride a train. I'll have to take Susie along."

Isaac Rouse met his daughter and granddaughter at the station in Fort Worth, so happy but looking so much older that it made Myrtie scared; there was gray in his mustache, and he climbed into the buggy heavily and slowly. He who used to leap into his saddle! If Paw was disappointed again, it might make him downright sick.

"I remember kissing Grandpaw!" I interrupted Mother's story eagerly. "His mustache prickled!"

"Rats!" Ike sniffed. What did I mean butting in? After all, this was *his* story. Wasn't he the one who was being born? "You were only three, too little to remember anything!"

My mother laughed. "You were right cute, Susie. You sat beside your Grandpaw on the front seat of the buggy; your legs were so short they stuck out in front of your dark-blue pleated skirt. Your Grandpaw Rouse looked down at your glasses kind of doubtfully and said, 'So you're a little Bostonian, Susie?' 'Oh, no,' you piped, 'I'm a Methodist!' "

Grandpaw's shouts of laughter frightened the mare so that even Isaac Rouse had his hands full for a few moments. The carriage tore down the main street of Fort Worth so fast pedestrians scattered right and left, and my mother held onto the side of the carriage for dear life and hoped there'd be a doctor handy in case she needed him.

But the new baby didn't arrive till the thirteenth of March, two weeks late; by that time not only Mother but the entire Rouse household was completely disrupted and decidedly jittery, waiting. "How soon will my little brother get here?" I asked at breakfast one morning. "Very soon now," my Aunt Gay said. I liked her best of anyone at Grandpaw's. She wasn't well so she still lived at home, but she was like her name, gay and uncomplaining, with a twinkle in her eye. I was glad I could sleep upstairs in her room. I persisted, "Well, why doesn't he hurry up?"

My Grandpaw Rouse looked up from the mountain of golden-brown hotcakes he was devouring, drowned in a lake of golden butter and syrup, ordering, "Take the griddle off, Susan, I'm through." He told me sternly, "The Isaacs are always late."

"But, Paw," my mother quavered, heavy, worried, almost in tears as she laid down her own fork. If he were disappointed after spending all this money to get her here. . . . She said, "If she's a girl, Paw, her name is 'Cynthia.'"

My Grandpaw snorted, slammed his chair back from the table, and stomped off angrily across the street to where Sylvia Doughty, Susan's sister, lived. His own family got on his nerves, always pointing out that the new baby didn't have to be a boy! He did, too, have to be. Isaac wouldn't see the next baby. This morning the pain in his chest had been so bad he like never to have got out of bed. He prayed, *"O Lord, is it too much to ask? I killed good men in Thy image at Gettysburg, but I've tried to make up for that. Texas is my home now. I've built a church here, helped to build a city. I don't ask for a miracle like Abraham's. I just want a son to carry on my name when I have to leave here. . . ."*

"The very next morning a strange thing happened," my mother went on, smiling down at me in the safe crook of her arm. "When Susie, here, woke up, she told her Aunt Gay, 'I heard the angels tapping on the window last night. Where's the baby?' As Aunt Gay stared, too startled to speak, they heard feet running downstairs. The front door burst open and your Grandpaw Rouse let out a real Texas rebel yell."

"'Isaac's come, Sylvia!' he hollered clear across the street from his veranda to Grandmaw's sister. 'You hear me? *Isaac*

Rouse is here! He's a buster. Weighs thirteen pounds. How's that for a Texas Cowpuncher?' "

"Bang! Bang!" Ike's cheeks were blazing red with excitement as he leaped from the big chair beside Mother, proudly crooked his finger to fire his .45. He shot Dad dead as he came through the bedroom doorway, but the lively corpse merely swept Ike up in his big arms, gun, cherub white nightgown and all, and flung him down upon his bed.

"Almost ready, Honey?" Dad asked Mother. "The church supper's at six. They can't sit down till I ask the blessing."

"I don't wanna go to bed!" the cowboy howled, as Mother left hurriedly to finish dressing.

"Dad, why did Grandpaw die?" Ike tried to string out the conversation a little longer.

"He didn't need to stay in Texas any longer," Dad explained. "He had his immortality, his Isaac."

"Does 'Isaac' really mean 'laughter'?"

"Yes. A time of great rejoicing, as we had when you were born."

"Will I always have fun? Because I'm an Isaac?"

"I wonder," my Dad said, sobering, "if anyone ever does." He looked down at his small, rosy, tousled son, lying there so young and vulnerable, Dad who had listened to so many people's troubles. "I hope so," Dad said. "But this I do know— if you fight the good fight as Isaac Rouse did, there is peace at the end. Good night, Son."

Chapter Three

HANGING ONTO OUR DAD'S COATTAILS

"THE terrible power of the unseen" was no news to Ike and me; we began each day by conversations with the Infinite.

After breakfast, as matter-of-course as folding our napkins, we four would kneel down by the body-warmed cane seats of our dining room chairs to discuss our plans for the day with the Lord. The fragrance of incense does not mean worship to me; but to this day the homely smell of a cane-seated chair is the very odor of prayer.

It did not occur to Ike and me that it might be presumptuous to bother the Creator of the universe with our small affairs. Though Ike did say he thought it queer of the Lord to pick out a sparrow to watch fall, those drab little fighters; Ike would prefer a bright-breasted robin. Our morning prayers were brief and to the point: Ike, worried over that D in English on his report card, asked help to remember that you "lay down" a book but "lie down" yourself. "Now, Sister," Dad prompted. "Mine is private today," I announced, so we all prayed silently for two minutes by Dad's watch that had Mother's picture in the back. I didn't want anyone else to know that I was begging the Lord, "Please, please, don't let Aunt Lizzie send me another Paris hat for Easter!" Aunt Lizzie was Dad's sister who ran a hat shop in Dallas, Texas, and supplied my hats free, but never bothered to wonder what they might look like on *me*. Wearing glasses was bad enough, but peering out of a halo of pink Parisian chiffon when all the other girls were wearing simple straw hats with daisies was pure hell.

Mother's petition was to keep her temper when the parsonage committee from the Ladies' Aid came today, saw

39

where Ike had spilled tomato catsup on the dining room rug; the Lord knew accidents would happen as long as boys had slippery fingers. Dad prayed for the wisdom of Solomon to decide which member of the choir should sing the Easter solo, the long one during the collection. He certainly was stumped, Dad admitted to the Lord; if Mrs. Brainerd, the lovely lyric soprano, sang the solo again, the tenor vowed he'd leave the choir. Tenors were as scarce as dollar bills in the collection plate, but Mrs. Brainerd was the wife of the church treasurer who wrote our monthly pay check. So the choice wasn't easy.

Then we all said the Lord's Prayer together, got to our feet to go our separate ways. But Dad was already beaming.

"I'll write them a duet!" he exulted. "For Easter."

Dad was a natural-born musician. He'd never had a formal lesson in his life, but he could both read and write music and could make our old upright piano, battered by many movings from parsonage to parsonage, stand right up and shout as mightily as any baby grand. We kids followed him excitedly into the back parlor where he screwed up the stool till it was high enough to accommodate his long legs, sat down, ran his big melody-wise fingers up and down the yellowed ivory keys. "A theme has been running through my head for days," he confessed. "Listen!" He flung back his bright head, began to sing and play:

> "The Lord is the strength of my life,
> Whom then shall I fear?"

In no time at all Ike and I had caught onto the refrain and were shouting the words with him, but Dad played on, improvising loudly. *Boom, boom!* went the bass under Dad's strong fingers, up soared our shrill trebles supported by his tenor, demanding, "Whom then shall I fear?"

Hanging onto Our Dad's Coattails

"Lee," my mother protested. "They'll be late to school. It's a quarter to nine."

The school was four blocks away but this was a lot more fun than finding the capital of the state of Minnesota. I pulled a dog-eared scrap of paper from the pocket of my plaid pleated skirt, so short it was only a frill, and announced, "The teacher wants me to sing this verse for Parent's Day. But it hasn't a good tune. She said, maybe you'd make up something more springlike."

"Certainly," Dad said. "I'd be glad to."

His sensitive fingers wandered softly over the keys, searching for the right notes, as he read the words I held up for him on the music rack on the piano:

> Under green hedges after the snow,
> There do the dear little violets grow;
> Hiding and nodding their beautiful heads,
> Under the hawthorn, in soft mossy beds. . . .

As he played he hummed and the tune grew: the quiet notes spread out as naturally as the violet's green leaves, as the soft blue buds opening, a child's music to fit the words. I can sing the gay little tune now; at least, I could if it weren't for the lump in my throat.

"Lee Nies, it's five minutes of nine!" my mother cried. "Which is the oldest, you or . . ."

"Get a move on, kids," Dad said hastily. "Didn't you hear your mother?"

So the choir got their Easter anthem and by the time Ike and I got home from school that afternoon, Dad had written out the new violet tune on a piece of music paper for me to take to the teacher tomorrow. All this was as unselfconscious as our morning prayers. Nothing was impossible. If you asked

41

the Lord to help you with your day, you expected Him to do just that. If you wanted to write an anthem, you sat down and began. After all, weren't things big or little according to the height of the vantage point from which you viewed them? Even the Washington Monument looks like a white pin from an airplane a mile up.

"The terrible power of the unseen" was no more astounding to Ike and me than a drink of cold water. Today's scientists are discovering what we preacher's kids knew all along, that you don't have to understand all about either an atom or a prayer to harness it. We knew from just watching the Stumble Brothers in our front parlor the explosive power of God in the human heart.

The Stumble Brothers were mostly "bums" who read Dad's name and address printed in gold letters on the sign on our church lawn, who came to cadge the price of a drink or a bottle but left full of good advice and black coffee. "Jesus Christ can help you lick this terrible craving," we kids heard Dad tell them. "But first you yourself have to *want* to be cured. God is a gentleman; He'll never force Himself upon you. If you mean business, get down on your knees!" Usually the cadger would gulp, "Yessir. Thank you, Father," and retreat hastily. But occasionally a Stumble Brother would really listen to what Dad promised, would kneel down by our big rocking chair, begin to pray himself through, to trust the terrible power of the unseen.

One morning, shortly after Nan left, I came into the front parlor with a fresh pot of black coffee, but the man kneeling there smelled so of vomit I could hardly bear to stay long enough to put down my tray upon the parlor table. "Faith can make the contact but only you can turn the switch," Dad was saying. This Stumble Brother looked terrible; his coat was torn and spotted; he hadn't shaved in days and his hands shook

42

so the rocking chair was going back and forth as he knelt there, groaning, "O God, help me!" he cried desperately, "It's no good. I can't get through!"

"Maybe," Dad said coldly, yanking a pint bottle of gin out of the kneeling man's back pocket, "now you'll have better luck." Dad handed me the bottle, ordering, "Here, Susie, take this out to the smashing rock."

The smashing rock was a huge hunk of concrete which the masons must have left behind when they fixed the parsonage cellar, and which frequently smelled pretty peculiar to be in a Methodist parson's back yard. But the gin bottle made a glorious *glunk*. I picked up the pieces of glass so they wouldn't ruin the lawn mower if Ike ever wanted fifteen cents badly enough to cut the grass, and sniffed at the bottom of the bottle. Gin looked like water, smelled like pine trees, but when I dipped in my finger, it tasted terrible. Whisky, as I already knew, smelt like someone's bad breath. Why did people drink this stuff? Then I remembered the time that I'd eaten a whole peach pie; I'd been deathly sick afterward, but it had tasted wonderful going down!

By the time I'd finished experimenting and came back into the house, Dad's Stumble Brother was splashing happily up in our big tin bathtub. A clean white shirt and Dad's second-best suit were lying neatly folded outside the bathroom door and Mother was in his study fussing at Dad. I stopped in the hall to listen.

"You can't give that suit away!" Mother argued. "It doesn't leave you anything but your dark-blue Sunday suit and your garden overalls."

"I can't wear but one suit at a time."

"Why not just give him the overalls?"

"Because they wouldn't do this guy any good. He is . . . was . . . sales manager for a big paper outfit up in Maine. He came down here for the convention, cut loose so badly he lost his job. He has to look decent to go back."

"That tramp? A sales manager?" my mother sniffed. "Then I'm an opera singer!"

" 'Shall I offer unto the Lord that which costs me nothing?' " It wasn't quite fair of Dad, I thought, to quote Scripture at Mother because he could always wrap her up in righteous texts. But she knew Stumble Brothers; she ought to, after thirteen years. But she made no more protest about the suit.

Two months later a package arrived addressed to Dad and postmarked from Maine. Inside was the only hundred-dollar suit Dad ever owned. (Someone had forgotten to take the price tag out of the little vest pocket so we knew how much the suit cost.) "I hope it fits," the paper-outfit man wrote Dad. "I had the best tailor in Portland copy your old suit. I'd like to keep that, if you don't mind, just to remind me. And don't worry, I can afford this. I got my sales manager's job back again."

"Cast your old pants upon the water and they shall come back to you a tweed suit!" Dad grinned, trying on the new coat, happily. "How do I look?"

"The shoulders fit wonderfully," mother admitted. "But you needn't act so smart, Lee Nies. You gave away four suits and got back only one! You'll need a new pair of shoes to go with this. Those you have on are terribly scuffed."

"I see by the paper they're having a sale tomorrow of English shoes in Boston," Dad agreed. Ike and I went through even our husky boots with the brass eyelets so fast that Dad always waited for the basement shoe sales to get his. He came home next day with a pair of English walking shoes, beautifully made but such a bright yellow you could hardly see what else he had on.

"There weren't any black ones in my size," Dad defended himself to my mother's gasp of horror. "But these are good shoes. Cost ten dollars originally and now they're only $1.98. The tag's right on 'em, see? *Made in England.* I paid only a dime for the black dye I got in the drug store; $2:08 isn't bad for a pair of shoes as good as these."

"The black dye will rub off," mother prophesied but Dad insisted stubbornly that was nonsense; he knew what he was doing. The black dye was so pungent, drying, it smelled up the whole house and every time we kids barged into Dad's study that week, he'd snap, "Look out for my English shoes!" He wanted them ready for next Sunday morning because he was planning to dedicate the individual communion cups which one of our official members who was a physician had given, insisting that the big silver chalice spread germs even when wiped off with a napkin.

It was raining hard the next Sunday. Dad put on his odoriferous new shoes and rubbers to walk the six blocks to the church, setting out under his big black cotton umbrella with the pine handle, with the rest of the family trailing anxious umbrellas behind him up the sidewalk. But mother's prophecy was justified; when Dad took off his rubbers at the vestry door, the toes of both his shoes were bright yellow suns.

"You can't wear those!" Mother wailed. Not with everyone kneeling at the communion railing, looking with bent heads right down to where Dad's shoes walk! "Susie, you go tell the organist not to stop the prelude till I get back. I'll run home for your old shoes!"

"No. Wait." Dad caught her arm. "There isn't time." He grinned down ruefully at his sunburst toes, murmuring, " 'Be sure your sins will find you out.' "

That Sunday the startled congregation was offered the newly dedicated communion cups by their preacher wearing his rubbers!

"Well, how did you like the little cups?" Dad asked at dinner as he served our favorite Sunday meal, browned calves' liver and crisp bacon, smothered in a luscious cream sauce and wiped up by Mother's baking powder biscuits so light you could eat a dozen and never know it.

"I don't like 'em," Ike said flatly, "You can't get but one swallow of grapejuice!"

Dad and Mother couldn't help laughing, but that didn't prevent Ike from having to read an extra chapter in the Old Testament for being so greedy.

Ike and I had both learned our alphabet before we were five from the proper names in the big family Bible. It was easy because the capitals were so large and the people they stood for were so exciting. "A for Abel, B for Benjamin!" I would cry, pinpointing the letters with an excited, triumphant finger. C was for Cain and D for Daniel; these were not merely crooked signs on a piece of paper, but red-hot drama. Had not C killed A, his brother? Imagine intrepid D walking around in a den of roaring lions! And the names had queer meanings. E for Ebenezer was a funny one. Ike used to double up with laughter because the boy next door to us was named Ebenezer Crooks. Who ever heard of a boy called "Hitherto-hath-the-Lord-led-us"!

Dad had promised that as soon as we could read a chapter aloud without making any mistakes, we could each have a Bible of our own. I chose the fourteenth of John because already from hearing it so often I could have recited it with my eyes shut. Small children love best the books they know by heart whether it be rabbits in Mr. MacGregor's garden or David slaying Goliath with his lucky stone. On my fifth birthday I stood up at the breakfast table, my heart pounding, read shakily aloud from the big Book propped up by the salt and pepper shakers on our dining room table, "Let not your heart be troubled; ye believe in God; believe also in me. . . ." When

46

Hanging onto Our Dad's Coattails

I'd finished the last excited word, Dad had pulled out my small new Bible from his lap where it had been hidden by the tablecloth and handed it to me.

"Congratulations, Susie," Dad beamed.

The book was bound in soft black leather and it had my name on the front in gold letters. I couldn't speak; there weren't any words big enough to say what I felt; I simply held the queer-smelling softness of the leather against my cheek, sniffing the heady fragrance of success. The whole world was mine for the taking; *I could read.*

From Ike's birthday on, each member of our family took turns selecting the reading for morning prayers till the Bible people were as flesh-and-blood to Ike and me as our playmates at school. We would chant together with small Samuel from his lonely bed in the Temple, piping "Speak, Lord, for thy servant heareth." We ran anxiously behind the little gray donkey upon which rode the lovely young Mary with the Babe in her arms, while Joseph urged the donkey to go even faster toward Egypt because he had been "warned of God in a dream"; we were never quite sure that the pursuing swords of the Herod's wicked soldiers would not catch up with us, and the Family. Our breakfast selections became subject to Dad's veto, however, after the morning when Ike put too much gusto into his rendering of the story of Jael and Sisera. Sisera, you recall, was fleeing for his life when the wily Jael opened her tent door to offer him shelter—and then, as he slept, she drove a nail through his temple. Ike got so excited, reading, that he let go with his knife, splintered his tumbler so that glass and water flew all over the breakfast table.

"I'm aware of the hazards of a preacher's life," Dad said wiping his face with his napkin. "But please remember, water glasses cost money. Five cents will come out of your quarter this week, young man."

From our weekly allowance we were supposed to give five cents to church, five to Sunday school and whatever we wished to the Junior League collection, so that actually our spending money worked out to about thirteen cents. But we were well paid by our reading the Bible aloud. Those early morning sessions set up measuring rods for all literature; we caught the rhythm and glory of great cadences as we never could have skimming the pages by ourselves.

Is it pure accident that since "reading readiness" and "remedial reading" have taken the place of the family's reading aloud together so many boys and girls consider books a nasty dose of medicine? "Gosh, I missed seeing the last show of *Moby Dick* and I need it for my summer reading list!" a neighbor's young son who attends an expensive private school moaned to me recently. He brightened. "I'll try the drugstore. Maybe it's in *Classical Comics*."

He was after the same adventure and excitement that Ike and I knew in Samson slaughtering his thousands with the jawbone of an ass, in the distracted Abraham binding his own Isaac for sacrifice. Ike never could bear to wait for him to find the ram, he always shouted, anxiously, "Hey, look in the bushes, Abe!" Cutting down a vocabulary to fit the child's age always seems to me like cutting off the baby to fit the crib. Shall we offer our children pablum instead of the red meat of real literature? Hand them lists of books we would shudder to read ourselves? The secret of Ike's and my joyous discovery of the Bible was that *our folks enjoyed it with us.*

To live intimately with a cultivated mind, as we PK's did, is in itself adventure. Most fathers leave home mornings in a flurry of burnt toast, only to return at night too exhausted to do much but moan, "Will you kids stop that awful racket?" But Dad was always home mornings. (What housewife wants a preacher to call till she gets her hair out of curlpapers and

48

washes the dishes?) And frequently when we kids got home from school we'd hear the pounding of his rickety typewriter in the study, where he was "making his sermon." The congregation didn't think it was getting its money's worth if the Sunday sermon was shorter than forty minutes, and "over four thousand minutes of talking a year takes a lot of spit and study," Dad used to chuckle when he laid his book down on his stomach to answer our questions. He used to read lying on the uncomfortable study couch because the lumps kept him awake no matter how tired he was.

Dad's study was literally papered with homemade bookcases he'd knocked together himself from unpainted pine, each box the same length and deep enough to hold his precious volumes. Whenever we moved to a new parsonage, the books didn't have to be repacked; the boxes were merely piled one above another in the moving van, to be set up later along the walls of the new study. Thus the furniture of his mind was always neatly at hand while poor mother was still struggling to unpack cereal and canned milk for our first night's supper in the new parsonage.

What a motley crew became Ike's and my friends, stepping down from those homely bookcases! Chaucer and Shakespeare jostled *The Complete Works of Sherlock Holmes* which Dad read nights when he couldn't get to sleep; there was nothing, he insisted, as soporific as a good murder. The fat volumes of the Bible Concordances and Commentaries stood by the thin red morocco volumes of his beloved *Journal of John Wesley* which Dad had gone without lunch for a month to buy, even secondhand. Balzac rubbed Parisian elbows with salty homespun "Cap'n Eri" of Cape Cod fame. Poetry ranged from Homer's wine-dark sea to the gay dangerous candle burning at both ends.

Ike and I were allowed to sample any of Dad's books we

fancied; we read anything our minds could chew. Words we did not understand we skipped or, if vital to the plot, looked them up in the big dictionary on its black iron stand almost as tall as we were. At ten I had devoured all of Dickens, wept with Little Nell, hungered with Oliver Twist, watched the terrible Madame Defarge knitting while guillotined heads fell into a bloody basket; I had galloped with armored knights, with the terrified wind in my hair, across the Scottish plains of Sir Walter; I had shivered through the Paris sewers with Victor Hugo.

"What horrible nightmares you must have had!" one of my friends shivered when I confessed to this highly seasoned childhood fare.

If Ike and I had nightmares, I do not remember them. Horror that has no basis in his experience rarely touches a child. There is plenty of blood in fairy tales too; the Wolf eats Grandma, and Jack kills the Giant, while even in the wonderful *Alice,* the Duchess callously throws the baby about. Only when I identified myself with the hero did my heart leap up, for imagination springs from the challenge of great ideas and ideals. I forgot the horrible Madame Defarge in the flaming cry of that man who gave himself for another, "It is a far, far better thing that I do. . . ."

What has become of the great shouts of literature? Of the declamation contests where Ike and I used to repeat in irony even a child could understand, the query of Southey's little Peterkin:

> "O tell us all about the war
> And what they fought each other for?"

> "Why that I cannot tell," said he.
> "But 'twas a famous victory."

Ike used to mount to the very top step of our back stairs to be as tall as he could to cry, "Fourscore and seven years ago. . . ." We were, at will, Lincoln, Napoleon, or Carrie Nation. Imagination could never atrophy for us to a shriveled useless appendix.

Ike and I learned too in Dad's study that "intolerance" is a sharp blade that cuts not only the victim but the hand that wields it. One morning, curious because of the author's queer name—Wigglesworth—I took down from the study shelf a thin brown volume of his verse. Horrified, I read his apostrophe to babies who had not been baptized before they died:

> Depart to hell,
> There you may yell
> And roar eternally. . . .

"It's a lie, isn't it?" I flung myself and the open book upon Dad's stomach as he lay reading. "God wouldn't do that . . . not to little babies like Nan's Jonathan!"

"Would you?" Dad put a steadying arm about me. "Would I? Then don't ask foolish questions about Infinite Love. Hey, what are you doing to Mike Wigglesworth?"

"Throwing him into the wastepaper basket where he belongs!"

Dad reached down, plucked out the thin brown volume, put it carefully back upon the shelf. "What people believe depends upon where and when they were born. It would be ridiculous for you to believe in witches as John Wesley did."

"I don't believe it!" Not the wonderful John who'd started our Methodist Episcopal Church! I knew all about his helping to avoid the bloody revolution they had had in France by substituting for England's common people "a revolution of the spirit"; about his brother, Charles, who'd written the hymns we sang in church; about their remarkable mother, Suzannah, who'd trained each of her eighteen babies to cry softly by the age of six weeks. . . . John Wesley believe in *witches?*

"You're joking!" I gasped to Dad.

For answer he handed me a red morocco volume of the *Journals*, open at John's own words: "Giving up witch craft, is, in effect, giving up the Bible. . . ." Dad took the little volume from my startled grasp, smoothed the soft leather as if it had been the hand of a friend. "To me it's very comforting that John was human, not just a great leader sitting in solitary grandeur upon a mountain peak. You see, Susie. . . ." He hesitated, ran his ink-stained fingers through his fair hair so that it stood up in untidy peaks like a schoolboy having trouble with his homework. "Truth is never static; it is always becoming something else. God does not change nor do the rules that govern his universe, but our *understanding* of truth changes as we ourselves grow in knowledge. The Methodist Discipline will read quite differently a hundred years from now."

But the Discipline was second only to the Bible in our house! I drew a deep shaken breath. "You mean, sometime it may be O.K. to dance? To go to shows?"

"Perhaps."

But it wasn't fair for the Discipline to be living yesterday and I today—I who had been born with rhythm teasing my feet, singing in my whole body! Why couldn't I dance as lightly, as innocently as tall grasses in Dorr's meadow out back of our house? But I knew why; because I was the minister's daughter in this year of our Lord, 1906, because I'd make Dad lose his job. And I loved my Dad. He glanced at my stricken face, sighed, put down his book and got up, suggesting, "How about making some strawberry ice cream? It's too hot to read anyway."

"O.K.," I agreed listlessly. But inside I was boiling with injustice that couldn't be righted in this world but maybe in the next. "The first thing I'm going to do when I get to heaven," I promised Dad fiercely, "is to take ballet lessons."

"Why not?" Dad grinned. "But look out for comets!"

Turning the crank of the old iron-bound freezer was a fine way to do what Ike called "running off the willies." The strawberries in our back garden were warm and sweet with sun as we kids picked them (eating every other berry). Mother washed them in the cool kitchen, added sugar, eggs, and cream; then Dad clamped down the top of the freezer tightly while Ike and I made a game of throwing in ice and salt, turning the crank round and round, round and round. It was hot work but when the time came to take out the dash, we had our reward. As we licked alternately it tasted deliciously of ripe sweet berries, salt, sweat, and cream, a mixture that dripped lusciously red and cool down our chins. We didn't have to wait till supper either to sample our wares; the instant the strawberry ice cream was frozen, we four would sit down under the shade of the great maple tree in our back yard, cooling our hands and throats with brimming bowls.

But the best part was "the last lick."

When Dad and Mother came home that evening from Wednesday night prayer meeting, Ike and I would be fast asleep up in our own rooms but the call would come up the back stairs, "Wake up, kids! Time for the last lick!" We would stumble down in our long white muslin nightgowns, blinking at the brightness of the kitchen gaslight, grab our spoons to dig into the cool ambrosia, while Dad and Mother sat there, eating too and smiling at the dreams still in our eyes. Homemade parsonage ice cream was not something to be devoured alone; Dad and Mother couldn't enjoy it even at midnight, unless we kids had some, too.

There is a gentle therapy in old and young working and playing together. Dad and Mother were more fun than any of the neighborhood kids our own age. From the Fourth of July when we were so small we shot off our firecrackers from a contraption Dad made by putting an empty spool on the end of a stick, till we were in high school, shouting down the mile-long hill nights on our homemade double-runner, our amusements were "do it yourself."

Our biggest family project was the skating rink we built the winter Ike was five in our Dorchester parsonage's back yard. Dad sank some two-by-fours into the ground before it froze, and Ike and I helped tote great buckets of ashes from our coal-burning furnace to mound up the wooden siding. After the New England temperature had dropped below freezing, we flooded the back yard with the garden hose night after night—and behold a skating rink that was the envy and playground of all the neighborhood small fry! I was old enough to have single-runner skates clamped onto my heavy boots, but Ike had, to his disgust, "double-runners." The older boys who swarmed the rink with hockey sticks and pucks used to tease Ike unmercifully.

"How can you play hockey with baby skates?" they sneered. But Dad said he couldn't afford to buy Ike new ones this winter; he'd have to make do with what he had.

"Lee, those big boys are knocking down the smaller ones with their sticks!" my mother protested, looking alarmed from the kitchen window. "You ought to send them away. It's dangerous!"

"No," Dad said. "Ike has to learn to fight his own way. A couple of good whacks won't hurt him."

Ike was determined to play hockey with the bigger boys or die—as he very nearly did. He'd skate after the rest madly, his cheeks flaming, shouting, waving his short stick; but he simply couldn't keep up on his double-runners. So one day he swiped my single-runners which were too long for him; they tripped him so that he fell on the ice, hit his head and lay very still. I rushed up to Dad's room where he was dressing to go out on his parish calls, yelling, "Come quick! Ike's killed himself!"

Dad's long preacher coattails floated out behind him as he ran, but when we got back outdoors Ike was just picking himself up, shaking his head groggily, practically standing on his wobbly ankles but upright and still game.

"Wait a minute, Son!" Dad went to strap on his own skates, slid out in an easy arc onto the ice where the older boys scuttled away to give him room. "Take hold of my coattails," he ordered Ike. "I'll give you a flying start."

Staggering dizzily, agonized at his failure before the others, Ike, trying not to cry, grabbed at Dad's coattails—and was off to a magic trip. Dad skated faster and faster, twirled and twisted on the ice, yet was careful not to make too abrupt a turn so that Ike would fall again. He ordered, "Now let go, Son." When Ike obediently released Dad's long preacher coattails, carried on by the momentum, he actually slid upright for a few seconds.

"Hey lookit!" Ike yelled. "I'm skating! Single-runner!"

And tumbled down, of course. But this time Ike started off again proudly on his own, while Dad quietly unbuckled his skates and went off to make his parish calls. Before that winter was over, Ike skated so well on my skates, which we used alternately, that he was undisputed captain of our scrub backyard hockey team. Wasn't it, after all, his yard? What Dad had given Ike was better than the skates he couldn't afford; it was again the terrible power of the unseen—Ike's belief in himself.

Yet who doesn't yearn for such security? For Someone's coattails to hold onto when the way grows dark and lonely? Ike was to find Dad's again later when he needed them most.

Chapter Four

WHEN IS A LIE NOT A LIE?

THERE are all shades of lies, black, orange, red, sneaky yellow, right down through the spectrum to white lies as transparent and tough to tear as cellophane; and everyone makes use of an evasion of some color at some time. It was especially bewildering to Ike and me, living in the midst of telephones, doorbells, and parish emergencies—a parsonage is a cross between a railroad waiting room and a hospital for broken dreams—to try to decide what was an "abomination-unto-the-Lord" lie such as had finished off Ananias and Sapphira and what was mere politeness. When the phone would ring after midnight, Dad would stagger sleepily to assure the anxious parishioner, "I was awake anyway. . . ." "Tact," Mother assured us PK's, "never hurt anyone." Yet she used to get annoyed with Sister Smythe's subterfuges. She was a bedridden widow who was always bullying her browbeaten spinster daughter into calling up Dad at odd hours to wail, "Mother's dying! Please come right over!" But when Dad got there, Sister Smythe would be lying there among her pillows in her best nightgown with a red paper rose pinned to her shoulder and a coquettish smile.

"She could die just as well after breakfast," Mother grumbled one day when Dad had had to rush over there at six A.M. so Mother had to get up to make coffee. "All she wants is to see a man."

"She's lonesome," Dad excused her. "Poor soul."

But if pretending to die just so you could see the minister wasn't lying, what was it? I used to wonder.

When Is a Lie Not a Lie?

Mrs. Newte, chairman of the parsonage committee, was one of those who always called a spade a spade. She'd been suspicious of the way the parson's kids were being brought up ever since the first day when she'd met us at the door of the Dorchester parsonage. It was late in the afternoon; Ike and I were not in our most amiable mood. We'd had a long, exciting day, up since sunrise tearing up rugs in the parsonage we were leaving, eating breakfast on top of the familiar packing cases, tying up the legs of the piano in old comfortables till it looked like an adipose old lady, scrambling excitedly to ride high up on the very top of the load of furniture. We pitied the other neighborhood children watching us wistfully; poor things, they might have to live in one house all their lives! Perched on our high seat, about to ride all of thirty miles, we put on all the airs of Christopher Columbus.

But the May sun had been unseasonably hot; Ike had dropped the sandwiches which Mother had provided for our lunch down into the tangle of furniture where they couldn't be rescued, so when we arrived at sunset at the new parsonage on Evans Street, Ike and I were hot, hungry, and in no state to be tactful.

Mrs. Newte was tired, too. She was a tall handsome woman whose big hips and ample bosom were clothed in expensive tweed and the lenses of her glasses were so thick you couldn't tell if her eyes behind them were friendly or as sharp as the petulance in her voice because we were so late arriving. She insisted upon taking us at once on a tour of the parsonage furniture to show us all the scratches the former preacher's children had made and to hope we wouldn't be such little vandals. That horsehair sofa, she announced, she'd had in her own living room for twenty years—"a genuwine antique"— before she donated it to the preacher's back parlor, and she pointed with pride at the "Joseph throw" of many colors which, folded neatly, covered the hole at one end of the sofa, a work of art which had been crocheted by her own remarkable eight-year-old daughter, Eloise.

"I'm hungry!" Ike wailed. "I want my supper!"

"Sh," Mother hushed him, listening politely to Mrs. Newte tell how clever Eloise was. Why she'd already collected twelve feet of pennies for the Sunday school contest!

"The Sunday school is raising money?" Dad asked, interested at once.

"A mile of pennies to paint the vestry," Mrs. Newte explained. "Each child is given a paper long enough to hold twelve pennies. When it's full he gets another. Whoever earns or collects the most cash gets a silver pen and pencil set."

"I've got twenty-four pennies in my donkey bank!" I boasted, eagerly. "I could use that."

Mrs. Newte inspected me coldly, pointing out that Eloise already had turned in a hundred and forty-four cents, away ahead of the rest of the parish children. "How old are you?" she asked Ike.

"I'm three, but I'm smart," Ike told her and Mother asked hastily if I couldn't find the cereal, sugar, and canned milk in that box out in the kitchen and fill Ike up.

Imagine the vast surprise two Sundays later when I turned into the Sunday school fund a hundred feet of pennies! The superintendent asked, startled, "Where did you get all this money, Susie? You're sure it's all—well—yours?" After all, I was only six.

"It belongs to the Lord," I said virtuously.

Eloise who was sitting down in the front seat sniffed angrily and wiped at her runny nose with the arm of her tan Sunday coat. She was a skinny child, with lank brown hair, a perpetual cold, and an eager-beaver air of wanting to be patted on the head. You could hardly blame her for hating me heart-

When Is a Lie Not a Lie?

ily when I retired, radiant, to my seat, clutching the coveted silver pen and pencil set, while everyone clapped madly for the new minister's daughter instead of for Eloise.

But later, back home at the parsonage, while Ike was trying out my new pencil on the nursery wallpaper and Mother and Dad were dishing up Sunday dinner together in the kitchen, she began to worry. "Lee, where on earth did Susie get *twelve dollars?* I know she's been running errands like mad the past two weeks but still. . . ." The cake pan in her hand fell with a tinny crash to the kitchen floor as she gasped, "The missionary collection I put up in your desk drawer for safekeeping . . . it was twelve dollars and fifteen cents. . . . You don't suppose. . . ."

But Dad was already racing up the stairs followed by Mother to his study. "Grace Susan Nies, you come right here this instant!" The ominous tone of Dad's voice brought both Ike and me running to the study door, but I stood there unafraid, small but sturdy in my dark-blue sailor suit, staring up inquiringly all six feet to Dad's red, angry face. My conscience was perfectly clear.

"Sure, I took the money. I just borrowed it for the Sunday school. What difference does it make? It all belonged to the Lord anyway." When Dad was too startled by this reasoning to speak, Ike loyally put in his two cent's worth. "She didn't even keep a penny for a lollypop!"

"But . . . but . . ." Mother gasped. "Oh Susie!"

"Let me handle this," Dad insisted grimly. He explained, "That money wasn't yours to give. You *stole* the Lord's money!" What, he demanded did I think the parish would do to a preacher whose daughter stole the missionary collection? Ask him to resign, most likely. We would all be disgraced for life.

"But I didn't know—I thought. . . ." Looking from the horror on Mother's face to the condemnation on Dad's, I was so scared I flung myself, sobbing, down on the study floor, buried my head in my arms. Ike began to howl too, in sympathy. Dad thundered, "Nothing ever belongs to you, Sister, except what you earn with your own two hands!"

"Salvation does!" I piped, frantically, between sobs. "Salvation's free. It belongs to everybody. You said so last Sunday, your very own self."

Mother and Dad looked at each other and then down at the young sinner they'd borne together and suddenly the corners of Dad's mouth twitched. He gasped, "All we like sheep have gone astray. . . ." Mother giggled and then both of them broke into roars of laughter. Between gasps, Dad told me that of course I'd have to give the prize back and return the missionary money, but I hardly heard. I hated so being laughed at; it was the one punishment I simply could not take. I rushed back to my own room, crawled, broken-hearted, under my bed, and refused to come out or to eat for the rest of that shamefaced day. I was thoroughly cured of "borrowing" what did not belong to me.

Eloise won the contest, of course, and the parish was torn between tolerance that "children would be children" and laughter. Only Mrs. Newte was shocked to her shinbones at having in the parsonage a child who not only stole but lied about it to the Sunday school superintendent, as she insisted I had done. She and Mother had widely divergent ideas on child training.

"I do not believe in telling a child any kind of untruth, not even fairy tales," Mrs. Newte told Mother, her eyes behind her thick glasses two fantastic pinpoints of light, "I assured Eloise when she was four that Santa Claus was a pleasant myth."

"Poor Eloise," Mother thought, remembering how I'd seen

heaven on Boston Common, but naturally she didn't dare say it aloud. Mrs. Newte would never believe that being laughed at was for me a far worse punishment than a licking. But it became apparent as the months went by and winter came on that if a member of the parsonage committee got too annoyed, all sorts of things could happen—or not happen—the hole in the parsonage roof went on leaking, cracked dishes were not replaced, the coal truck didn't arrive till the kitchen pipes were in danger of freezing because the driver hadn't been paid yet for the last load. Mrs. Newte would never let the parsonage pipes or the preacher's family actually congeal, but she wasn't above making us put on two sweaters.

"She just can't help being literal-minded," Dad diagnosed when Mother, who had a fiery temper she found it hard to control, sputtered that she guessed her children with all their imagination that got them into scrapes weren't any worse than that smug little Eloise! Dad pointed out that Mrs. Newte had one redeeming quality anyway; her voice was startlingly rich and beautiful.

"Her voice is as unexpected as a blossom on a cactus plant," Mother admitted. "And Eloise isn't so bad really. I took her with the children to the Franklin Park Zoo yesterday. You know, Lee, if He can make a creature with a neck like a giraffe, the Lord must have a grand sense of humor!" She sighed, "If only He'd given Lizzie Newte a little!"

Mrs. Newte's ideas of child training and Mother's clashed again that day at the quilting bee in the church vestry where I'd come to help pull out bastings. The Ladies Aid were piecing together a star-quilt out of blue, red, and white triangles to sell at the fall fair. This seemed to me the essence of stupidity. Why cut up good cloth just to sew it together again? Not that anyone cared whether I approved or not; and I knew better than to speak until I was spoken to. One of the

sewing ladies kindly asked me if Ike had been born in Townsend, Massachusetts, as I was?

"Oh no," I beamed. "He was born in Fort Worth, Texas.
Mother and I were there too. I heard his angels tap on the
window to let Ike in."

"Angels!" Mrs. Newte gasped. She bit off her thread, glared
across the quilting frame at Mother stitching neatly on the
other side. "Now, I ask you—what will Susie think of you when
she grows up? If she finds out she can't believe what her
own mother says?"

My mother's cheeks grew pink. "Would you prefer the
stork?" She shot a warning glance at me, all ears, a basting
thread idle in my hand.

"Nature tells no lies," Mrs. Newte snapped. "That's why
we bought Eloise so many dear little pets—puppies, and kittens, and guppies."

What had guppies to do with it, I wondered, yanking at a
basting. I'd already inspected Eloise's fish bowl, and what
good were silly little fish you couldn't hold or pet or hardly
even see?

"Maybe you're right," my mother admitted honestly to
Mrs. Newte. "Perhaps we do need some pets at the parsonage."

Mollified at having won her point, Mrs. Newte beamed that
they had a big yellow cat they could easily spare; her husband
had named it Limburger because its fur was exactly the color
of cheese. Another parishioner spoke up quickly, "How about
a couple of white rats?" Mother, always careful not to show
preference between parish gifts, had to accept both offers.
But this was not the end. The parishioners were lavish with
pets they were glad to get rid of to teach the preacher's kids
biology. By the end of the week Ike and I had collected happily not only Limburger and the two white rats, but a couple
of gold fish named regally Antony and Cleopatra, a canary,

When Is a Lie Not a Lie?

a mangy parrot, a mongrel pup which after one dubious look Dad christened Hash, and a chameleon a rich parishioner had just brought back from Florida, which expired fifteen minutes after it arrived, in the bottom of our bathtub. Mrs. Newte dropping by to inspect the parsonage menagerie, said smugly that taking care of all these pets ought at least to teach Ike and me a sense of responsibility.

"*If* they take care of them," Mother moaned. "I have an awful feeling. . . ."

"If you're any kind of parent you'll see that they do," the parsonage chairman interrupted firmly. "We bought Eloise an alarm clock. When it goes off at six she gets up and does all her chores."

Ike and I did pretty well for a time. I fed and cleaned out the cage for the parrot and for Yelly Belly, the canary, and gave Limburger her milk. Ike picked up the shoes Hash chewed, hid them so the puppy wouldn't get scolded, scattered white stuff in the goldfish bowl, and fed the white rats whom he named Mr. and Mrs. Abou Ben Adam because their tribe increased so rapidly. Dad and Ike had to keep adding new cages down cellar almost as fast as they could build them out of packing boxes; but Ike loved every little pink-nosed baby. I hated their long scaly tails; nothing could have persuaded me to carry a snake-tailed rat around in my pocket as Ike did. He even carried them hidden in his sailor blouse, until the harassed teacher told Ike either he or the rats would have to stay home from school.

But it wasn't long before Mother began to complain that we children dawdled too long over breakfast and strung out morning prayers deliberately so there was no time left before school; if we thought she was going to feed all our menagerie. . . . Ike and I knew perfectly well she'd never let an animal go hungry, so, while she was still talking, we and our sense of responsibility would slide quietly out the kitchen door. We did acquire some practical biology from our animal friends; and we learned about lions from the missionary bishop who came to lunch one noon before he was scheduled to speak to a group of ladies from both our own and the neighboring churches about "Roaring Lions, Black Babies, and Sin in a Dark Continent" (a subject which seemed to include almost everything). He told us kids how a lion had come right into his missionary compound in Africa, had carried off a little black baby before anyone could stop him, and had presumably eaten it, for all the hunters found were a few small bones nearby.

"If I'd been there, I'd have shot him!" Ike cried, his blue eyes wide with excitement. "My Grandpaw could draw faster than Jessie James. So could I too, if I had a .44. I was born in Texas!"

"Ike!" Dad reproved. "That will do."

"The children wouldn't be such awful little show-offs if the parish would just ignore them," Mother lamented to Dad that evening when by some minor miracle they had a night alone. "Why do we always have to sit down in the front pew? Exhibit A?" I was going by the study in my bare feet on my way to the bathroom for a drink; by being thirsty at the right time, you learned a lot of useful things. Mother was sitting there by the crooked-neck desk light darning socks, ready to smile at Dad whenever he looked up from his eternal book, as he lay there reading on the study couch. "If only we could afford to send the children to camp this summer!" Mother worried. "There they'd be just anybody."

"They'll come out all right." Dad laid his book down on his stomach, reached for her small busy hand with his big warm one. "You're their mother, Sweet."

I went back to bed, a warm feeling wrapping me in a

When Is a Lie Not a Lie?

blanket of content, because my Dad loved my Mother so much and they loved me. As I drifted off to sleep I heard Mother say the parsonage committee had been here today to see what she absolutely had to have, and when she'd said that the broken spring on the old sofa was a menace, Mrs. Newte had snapped, "I guess if that sofa was good enough for my front parlor for twenty years, it'll do here a little longer! Some people seem to think the Aid's made of money!"

"O well, they didn't make as much as they expected at the Fair," Dad reminded her. "Sofas are expensive. Lim certainly adores the Joseph throw. You can hardly shoo her off it. We might put up a sign LOOK OUT. THIS REAR END RESERVED FOR LIMBURGER."

Who could have the faintest idea that the old horsehair sofa was going to be the cause of Mrs. Newte's telling a lie? Did Mother tell one, too? I never was able to decide. The whole trouble started at Eloise's ninth birthday party to which neither Ike nor I wanted to go. As Ike grumbled, Mrs. Newte would call us "little vandals" and make us behave, so no one would have any fun.

"That Eloise is a wart," I chimed in. "She tattles like her mother."

"You're both going," Mother announced grimly. "How would it look if the preacher's children didn't show up at the birthday party of the daughter of the parsonage committee chairman? It'd be all over town before supper."

On the day of the party Mother called us up to the bathroom, scrubbed us even behind the ears, put on our best clothes, and handed us a pink-wrapped parcel to give to Eloise. "It seems pretty sneaky to me to call a girl a wart and then take her a present," Ike remarked. He kicked at the wet bath towel on the floor. "Happy birthday! Rats!"

"Speaking of rats—Ike Nies, if you take any of your pets to

65

the party and scare the girls. . . ." As Ike avoided her eyes guiltily but Mother swung him to face her. "Promise," she ordered. "You promise me solemnly you won't even go down cellar before you go!"

"I promise," he mumbled, relieved. "Come on, Susie, let's get it over with."

We must be sure to tell Mrs. Newte we'd had a good time when we left, Mother called warningly after us, whether we did or not—if we knew what was good for us!

As we went gloomily down the street, stepping carefully to keep our newly-whitened party shoes clean, clutching the pink-wrapped package, Ike murmured, "So now we gotta drop dead. Like Ananias and that Sapphira."

"You can cross your fingers," I reminded him. "There's two kinds of lies—the polite ones people know you don't mean and the 'abomination-unto-the-Lord' one Ananias told."

"What's the sense in being polite if people know you don't mean it?" Was there a suspicious bulge in Ike's blouse? He began to run down the street toward the Newtes' house so fast I couldn't tell if the bulge moved or not. It might be just his handkerchief; it must be because he'd solemnly promised Mother. And a promise wasn't taken lightly at our house; our folks trusted us.

The party didn't turn out as badly as we'd feared. Every one we knew was there and even if we didn't play rowdy games I got a prize—a celluloid bar pin for pinning the tail on the donkey. It was when they lifted the blindfold from my eyes that I looked directly up and noticed the great lion lashing his tail, glaring at me from the parlor wall. The sepia picture was at least three feet long, so the lion looked almost as large and ferocious as if he'd been in a cage instead of only a brown frame. As I stood there, staring terrified, my heart literally stood still, and then began to pound furiously. The

When Is a Lie Not a Lie?

missionary bishop had said that day at lunch that if you looked a wild beast in the eye, it would usually back away from you, not hurt you at all. Mrs. Newte said, "My goodness, he won't bite you, Susie."

I yanked my eyes away. "He—he roared at me!"

"None of your fairy tales," Mrs. Newte snapped. "Now, children, let's march into the dining room." This was the real party, the part that counted. The cake had nine candles and after Eloise blew them all out, sneezed them out actually, for she had a cold as usual, we each had a big piece of angel cake. Ike's disappeared very fast, but it didn't dawn on me why until I saw the growing ring of crumbs around his chair. Oh my goodness, I thought, I'd better get Ike out of here! But Eloise saw the two little pink noses poking greedily out of the front of Ike's blouse, too, and screamed.

"Mama! Mama! That awful Isaac Nies brought his white rats to my party!"

At the word, "rats," all the other little girls began to run about, squealing, and Eloise stood up on her chair, still yelling. Mrs. Newte grabbed Ike by the ear, propelled him toward the front door, ordering, "You get right out of here, you—you awful boy. Susie, you too! The truth is not in you!" The front door slammed behind Ike and me and Mr. and Mrs. Ben Adam; we preacher's kids were in disgrace again.

"Now you've done it," I said.

Ike let his pink-nosed pets run up his sleeve, nestle cosily in his warm neck, pointed out defiantly, "I didn't promise Mother I wouldn't bring 'em. *I said I wouldn't go down cellar.*"

Usually I stood by him but this was too much. "You knew perfectly well what she meant. You already had those rats in your blouse, Ike Nies. You said an 'abomination-unto-the-Lord' lie!"

Mrs. Newte had phoned before we got home; she said she didn't like to tell tales out of school, but really. . . . "Don't worry," Mother promised her grimly, "he'll be punished." Ike was sent up to his room to be alone, to ponder the enormity of his crime. The words you said didn't matter so much as what you had in your heart, Mother told him sorrowfully; Ike had intended to deceive her and that was the worst kind of a lie. Would he pay the extreme penalty, as Ananias and Sapphira had? Worried, I kept running up to his room, peeking anxiously through his keyhole all afternoon but I could hear him moving around healthily. With so many kinds of lies, how could you ever be sure which one you'd be punished for, or how? What would they do to poor Ike? When Dad came home and heard the news, he went into Ike's room, stayed there a long time, and finally Ike came out very subdued but alive.

"You get a licking?" I whispered.

Ike shook his head. "Dad says he'll have to think it over— how to punish me." His eyes were red and his mouth drooped down at the corners, for this uncertainty was the worst punishment that could happen; it hung over you in a black cloud.

All the next week our entire household was gloomy; Dad no longer sang in the bathtub nor did Mother hum about *La Paloma*, the gay little dove, when she was cooking in the kitchen. Dad read sternly at morning prayers, "As a man soweth, that shall he also reap. . . ." Ike and I were careful not to slam the back door, tried to be as inconspicuous as possible. A breathless ominousness hung over the whole parsonage till Dad made up his mind how it would be fair to punish a boy who'd deliberately deceived his own mother.

The tension was not eased by my own strange behavior. Every day on my way home from school I'd stop at Mrs. Newte's house, ring her doorbell to ask, "Could I see your

When Is a Lie Not a Lie?

lion, please?" I'd stare at the sepia lion on the wall for a long time, shiver, and then run out the door; but the next day I'd be back again. I got to be such a pest that finally Mrs. Newte told Mother about my queer visits. "She looks uncanny!" Mrs. Newte said in her beautiful voice. "I can't think what she sees. It's only a picture."

"What next?" Mother sighed. "I'll forbid Susie to come to your house again until you ask her. I'm so sorry she bothered you."

She did forbid me; but the very next day I stopped at Mrs. Newte's again. I had to. When Mother asked why I was late home from school, I said I'd had to stay to study spelling. Mother looked at me so sadly that I knew Mrs. Newte must have phoned her before I got home. I added wildly, "I didn't go inside! Truly I didn't. The lion came to the front door!"

"What's got into you two children?" Mother wailed. "You never lied to me before!" Her face hardened into resolution; she went out the back door to the lilac bush, broke off a twig and told me to hold out my hand. She flinched every time she hit my reddening palm; she was hurt a lot worse than I was, though I sobbed loudly enough. Finally Mother couldn't stand it any longer; she tossed the twig onto the kitchen floor, gathered me, sobbing, into her arms, urging, "Susie, Susie, tell me!"

"The missionary bishop's lion in Africa!" I confessed wetly to the back of her soft neck. "The one he told about that ate up the little black baby! Don't you remember? Every time I looked at Mrs. Newte's lion, *I was that baby!*"

"I see," Mother said slowly. "You make up stories in your mind and they become real, don't they, darling? Is that what you do out in Dorr's Meadow?"

So she knew about that, too! Dorr's big barn was out back of our house beyond the great lush field where we kids were forbidden to go because we beat down the hay intended for

69

Mr. Dorr's cows and goats. But what warning ever kept a child out of a tempting green sea like that? I used to creep low under the kitchen window where Mother'd be at the sink washing up, wriggle my way out through the tall, sweet-smelling grass to my nest in the middle of the meadow where I could lie flat on my back, watching the clouds go by in the great blue highway of the sky. That large fluffy cloud was Jason's magic fleece; the white sail was the *Mayflower* setting out for our rocky Massachusetts shore. Oh, I sailed the seven seas lying there flat on my back; and I found in Dorr's meadow something even more precious than adventure; I found my own self.

"Yes," I told my mother. "There's people in Dorr's meadow."

Mother kissed me, gave me a little push. "Run up to the bathroom and wash your face, dear. There's cold lemonade in the icebox."

She must have had a talk with Dad, for the next day he handed me a pad of ruled paper and suggested that whenever I felt a story coming on, I write it down, get it off my chest. That spring a jingle of mine about a knight riding his horse across "the daisy-spotted mead" won a prize in a contest for schoolchildren at the Boston Public Library. So now I was getting prizes for my "lies" only they were called "compositions"! It was all very puzzling.

When Dad finally decided upon a punishment fit to suit Ike's crime of lying to his mother it was one neither of us PK's would ever forget. One afternoon when we came home from school, Ike went down cellar to play with his white rats, and not a single member of the Abou Ben Adam family was there! Frantically Ike and I looked all over the cellar, the house, the attic, and even out in the back yard, but all we could see was Lim rolling happily in the catnip bed Dad had planted for her. Mother wouldn't tell us anything, but when

When Is a Lie Not a Lie?

Dad came home from his hospital calls that afternoon he led us both over to a small mound of newly-turned earth under the rosebush.

"Abou and his tribe are all sleeping there," Dad explained sadly, for he hated to hurt us even when he felt he must. "I'm sorry, Ike. But I had to teach you a lesson you'd remember. You know the poem? They're just 'in a deep dream of peace.'"

Ike gulped, "You mean, they're all gone to heaven?"

"Well, not exactly. There were getting to be so many of them, anyway, either they had to move out of the parsonage or we did."

Ike, who'd been secretly getting pretty fed up with the endless feeding and watering of his tribe, grinned suddenly. "Is it a white-rat heaven made of cheese?"

Dad said, relieved, "Heaven is what you want most I reckon."

Ike and I didn't blame Dad for what he'd done. But we did feel pretty bitter about that tattletale Mrs. Newte; both the lion and white rat incidents might have blown over harmlessly if she hadn't kept nagging at Mother over the phone, asking how we were to be punished. We hoped she was satisfied.

Strangely enough, the instrument for the downfall of Mrs. Newte was the yellow cat, Limburger, whom she herself had contributed for Ike's and my biological training.

One afternoon about a month after the demise of the Abou Ben Adam family, our Methodist Ladies' Aid was entertaining the Women's Alliance of the neighboring Unitarian Church at tea at our parsonage. There was quite a bit of friendly rivalry between the two churches and Mother was in a stew lest something go wrong. She had us children help her move the furniture around in the front parlor, to be sure the wobbly rocker that tipped over if you bent too far backward was safely propped against the wall, that the center table was over the mended hole in the rug, and that the Joseph "throw" of many colors was draped in such a manner as to hide the hole in the horsehair sofa. "I wish to goodness the committee had at least mended the spring," Mother worried, "even if they didn't re-cover the sofa. If one of those Unitarian ladies was to sit down on that, we'd never hear the end of it." She grabbed up Lim who'd just walked into the front parlor and was making for her favorite perch on the Joseph throw. "No, you don't," Mother snapped. "I won't have cat hairs all over my clean parlor. Here, Ike, put Lim down cellar. And keep her there."

A spark flashed suddenly into Ike's blue eyes; I should have known he was up to mischief when I saw him picking something out in the garden and then sliding into the back parlor, but I was too busy helping Mother wash teacups and polish silver to pay much attention.

It was a very grand party. Sixty ladies dressed in their best clothes and manners, both Methodist and Unitarian, left their coats in Mother's bedroom where she'd put on the bedspreads it had taken Grandmaw Rouse six months to crochet. Ike and I passed sandwiches on the wedding-gift silver platters that I privately thought looked like collection plates and lied politely that yes, we liked school. (Maybe in the winter but certainly not now it was spring!) Mother at the parlor table poured tea out of the Ladies' Aid's silver teapot, sunbright for the big occasion, and Dad came down from his study to keep the ladies laughing at his stories.

Mrs. Newte, as chairman of the parsonage committee, was in her element; she had on a changeable silk dress that shimmered as she moved, and a pansy hat. You could see she was proud that we Methodists were really putting on a good party; she guessed this would show those Unitarians we knew

When Is a Lie Not a Lie?

how to do things! I heard the chairman of the Unitarian parsonage committee tell Mrs. Newte, "Our Alliance just bought our minister a new suite for his front parlor. Two chairs, and a sofa, with lovely tapestry, rosebuds on light blue."

"I prefer antiques," Mrs. N. said loftily, glancing at the old horsehair sofa to be sure the Joseph afghan was still safely in place. "Do have some more tea. How about a lobster sandwich?" She patted the Unitarian lady on the shoulder, moved graciously on to the next group.

"You'd think she was the hostess here instead of Mother!" I whispered, disgusted, in Ike's ear.

"Just you wait," he grinned. "I'll fix her."

"Ike Nies, if you dare to upset the party . . ." But he'd disappeared. I heard the cellar door open and a yellow arrow shot into the back parlor and onto the Joseph throw. Lim stood there, kneading the soft wool with her sharp toes and purring.

"Why, it's the nice kitty I gave Ike and Susie!" Mrs. Newte beamed. "Here, kitty, kitty!"

Lim paid her no attention at all. Instead she made a growling sound deep in her throat, began to claw frantically at the Joseph throw. As it slid to the floor, the hole in the sofa with the broken spring sticking through were plainly evident, with Lim digging desperately into the hole, scattering its hair innards.

"Stop that!" Mrs. Newte made a frantic dive for the cat. "Limburger!"

Lim clawed aside her hand, and dug even faster. As the ladies crowded around to see what all the excitement was, the humiliating wreck of the Methodist sofa was clear to every smiling Unitarian. Mrs. Newte turned a deep red; her lips were going in and out and her hands were trembling, and she didn't dare look at the Unitarian parsonage chairman she'd boasted to about antiques. Even when Dad came to the rescue, grabbed Lim and thrust her yowling back down cellar, Mrs. Newte looked as if she'd like to sink right down through our back parlor floor, pansy hat and all.

Mother said, trying to smooth things over, "I can't imagine what's got into that cat! Won't you all have another cup of tea?"

"It doesn't matter, Mrs. Nies. The new sofa'll be here tomorrow anyway." Mother stared unbelieving at Mrs. Newte, but her voice had never been so bland, so dulcet. "You can give that old couch thing to Morgan Memorial! Didn't Hellman's phone yet to ask what time they could make delivery?"

Hellman's was the biggest and best furniture store in town. "Why, no," Mother gasped. "Not—not yet!"

Mrs. Newte dazzled Mother with her too-bright smile. "It *was* the green velvet covering you wanted, wasn't it? The expensive one with the deep pile?"

She was lying. I knew it and so did Dad, Ike, and Mother. The Methodist ladies must know too that no sofa had been ordered; but though the Unitarian ladies might suspect it, they couldn't be sure. I drew in my breath sharply at Mother still sitting there, her hand frozen to the teapot handle. Would she let Mrs. Newte get away with this? At first I thought my mother wasn't going to answer at all; then the twinkle began in her violet eyes and I remembered what she'd said about the giraffe and the Lord having a sense of humor.

She told Mrs. Newte sweetly, "The green velvet will be fine."

When I let out my breath, all the other Methodist ladies did, too, a regular gale of relief. We could still hold up our heads before the Unitarians. And we had a new sofa! Would Mrs. Newte have to pay for it? Serve her right if she did, not for shading the truth—anyone would have tried to save the

When Is a Lie Not a Lie?

honor of us Methodists—but for being so penurious, for refusing to have that spring fixed for Mother, for *hounding* us kids. . . .

After the company had all gone, Ike and I tried to sneak outdoors, fast, to avoid washing the dishes, but my Dad called us both to him. He stared down at me in my frilly white party dress and then at Ike's sparkling blue eyes under his brown Dutch clip. "By any chance," Dad asked, "do either of you know what interested Lim so in that hole in the sofa?"

Ike grinned up happily at his tall Dad. "Sure," Ike said. "Catnip."

Chapter Five

SALT-WATER SUMMERS

THE hardest thing to understand when you're a very small preacher's kid is that, in times of crisis, the parish always comes first; if anyone is sick or in trouble, getting born, married, or buried, your bumped knee or broken heart has to wait till the parson and his wife have time to become your parents again. Once while Dad was marrying two people in our front parlor, I burned my left arm badly trying to get lunch in the kitchen, but when I cried, Mother hissed reprovingly, "Will you be quiet, Susie? You'll ruin the wedding!" I carry the white scar still across my arm, though Mother dressed the burn, clucking with distress, as soon as she was free from being a marriage witness as the state law required. As long as we were in the parsonage, duty came first.

But up in Maine, summers, everything was different. For two long, leisurely, salty, and glorious months our parents actually belonged exclusively to Ike and me. We were a *family*. Dad and Mother turned into enchanted companions, hardly older than we were, who fished off the yellow cliff with Ike... "Hey, Son, what a whopper of a cunner!" or read without smiling my fairy tale about the little mermaid whose brown seaweed hair got left behind on the rocks. There was not even a telephone by which the parish could reach us except in dire need. (The many subscribers to the black wooden box with the handle to ring that hung on the wall of the village store, where interested listeners were always hanging around, made private conversations a series of public yells.)

76

Salt-Water Summers

Nobody could stop our doing things together—reading aloud, walking the sweet-fern-scented paths, or just lying silent side by side upon the sunwarmed rocks, with the sea murmuring, whispering, or thundering down below.

"Isn't it nice?" I said dreamily one bright Maine morning, as I looked up and down the empty shore. "If anyone decides to die or get married, what do we care!" I glanced at Dad and Mother standing there beside me, holding hands, watching Ike feed bits of fish and garbage to his pet sea gull, whom he called John. The instant Ike came out onto the rocks with his pan, John would circle overhead, screaming, drop down in an almost frightening swoop. But now he waddled up to eat tamely from the pan still in Ike's hand. I announced happily, "I like being all alone with John!"

"All alone—*together*," Mother amended, smiling at me.

When we four first discovered the peace that was Southport Island, Maine was not in Boston's back yard, a few hours away by chrome-bright car. To get there in 1907 meant an overnight voyage by boat to Bath, where we had to get up at four on an icy, sleep-drugged morning to change to the mail boat. This sturdy tug wandered for busy hours downriver, rousing the fog-wreathed, dreaming islands with its warning blast, "Wake up, sleepyheads! Company's coming!"

Ike and I looked forward to this hegira every July with as much leaping excitement as if we were going to Tibet. First Dad would get down the steamer trunks and suitcases from the dusty attic and we would wrangle happily over what to take. Fishlines, hooks, and sinkers were all Ike wanted; I piled up writing materials and my fiddle in its black-painted wooden case and laid on top the oilcloth cover to keep out the damp of the Maine woods. (The family insisted I practice outdoors summers to give them a vacation from my squeaks.) Dad appeared staggering under the mountain of books he meant to read. No clothes would have been packed except for Mother who sorted both thin and heavy clothing to meet the fickle Maine weather, for an icy August fog could chill to the bone without proper sweaters. The bathing suits took a whole suit-case to themselves; Dad's and Ike's were black knitted wool, rather like knee-length underwear, but Mother and I wore heavy blue-cloth sailor suits with bloomers and skirts; her long black cotton stockings were held up by garters and we all wore sneakers for the sharp rocks. When we were fully equipped for swimming we were practically water-logged already!

The trunks were sent ahead by express, but we took the suitcases with us on the streetcar from Dorchester to Boston, panting and tugging when we had to change at Scollay Square; at last we'd stagger, perspiring and exhausted, onto Atlantic Wharf where the sign said, "Boat for Bath, leaving five-thirty P.M. Keep your stateroom keys with you."

Ah, that first smell of the sea and the ship as you went aboard! The smell was compounded of the wet deck, the sullen gray harbor water rubbing half-eaten oranges and other rubbish against the sides of the ship, clifflike as we peered down, of the greasy but delicious aroma of fried clams for dinner coming from the ship's dining room, and of the excited sweat of our own weary bodies—taken all together, it was the very perfume of freedom. Not a single person aboard knew that Ike and I were preacher's kids! We might be anything, a circus clown's son and daughter, a college professor's; we night be pirates! Ike and I, our cheeks very red, would dump our suitcases in the little cabin with its open space along the top where you could peer into the lighted saloon from the upper berth when you were supposed to be asleep, and then we would dash outside. Around and around the deck we would tear as fast as we could till we barged into some irate

78

old gentleman or one of the deck hands bawled, "Quit that, ye spalpeens!" We weren't frightened. He certainly didn't belong to our parish! But suddenly we were ravenously hungry and dashed into Mother's cabin, yelling, "When do we eat?"

Mother always brought a lunch in the big basket and a bottle of milk with a wet newspaper wrapped around it to keep it cold. Dinner in the ship's dining room would have cost a dollar apiece, a fantastic sum when we could board for ten dollars a week for adults and five dollars for children, at Cosy Harbor Boarding House! Our sandwiches were large and filling, but the smell from the dining room sifting through the open grill of our cabin was wistfully ambrosial.

"Some day when I get rich," Ike dreamed, sniffing enviously, "I'm going to buy me *two* big steaks! With french fries *and* ice cream. And eat every bite myself."

"You'll be sick," I warned. "Like you were when you ate all those lobster salads last summer."

Cosy Harbor boardinghouse where we stayed because it was inexpensive and the almost landlocked harbor allowed safe rowing for small children, had about twenty guests, mostly teachers, secretaries, or ministers and their families. It was run by a retired minister and his wife and we all ate family-style at a long table. Every Friday supper we had lobster salad which Ike adored so that once, staring hungrily through the screen at twenty tempting salads all lined up in a row, Ike had yielded to temptation. He ate his way all down one side of the table before he became deathly ill. Ike glared at me now for reminding him.

"Well, anyway, I don't sit on the rocks and write drippy poems about 'Why the Seaweed Weeps.'"

"Children, if you don't behave, you can't sit up for the band concert tonight," Mother warned, separating us to prevent mayhem. Just then the band crashed into "The Stars and

Stripes Forever" and Ike and I rushed to capture two red plush seats in the saloon, scrunching down so we'd be inconspicuous, so mother wouldn't remember we ought really to go to bed because we had to be up so early next morning.

Getting up before sunrise to change to the mailboat at Bath was always, at first, a nightmare, with our eyes still glued half-shut with sleep. The tiny electric bulb in the cabin ceiling gave only a dim glow by which we had to stagger about, stuff our nightclothes into the bulging suitcases, try to put our left foot into our right shoe. Ike refused flatly to wash his face, for who could see the dirt? He and mother argued so long that we almost missed the mail boat.

That sail downriver was like being born again. At first, wrapped in the dark womb of the morning, we were too uncomfortable to stir, sat hunched upon the canvas deck seats, but gradually as the sunrise neared the chill would pass; the white veil of the fog would lift to show us how thrillingly near the dark rocky shore we were. It almost seemed as if you could reach out your hand, touch the bank slipping by, the river ran so narrow and swift. We children would edge close to the rail to watch the red glow deepen over the tops of the dark pines, to look down, shivering more with excited fear than cold, at the angry foaming water of the river. The whirlpools at Hell's Gate where the river narrowed had, as we knew, swamped many a small craft. We stared down at the frightening oily funnels in the black water; and, as we bucked the swift-running tide, we could hear the bells ring in the engine room, feel the boat seem to hesitate, to shiver, too. Then she'd spurt ahead triumphantly, going faster and faster, till we were steaming along easily. Hell's Gate was behind us for another year and ahead the glorious red sun was burning the tops of the tall pines. We had been born into a new day, a new Maine summer.

Salt-Water Summers

Sun-warmed, we settled down to enjoy the winding trip among the endless little islands, distributing mail and passengers at sleepy wharfs which appeared mysteriously from around the bend in the river. When the warning ship's whistle would sound, relatives would erupt from the cottages along shore, their clothes hastily flung on, their hair uncombed but with their faces bright with welcoming smiles. "Hello, Tom! Had a good trip, Sally? The bacon's sizzling. Here, let me give you a hand down the gangplank." We screamed greetings ashore at friends we saw only once a year, waved violently back at perfect strangers; but we were all akin, members of the salt-water fraternity who'd get up gladly before sunrise to greet a bright Maine morning.

By the time we arrived at the Southport landing where we disembarked Ike and I were so ravenously hungry even the crusts of last night's sandwiches tasted marvelous. Cap'n Hiram would be waiting for us on the wharf with his buckboard drawn by two spanking big black horses. He always said exactly the same thing:

"Mornin', folks. All them suitcases yourn? Great jumpin' Jehosaphat. Lucky the turkle carries his suitcase on his back. Ike, I got some split-gut fishhooks for you down't the boathouse. You'n Susie kin sit on the front seat but leave them reins be!"

No foolishness about, "Did you have a good winter? How are you?" Cap'n Hiram took right up where we'd left off last year. It was a wonderful feeling, as if nothing had happened since we'd been away, as if Maine had been here all winter waiting for us.

The black horses pawed the gravel; the suitcases were tied on the back; we bounced, impatient on the hard seat and then were off, right into the heart of the dewy morning where the birds were singing like mad and the smell of sweet fern and

81

salt water made you ache for the breakfast waiting at Cosy Harbor, a mighty breakfast of bacon, country eggs, and milk so yellow it was almost cream. Ah, me, it would be heaven indeed to hear again the river boat whistle around the bend, to see Dad and Mother sitting there behind us smiling at each other on the back seat of the buckboard! To hear the gay clatter of the black horses' feet along the yellow gravel road, saying over and over, "You're home again, home again, home again!"

Dad and Mother frequently slept luxuriously through breakfast, so we kids were free as air to do as we pleased. Ike made a beeline for the harbor; laden with fishhooks and gear, he'd drop into his green dory, push off, and come ashore only to eat or sleep. One summer he caught a thousand cunners, all in Cosy Harbor! Occasionally I could get him to row me across to Pratt's Island which formed the outer rim of the little harbor. The southern point of land looked directly out to sea so that on what Cap'n Hiram called "a pretty day" you could see clear out eleven watery miles to Seguin Lighthouse on its barren turtle rock. ("Seguin" is Indian for "turtle.")

My favorite path in all the world was Cathedral Walk which led from the harbor side of Pratt's Island down to the open sea, to the abandoned house on the beach which we called our "castle." Tying the dory securely to a rock, Ike and I would scramble ashore, crushing slippery brown and gold seaweed under our feet, climb up through the hot meadow where the crickets were sawing away like crazy, enter the grove of great pines so tall they seemed to hold up the blue sky. Cathedral Walk was indeed like the aisle of a vast outdoor church. Above us arched the great arms of the ancient pines stretching higher and higher in silent prayer, and down below where the sunlight filtered through in golden patterns, the thick carpet of the moss fitted close about their roots, where mice and men

Salt-Water Summers

scampered for a few generations and then were gone into the vast silence. The stillness in here at first was almost frightening. No matter how loudly the sea crashed against the yellow rocks outside or the gulls screamed overhead, or the crickets shrilled in the outer meadow, Cathedral Walk was always hushed, cool. When Ike and I entered, it was as if a thick padded door closed behind us shutting out the clamor of the world.

Awed by the quiet, Ike and I would unconsciously move closer together for protection from we knew not what, and the muffled beating of our hearts was louder than the distant murmur of the sea. We stood so motionless, so enchanted, we could see the motes dancing in a broad beam of sunlight, knew that we ourselves were no more important and were content that this was so, to be a small part of this soundless prayer of the great trees. Suddenly a gray squirrel would begin to chitter, scolding high up on a branch, relieving us from the spell that held us. Then we would run, shouting, down the path to the sea and our castle.

What a pity children today too often are cheated of such peace! They are so busy tying knots, "souping up" their jalopies, roaring over the sea with outboard motors, so conditioned to racket that some of them cannot even study without the radio, TV, or the latest bebop record going full blast! There is no time just to stand still under the cathedral pines, to listen to silence and the deep primeval peace. Yet there is a universal language that speaks only to the quiet heart. I sometimes wonder if we wouldn't get closer to international understanding if, instead of "summit" conferences and alphabetical treaties, we all sat down on the shore of the Maine sea and listened to eternity roll.

Another path we four always liked to take together led to the little cottage perched like a gray gull on the shore above the sea cove. "Anyone want to walk over to Good's with me to buy some sugar cookies?" Dad would call and Ike and I would yell, "Me! Me!" Mrs. Good's cookies were not bakery airy-fairy nothings; they were large enough to stick to your ribs, dripping with sugar. We'd sit on her sun-warmed back steps to eat and to listen to her six-foot captain husband's salty humor. When Ike asked him how old he was (why not, when everyone asked us kids?) Cap'n Good's blue eyes twinkled in his sea-wrinkled face.

"Wal, Sonny," he drawled. "I was eighteen when I fust dropped anchor with my good wife, here in this very house. 'N I been here, off'n on, ever sence. Figure that one out by algebry!"

"Off and on" was right. Like many of the village men, Cap'n Good had sailed around the world but had found nothing so lovely as the little Maine village where he was born. Now he was ashore for good, and since his heart got "too dickey" to haul his lobster pots, he eked out the family income chiefly by picking berries for the hotel. Odd to be master of a ship, with the power of life and death almost—and to end up picking blueberries! "It ain't what you do; it's how you tackle it," he'd explain to young Ike who loved to help pick and to listen to the cap'n's sea stories. They were a funny pair, the big wise man and the small sneakered boy. I never saw Cap'n Good without his great sea boots; I used to wonder how he managed them in bed. Ike would grab a pail, walk spraddle-legged down the path after the cap'n as if he too wore heavy boots. They'd tackle the high-bush berries first and then squat down in the hot meadow to pick the smaller ones. The old man never tired of making Ike's blue eyes pop out as they worked. He told about the terrible storm where more than eighty fishermen from Southport were lost at sea so that there was black mourning in every snug little house along shore; of the big blow where a sailing vessel "walked herself right up the rocks at Newagen Harbor." But the story Ike liked best was about the big brown bear who'd attacked the Cap'n one day in the deep woods.

"When he come at me, his mouth slaverin' and breathin' through his jagged teeth," the cap'n would roar, illustrating frighteningly, "you know what I done?"

"No!" Ike gasped. "What?"

"I reached right down inside his mouth, grabbed his tail— and turned that crittur inside out!"

"You think he really did, Dad?" Ike asked that night as the four of us sat around the Cosy Harbor living room fireplace, reluctant to leave its warmth for the sea-damp beds.

Dad's eyes twinkled as his big hand ruffled Ike's brown Dutch clip. "Ask the Cap'n. Maine people have real salt in their veins, salt that hasn't lost its savor. You're lucky to have a friend like that to anchor to."

It was a desire to get to know these salty Maine people, to make them our real friends, that led Dad and Mother to buy the tiny shell of a house on the sea end of Southport Island, called by the early settlers "Newagen." The first settlement died out, killed either by cold, starvation, or Indians, leaving behind only banks of empty white shells to mark their passing; but Newagen, the town, returned, hardly more populous now than in pioneer days. The dozen or so white or gray little cottages were scattered hit-or-miss along the shore or winding gravel road. If one man wanted to face the ocean, he did; if another disliked the sea prying in his windows, he turned his house toward the road, where the neighbors sauntered by.

"Newagenites are as independent as the sea itself," Dad used to chuckle. "They won't accept us just because we've moved in next door. We'll have to prove ourselves worthy neighbors. I sure hope we can."

The cottage on the shore was a tight fit for us four. There was only a tiny living room downstairs and a dark closet of a kitchen, while upstairs was an open loft where we all slept, with green curtains hung in between the cots. There were cracks in the outside walls where you could see the sky, and when it rained the water ran in a brook underneath the front door. We were so close to the sea the villagers used to shake their heads, warn us that sometimes on a flood tide, in a bad blow, the waves could lap our front steps. But we loved the beat of the rote in our ears, a great clock ticking away the lazy hours. From our screened front verandah, the real living room of the house, we could watch all the ships going by on their way to Boothbay Harbor or inching along the horizon to Spain, perhaps? The sea was our nearest neighbor and it didn't belong to our parish.

The first evening when we moved in was cool for August and the four of us huddled around the wood fire in the small iron stove where we could watch the fire flicker through the cracks. Mother glanced up at the rack where the kerosene lamp shed a faint golden glow down upon our drowsy faces and sighed with content.

"Lee," she said dreamily, "do you realize this is our first real home? The first time since we were married when we've had a front door we can shut—and open it only when we want to?"

We may have lived in a shack, but we were rich. We owned the yellow cliff outside our door, the blue mysterious arch of sky and sea; and the salt-sharp intoxicating air. Best of all, our Maine neighbors slowly came to call us friend. We weren't sure they'd actually adopted us till one night when Dad had gone back to Dorchester to preach for the weekend. (All four weeks of July were vacation for him, but in August he went home to preach in Dorchester each Sunday, visited the sick in the parish, and then rushed back to Maine as fast as he could.) This very stormy night Mother remembered uneasily what the villagers had warned about our house not being above the flood tide all year; she lifted the lamp anxiously to the window to watch for the encroaching dangerous water—and saw, huddled on our back steps, the dark, mysterious figure of a man. Her heart turned over with fear. Who could this be, with Lee away? Then the man, huddled in his oilskins against the rain and wind, turned his face up to the light.

"I figured ye might be nervous, alone, so close to the sea," Tom Perkins, our next door neighbor inshore, explained sheepishly when Mother made him come inside to dry off by the stove, to sample her coffee and cookies. "I thought I'd just watch the tide turn, be sure ye were all right. I didn't heave out a yell for fear of frighting ye."

Tom's wife, Temperance, became Mother's closest friend at Newagen and we learned from her what Maine people were really like, as loyal as the granite upon which their homes were built and about as reticent about their own business. They had their own set ways of doing things, such as putting up bars at the parlor windows when a member of the family "went queer" and taking care of him themselves, instead of sending him up to Augusta to an institution, and marching three times around an open grave before letting down the lonely coffin. Dad commented, "They're just themselves, take 'em or leave 'em."

Temperance was a round, plump, little woman, crisp as the starch in her fresh cotton dress; she wore her knot of fine black hair pinned on the top of her head and her black eyes snapped and shone when she chuckled, but always quietly. She was a wonderful cook and immaculate housekeeper; she and Mother started by swapping recipes for fish muddle and crochet patterns and ended by exchanging deep confidences. Temper ance confessed to Mother than her great wish was to go up to Augusta to visit her Aunt Emily whom she hadn't seen or written to for ten years.

"Why, that isn't far, less than fifty miles," Mother cried. "I'll drive you up in the Ford."

We'd had a car now for about two years—one of those open touring cars with the little cathedral isinglass windows in the back—but the roads from Bath to Boothbay were so rocky and rutted that we seldom used the Ford except for the trip up from Boston and back. At the top of the great hill outside Boothbay, Dad used to grit his teeth, slam his foot upon the gas pedal and down we would roar, rattling over boulders, churning the mud in order to be sure we would make the top of the next tall hill. Once, in this mad rush, our car slid off the road and we had to be ignominiously hauled back by a farmer who was ploughing with a horse in a nearby field. When we were safely back on the so-called road, the horse turned his head, looked back at us—and kicked out the Ford's left headlight, as if to say, disgusted, "There, that to you!" Not even horses take kindly to change in Maine.

The state engineers had been rebuilding this road so long that the surveyor's stakes by the side of the road had sprouted leaves. But this summer that the road was actually black-topped, in a second miracle Mother had achieved her driver's license. Dad shuddered at how the state examiner could possibly have given her one; he supposed Mother must have smiled at him. She'd always start off in a series of bunny hops, race the engine, and then finally roar away in a burst of smoke and fumes. Dad begged her to keep her eye on the road and not turn to talk to anyone in the front seat, but Mother said tartly that she always seemed to get where she was going. Maybe, Dad moaned, this was because everyone except inanimate objects took one look at her wobbling down the road and went rapidly elsewhere. But Temperance Perkins had perfect faith in Mother and accepted her invitation to drive her to Augusta.

"Hadn't you better write and tell Aunt Emily we're coming?" Mother suggested.

"We never write," Mrs. Perkins said comfortably. " 'Taint needed between blood kinfolks. We'll just take up visiting where we left off. Will there be room in the car to take her some of my canned things?"

"Plenty of room," Mother said, "with just the two of us on the front seat."

But it turned out there were three of us. Dad insisted that if Mother wouldn't let him drive them to Augusta, they had to take me along. "If you have an accident, Susie can at least walk to the nearest telephone to call the ambulance—I hope," he said. We three set out about five in the morning. Mother had protested this seemed kind of early but Temperance said, "Sun's up. No need to be no lazier."

She was all ready and waiting by her front door when our whole family stumbled up, sleepy-eyed, preferring to follow Mother on foot down the rocky path from the cottage to the main road rather than risk riding. Temperance was neat and perky as a blackbird in her black Sunday wool suit, black sailor hat pierced with a silver hatpin to hold it to her neat knob of hair, and black kid gloves. She was almost entirely surrounded by big brown paper cartons of jars—canned lobster, strawberries, venison, blueberries, and canned honey to take to Aunt Emily—and she carried a big bunch of bright-colored dahlias wrapped first in a wet newspaper and then in a dry one.

"To put on Uncle Fred's grave," she explained. "He's Aunt Emily's husband. He's been dead these ten years, but it would please Aunt Emily. We go right past the cemetery on our way into Augusty. And this basket here has lobster sandwiches for our lunch."

Dad piled all the stuff into the back of the Ford, offered again to drive us to Augusta, got turned down flatly by Mother who bunny-hopped off indignantly—and then repented enough to wave him good-by. "Put both hands back on the wheel!" Dad yelled. "Keep your eye on the road—oh, merciful heaven!" An ice cart had just rounded the bend in the narrow gravel road, but the driver took one look at the Ford and ran off into the ditch as Mother roared by, still waving.

"Get into the back seat if you're nervous," she told me coldly when I yelled, "and close your eyes." I tumbled weakly in among the cartons but my eyes were glazed open. We careened around corners, blowing the horn madly; in the narrow streets at the Harbor, Mother scraped the paint off a truck, by favoring the middle of the road, but when she asked the pursuing policeman how was his dear little daughter who sang such a nice solo last Sunday in the choir? he remembered that Dad had preached in his church and let Mother off with only a warning. Out on the open highway Mother insisted upon straddling the middle at twenty miles an hour on the theory that a line was the shortest distance between two points, so that a loud sound of impatient horns hooted us most of the way to Augusta. To add to our joys, the day turned out to be very hot. As we neared the city Mother and I were dripping with perspiration and impatience to arrive—but not so, Temperance. She sat cool and unruffled on the front seat beside Mother, with her black-gloved hands folded loosely in her lap. She didn't even turn a black hair when a yellow cat disappeared under our car and then ran yowling out the back. "When you live all your life by the uncertain sea," Dad explained to me later, "you learn to take even your mother's driving as an act of God."

Salt-Water Summers

At the big cemetery just as we neared the city, Mother asked if this was where Uncle Fred was buried and Temperance said, Yes, but not all of him; he'd been lost overboard from his dory and all they'd ever found was his arm tatooed with a mermaid. Uncle Fred had always loved her dahlias, so that was why she'd brought him some. "Couldn't we go first to get a drink? At Aunt Emily's?" I wailed thirstily from the back seat, but Temperance said it was too near lunchtime; she didn't want to barge in for a meal without warning. We'd eat our lobster sandwiches first by Uncle Fred.

Mother headed for the cemetery's granite posts, escaped both by a minor miracle, began to drive round and round the narrow roads, looking for Uncle Fred. When we finally found the Perkins lot, Temperance got out carrying her bouquet, but Mother and I waited, exhausted, to be assured this was the right place. "Here he is!" Temperance called, triumphant, leaning down to peer at a gray granite headstone. She laid the dahlias down slowly on his grave, turned to stare at the new white stone right next to Uncle Fred's. Mother called, "You'd better put those flowers in water. There's a jar and a water faucet right over there." But Temperance didn't answer or move. She stood there, staring down for quite a spell, then she came slowly back to the Ford, climbed into the front seat, and slammed the car door.

"Turn around," she told Mother. "We might as well start back right now, so we git home before dark."

"Temperance Perkins!" Mother gasped. "Have you gone crazy? I thought we were going to visit your Aunt Emily!"

"You're visiting her right now," Temperance told her calmly, pointing to the new headstone. "She's been dead and buried for two years."

Dad teased Mother all summer about her rapid round trip to Augusta but they never laughed where Temperance or any of the neighbors could hear them. "Never laugh *at* anyone, just *with* him," Dad warned Ike and me. "Mrs. Perkins probably thinks you do a lot of queer things too; going to church without a hat or gloves, for instance."

But Maine people are hard only on the surface; they have an inner core of gentleness shown shyly to those they love. One day as I was practicing my fiddle out in the pine grove beyond the cottage so the family couldn't hear my squeaks, I discovered the real meaning of the words I'd heard Dad say so often in our front parlor, "In sickness and in health . . . forsaking all others. . . ." The wife of one of the Newagen fishermen had suddenly lost her memory. She used to wander the fields daytimes picking berries, murmuring to herself, and nights she'd carry round a lighted lantern looking for her son whom she imagined lost. It was startling on a foggy night to be going down a dark path, have a lighted lantern thrust into your face as she demanded anxiously, "Have you seen my Johnny?" But we all loved the gentle soul, and her fisherman husband would never admit in so many words that there was anything wrong with his Lucy.

That day as I was playing *Träumerei* on my fiddle, I heard a rustling behind me and turned to see who was there. At first I didn't see anyone and then a tall blueberry bush moved and I saw Lucy, squatting there in her gray gingham dress with her berry bucket beside her, listening to me play. As we stared silently at each other, a fisherman's big sea boots thumped down the mossy path. It was her husband.

"Come, Lucy." He held out his hand, drew her to her feet, then turned to me, bristling loyally, "Some likes to berry and some likes to fiddle. Guess the squirrels don't mind much which." I watched the two of them go off together down the dim path, those middle-aged lovers whom sickness could not part. I hoped that sometime someone would love me as much.

Salt-Water Summers

Even as a child, I liked to listen to Maine people talk, to find how their minds ticked. I used to tag after Dad, a small-girl shadow, as he went down the path through the sweetgrass to the harbor to sit and visit with his fishermen friends; and sometimes just to sit. Then I would be quieter than a red bunchberry growing in Cathedral Walk, for I knew the smallest movement might break the spell, make Dad remember there was some language too strong for a small girl's ears.

That was how I happened to be there one hot August day when Johnny Snowman told Dad about his "sea monster." I liked Johnny the best of all Dad's friends. He was a big-shouldered, slow-talking man whose shrewd blue eyes twinkled out of a sun-wrinkled face as he stood there slapping paint on the bottom of his dory upturned on the tiny beach near his cottage at the cove in Newagen Harbor. Dad and I sat there on the pebbly beach, watching Johnny paint, listening to the whoosh of the waves as they sucked along the shore.

"You believe the Lord takes heed of the likes of me, Mr. Nies?" Johnny asked, painting busily. "A man's got to sail his own craft. If he runs her up on a ledge, thumpity, ain't no one to blame but himself, says I."

"But who gives you the strong right arm and the wits to sail her?" Dad countered, not arguing, just stating.

Johnny couldn't think of any good answer to that so he just went on slapping on paint, and the waves slapped too against the shore and the gulls screamed out in the harbor. Finally Johnny asked again, "You believe in miracles? That God would pass one to help out a feller who needed it bad?"

"I believe there are happenings we can't explain because we don't know enough yet about natural laws," Dad said slowly. "I believe the Book that says 'I have not yet seen the righteous forsaken nor his seed begging bread.'"

Johnny stared at Dad, laid down his brush. "I got something

to show you," he said. He marched up to the house, came back with a flier printed on cheap gray paper that screamed along the top in black print "*Sea Monster at Harbor. Come one, come all!*" And this is the story Johnny told us as we sat together there on the pebbly beach at Newagen Harbor, a story that was to haunt me for years, wondering what was the real answer to Johnny's query about miracles.

The preceding spring, Johnny said, he had run a rusty fishhook into his hand and blood poisoning set in. He told Dad earnestly, "The poison run right up my arm, over my shoulder, and down my back. I was some swole up." They took him over to the hospital at Boothbay Harbor where he lay burning up with fever till one morning Big Doc told him honestly, man to man, "Johnny, you got anything you want to do, do it now. You're going to die."

"Not here, I ain't," Johnny retorted. "Gimme my pants! If I'm gonna die anywheres, I want to be home." In his small brown house set close to the shore, he could hear the waves run up his cove, whisper, yell, and sing; a lobsterman shouldn't die out of sound of the sea. When Big Doc wouldn't hear of his going, Johnny called a taxi and went anyway. He fainted on the way home, had to be carried to his bed.

"For days I laid there like a dead corpse," Johnny told Dad, looking out to the Harbor where a powerboat was chugging in, the gulls yelling like crazy over the bait barrel. "Then a queer thing happened. Something—Somebuddy—said inside me, 'Johnny, you're gonna git well.' And I did. The poison ran right back up my back, over my shoulder, down my arm and out my hand."

Of course, he was pretty weak yet, too weak to overhaul his gear, to haul lobsters, or to fish; all his savings were gone and he still owed Big Doc a hundred dollars for the hospital. Johnny wished he'd thought of coming home sooner but he hadn't known he could, and a debt was a debt. But with the good fishing season over and the lobsters getting scarcer, how was he ever going to pay up? It worried him something terrible. As soon as he could stagger around, Johnny asked his neighbor, Dec Nelson, "How about us taking my powerboat and gear, going out, fifty-fifty after swordfish?" Dec was willing. They went out every day for a week but they had no luck at all. Gasoline cost money, and Johnny didn't have any. Weak, in debt, he tossed on his bed, wondering what he could do—and remembered what he'd learned in Sunday school about the righteous having bread. Johnny hadn't gone to church regular for years, and certain sure he didn't set himself up as righteous. He was a little ashamed to be bothering the Lord at this late date, but he was desperate.

"So I prayed," Johnny explained, half defiantly. Dad nodded and Johnny told his prayer. "I've done all I can, Lord. Now it's up to You to help me a little. I ain't a church man but I never cheated no one as I know of. You sent a big fish for Jonah. *Send us a swordfish tomorrow.* Amen."

But the next day when he and Dec went out, it was just the same—not a fin in sight. They cruised around all day, using up good gasoline, and were just starting for home when Johnny asked, "Dec, you see what I see out there? What's that post swimmin' along?"

"It's a turtle!" Dec said, looking where Johnny said. His voice quickened to excitement. "A whale of a big turtle!"

Johnny reached for his dart, threw it, caught the back of the turtle's neck, and had the creature on his line. "Reverse the engine," he ordered. "Let's haul her in, take a look at her." But instead, the turtle was so strong, it began to haul *them,* powerboat and all, out to sea; it sure must be a big feller! They didn't want to cut the line, lose their dart, so they raced the engine and caught up with the crittur.

95

"That ain't no ordinary turtle!" Johnny cried. "She's got a shell and flippers all right, but lookit her long neck! Like a snake." Seaweed and barnacles, all sorts of sea stuff had attached themselves to the huge shell, so that her little red eyes peered fearfully out of a mass of green and brown. "Let's lasso her flippers and tow her ashore," Johnny told Dec. "She's somethin' to see!"

So that's what they did. When they lifted that queer turtle up on the wharf at Newagen with the hoist, it weighted over sixteen hundred pounds, measured fifteen feet from flipper to flipper. Johnny kicked at the great shell with his big sea boot. "Why wasn't you a swordfish? Worth some cash?" People came running from all over to look at what Dec and Johnny had fished out of the sea, people from the hotel, from the village, from the cottages, all crowding onto the wharf, gaping. For the crittur didn't act like a turtle at all; it kept craning its long neck, blowing off water through two holes in its head more like a whale, making the crowd jump back so they wouldn't get wet.

"If we had ten cents for everyone that's come to see our monster," Dec joked, "we'd be rich."

Johnny stared at Dec. A sea monster! Maybe the Lord didn't always answer prayer in the way you expected; maybe you had to have sense enough to use what He sent! Johnny slapped his big knee, yelling, "Dec, you said it! Ten cents ain't much to pay to see a real live sea monster!"

So he and Dec towed that snake-turtle or whatever it was over to Boothbay Harbor, hauled it onto the wharf, put a tent over it, charged people a dime a look. They did it up brown, got out fliers, SEE THE SEA MONSTER, NELLIE G. WHARF. ONLY TEN CENTS. The editor of the local newspaper came down, saw the big creature, and ran a piece in his paper. The headlines shrieked, SEA-SERPENT, TURTLE,

Salt-Water Summers

OR WHAT? Sea monsters were always good for a stick. People came a-runnin' to look. Thirty thousand people live, summers, in and around the little islands near Boothbay Harbor and most of them came to see Dec and Johnny's monster. They came in sailboats, motorboats, cars, buckboards, and on foot, and they all had ten cents. The dimes rained into Dec's derby hat so fast that he had to keep emptying it; and nights when it was too late to get to the bank, he and Johnny took turns sleeping at the tent door, to watch the money and their strange silver mine that had erupted from the sea. Johnny paid back Big Doc all the money he owed and still had some left for the new gear he needed, he told Dad. He couldn't help wondering. . . .

Johnny Snowman stopped talking abruptly, got up from the beach, began slapping on paint violently on the bottom of his dory again as if that were the end of his big fish story, but even I knew that it wasn't; there was still the burning question in his mind. Johnny wouldn't rest easy until he knew the answer but he wasn't one to back Dad up against a wall, make him explain the Lord's way if he didn't want to. Johnny was a gentleman.

Dad helped him out. "What happened to the—er—sea creature? Did you put it back into the ocean?"

Johnny finished a line of green paint carefully before he mumbled, not looking at Dad, "Sold her to a feller from that place where they keep queer critturs. He come clear to the Harbor to see was she a sea serpent. Smith . . . Smith. . . ."

"Smithsonian Institution?"

"Ayuh. Maybe they stuffed her. I wouldn't know." Johnny slapped on more paint, still not looking at Dad. "Mr. Nies, you think she was *sent?*"

"You're the fisherman," Dad countered. "Was she a monster? Or just a heck of a big turtle?"

"You're the preacher!" Johnny flung back. "Was she a miracle? Or just a happenstance?"

When their eyes met at last, I saw that Johnny's were as blue as Dad's, as blue as the little waves dancing out there in the harbor, and the twinkle, flashing from one to the other, was bright as the sea foam sparkling in the sun. Suddenly Dad began to chuckle and then to laugh aloud and Johnny threw back his head and laughed, too; the two of them joined together in great shouts. I giggled too though I wasn't sure what was so funny; grownups laugh at the queerest things. When he could speak again, Dad wiped his streaming eyes, said, "I guess there are some things we won't find out for sure till maybe we get to heaven."

"I could use a good-marked chart to Upstairs," Johnny admitted. "You gonna preach next Sunday up to the Harbor, Mr. Nies? I'll be there."

It's my guess that they both made it, to Upstairs. Whenever I watch the lightning flash, hear the roll of thunder across the tiny harbor at Newagen, I wonder if Dad and Johnny Snowman aren't sitting up there, telling the sea tales they both loved, giving their great homeric shouts of laughter, not *at* each other but *with* each other. Maine isn't so far from heaven, after all.

Chapter Six

MOTHER PLAYS CUPID

Money may be the root of all evil but it never stayed long enough in our family to put forth either roots or leaves. During the years we children were growing up, Dad's salary seldom averaged over three thousand dollars (his first church paid him ten dollars a week), but even this modest sum was misleading, for he promptly gave back to the church 10 per cent of his gross income. The "Tithe for the Lord" was taken out of Dad's monthly pay check first; then the remainder was divided equally between Dad and Mother, her portion for food and household running expenses, Dad's to pay for clothes, carfare, books, medicine, and all the rest. By the end of the first week neither of them would have much left in their pockets. Conversation at the breakfast table would run cautiously.

"Lee, could you lend me a dollar? The Ladies' Aid are meeting here this afternoon and I need a pound of butter and some tea."

"But, Sweet, I just gave you. . . ."

"I know, I know. But I met Sister 'Iggins at the grocery store. Lee, she's 'expecting' again! She looked like someone had drawn her through a knothole. I simply couldn't go on buying pounds and pounds of food for us and not. . . ."

"Of course you couldn't, Darling," Dad would agree.

We all knew Sister 'Iggins. She was a Cockney who told us every Wednesday night at prayer meeting how she'd come 'ere from Hold Country to this church which, praise God, had

99

never let a body go 'ungry for her cuppa tea! Her six children were at once our responsibility and exasperation; everyone saved their own children's outgrown clothes for the 'Igginses and whatever food was left over from a church supper went to them as a matter of course. But sometime it did seem as if Mr. 'Iggins could do something more than keep Mrs. 'Iggins constantly "expectin'."

"I got her duplicates of everything I bought us and that's little enough for eight people," Mother explained half-defiantly, to Dad. "It's her seventh baby in nine years and heaven knows she's entitled to her 'cuppa.' You know what she said? I asked if she was going to have her baby at home and she said, shocked, "Aow, no, Mrs. Nies! In the 'orspittel. Them two weeks is the honly 'oliday I 'as!" Mother, smiling, held out her hand to Dad, urging, "Give."

Dad put his hand into his pants pocket, drew out four dollars and sixty-five cents, admitting it was all he had left for the rest of the month. He'd been calling on Jed Steel yesterday in the hospital, he explained. "He's almost over his pneumonia bout," Dad explained, "but he's worried sick over his big doctor's bill, so I made him a little loan. You ought to see how much better he looked right off!"

"I'll bet," Mother said coldly. "Well, that's that." She reached over, filched a dollar from Dad's little hoard. "I'll simply have to get that tea for this afternoon. And a loaf of bread. Someone always forgets what she's supposed to bring. Remember the time Mrs. Hanson forgot the bread for the missionary society and I had to cut my one loaf into sandwiches about as big as ten-cent pieces? Talk about the miracle of the loaves and little fishes!"

Hearing all this, Ike made a face at me, over the breakfast table, knowing we'd have chewed-up meat for dinner the rest of the week. Or cereal.

Mother Plays Cupid

The only thing that could save us at this time of the month was when Mr. Hunter at the wedding license bureau sent Dad over a "stray couple." A prospective bride and groom who had no home church would often ask him to recommend a minister to marry them; and since Mr. Hunter went to our church, he would send them to Dad. The strays were of all creeds—all kinds of Protestants, Mohammedans, Spiritualists, and once a Chinese laundryman with his cute, sloe-eyed little bride who said, smiling up at six-foot Dad, "We pray to Buddha. But you marry us? All samee 'Melican God, yes?" The Chinese gave Dad a wedding fee of two dollars in dimes.

The wedding fees all belonged to Mother; Dad always handed them over to her the moment the front door closed behind the happy couple and he never asked her how she spent the money. In all her forty years of married life, this was the only money Mother ever had of which she did not have to account for every penny. It meant far more than cash to her; it was the very breath of independence, her chance to play Lady Bountiful. For usually she spent the money for little luxuries for the family, a new dressing gown for Dad to lounge in when he studied so he wouldn't wrinkle his good clothes lying on the humpy couch, a party dress for me, once a secondhand policeman's hat bought from Johnny Guptile's father because a thief had shot a hole through it. Ike told Mother passionately that if she bought him that bullet-hole hat, he'd never ask for another thing as long as he lived! Naturally, the whole family could hardly wait till the wedding couple got out the front door, to see how much of a fee Mother got this time.

Dad never asked anyone to pay him for a wedding, especially not our own parishioners, but usually the groom handed Dad either two one-dollar bills or a single five. "Just a little remembrance, Pastor!" the happy groom would say and thrust a small sealed envelope into Dad's hand; or perhaps, if he was flustered, the groom would just gasp, "Here!" and rush out the door. Only wealthy parishioners who'd asked Dad to come to their home to perform the ceremony or had a big church wedding gave a fee as large as ten dollars; but when Aunt Laura's only daughter was married, Dad received twenty-five dollars!

"Oh!" Mother gasped when Dad (rather reluctantly but magnanimously) handed the check over to her. "You can have that Stanley Jones book on prayer you want, Lee!" Her eyes grew wide and soft with happiness. "And I can have a new dress for the bishop's wife's reception!" Her face clouded; it was terribly selfish to spend so much on herself, but she hadn't had a new dress for. . . . "Lee, do you think I'm an awful pig?"

Dad looked down at his small pink-gingham wife. He couldn't ever remember her spending any of her wedding money on herself before. "A flower needs its petals and a bird its plumage," he said. He laid his cheek against her soft curls. "My Sweet, did I ever happen to mention that I love you?"

Seeing there were to be no dividends for us in this wedding check, Ike and I tiptoed out of the room and left them to what Ike called, "That gooey stuff." It had never occurred to us that all husbands and wives weren't as much in love as our Dad and Mother. So the gold of experience slips through your fingers without your ever knowing what riches you hold.

Both Ike and I got pretty fed up at being asked to be in the parish wedding parties. Ike loathed the little light-blue satin suit with lace at his wrists and on the bottoms of the trousers which Mother made for him to wear as ring-bearer, and the starch in the white dress Mother embroidered for me to blossom out in as flower girl tickled the backs of my bare legs. Weddings were stupid, we decided, except maybe for the bride and groom. Who wanted to balance a slippery ring on a silver tray or to throw out flowers for someone to step on when

Mother Plays Cupid

outside the June sun was golden and sweet in Dorr's Meadow and the boys in the street were playing baseball? I told Ike passionately, "This being a preacher's kid is pizzicato!" I'd read the word in a music book and had no idea what it meant, but it sounded just the way I felt wobbling slowly down the hot aisle, trying to keep in step with the organ and at the same time see who was there.

"Aunt Ella's" wedding was the last one at which Ike and I were asked to officiate as ring-bearer and flower girl—and with good reason. We always called all Mother's intimate friends who were too old for us to address by their naked first names "Aunt." Aunt Ella had baby-sat with Ike and me many times and she insisted that she wanted "those two imps" in her wedding party even if Ike's blue satin pants were getting a bit tight for him. "Don't you dare sit down, Ike, before the wedding!" Mother warned, "or you'll be sorry."

"I won't wear 'em!" Ike stormed. "They're girls' pants. If you make me, I'll throw the ring at—at. . . ."

"You'll throw nothing and you'll act like a perfect gentleman," Mother said grimly. She bribed, "If you'll just do this for Aunt Ella, I'll let the barber cut off your Dutch clip."

Ike hated his hair cut long with the bangs, but up to now Mother never would agree to her baby's looking like a man, even if he was almost six. So now they were both, if not happy, at least agreed. Mother got him safely into his skin-tight pants and he marched down the aisle, stiff-legged, with the ring, while I followed, tossing roses out of a pale-blue basket, before the bride. But during the ceremony, after he got rid of the ring, Ike got bored, decided to do a clean-up job. Amid the grins of the wedding guests he wandered back down the aisle, picked up every rose I had thrown out. Hearing the crescendo of giggles, Dad looked up from his prayer book just in time to see Ike emerging from under Aunt Ella's long white train, clutching the last rose, beaming, "Lookit! I got 'em all!"

As we grew older, Ike and I had to act as witnesses for all the "stray" wedding couples who arrived without friends at the parsonage, as the state law required two names signed to the register. We discovered, with a sense of shock, that there were all kinds of brides and grooms. At first we had thought all of them were marrying for love as Dad and Mother had, but before long we found out there were other reasons for matrimony. "Effie's Home Restaurant" was just around the corner from our house, an excellent eating place, although the cooking was neither home nor Effie's. The cook was a tiny wisp of a man in a dirty white apron with magic in his hands when it came to pastry. He could have made much more money in a big hotel kitchen had it not been that he had a passion for gin. One morning Effie, who weighed easily two hundred, arrived at our parsonage front door with a wedding license and her midget cook in tow. After the ceremony when we all congratulated the happy couple, Effie said frankly, "I just had to marry him, Mr. Nies. It's a lot cheaper than paying wages. And if I keep him under my eye, night and day, he'll stay sober!"

Ike began to giggle but I kicked him on the shin, muttering, "Effie ought to be good for a real fee. Maybe you'll get the football you want." But when we all rushed to see Mother tear open the envelope Effie had handed Dad, it held merely a card entitling the bearer to ten meals (numbers to be punched) at Effie's Home Restaurant. "Well, anyway, we won't have to eat chewed-up meat at the end of *this* month," Ike said.

The bridal couple who really burned us up, however, were the middle-aged man and woman who woke us up at two A.M. for the ceremony. We were all sound asleep when the pounding began on the parsonage front door and Mother shook

Mother Plays Cupid

Dad, urging, "Get up, Lee. Someone's in trouble!" Dad groggily put on his dressing gown over his nightshirt, went to the door. The couple who stood there were gray-haired, well dressed, and very nervous. If they'd been teenagers Dad might have suspected they were eloping, but this middle-aged man and woman. . . . "Please marry us right now," they insisted. "We have a license."

When the groom thrust it at Dad he saw by the hall light that the groom was sixty-seven and the bride fifty-eight—certainly old enough to know their own minds, but too old to be breaking into other people's sleep. Dad yawned, "Couldn't you come back later this morning? I'm not dressed and I'd have to wake up the family to get two witnesses. . . ."

"No, we have to be married right now," the groom said, flatly. "I know it's an imposition but there just isn't any other way. If you won't help us, we're sunk."

"Well, come in," Dad gave in.

"What's the big idea?" Mother asked Dad indignantly when he told her she and I had to get dressed. We didn't get the answer until Dad pronounced the gray-haired couple husband and wife, and the groom sighed with relief as he turned to give his plump bride a loud smack.

"Well, we did it, Sally!" he exulted. He explained, "We had to elope from our children. She's got two and I have four. They didn't want us to marry for fear they'd miss a nickel when I die. So we crept out while they were in bed. Sorry to put you folks out this way, but it sure was worth it!"

He handed Dad a bill and went out with his Sally. Dad gasped and handed it over to Mother who cried triumphantly, "I'd wake up any night for a ten-dollar bill!"

This was the bill Mother paid down for the green suit I wanted so badly that I literally ached with longing. I was sixteen; up to now I had worn Mother's old skirts cut down to my size with a shirtwaist and sweater. We saw the suit first in the window of a Boston store so expensive we usually just looked through the plate-glass window and walked on. But today . . . "That is *my* suit!" I cried impulsively. "Look, Mother!" The suit was a soft deep green, the color of the smooth leaves that cradle the lily of the valley; and I knew without trying it on how becoming it would be. It was the sort of suit Sylvia Meadows might wear, Sylvia expensive and silken like her name, who sat beside me in high school, who had everything she wanted, new clothes, an English bicycle, money to buy her lunch noons at school, instead of carrying sandwiches in a greasy paper bag. In this soft green suit, I would look like other girls who didn't live in a parsonage, well dressed, sure of myself, maybe even pretty. Mother saw these thoughts chasing themselves across my thin yearning face and said abruptly, "Let's go inside, see how much it costs."

The price was forty dollars. Not even Mother had ever paid that much for a suit; for a winter coat, maybe, but not for a suit warm enough to wear only a little while, spring and fall. I knew I couldn't possibly have the lovely thing but I made the mistake of trying it on. I looked in the mirror and gasped. There was something about the color that brought out the faint pink in my cheeks, the gold in my hair. For once in my life I was *beautiful*.

I didn't beg for the suit, there was no use. But I saw in the mirror Mother's eyes and I knew she thought, as I did, that this was the most becoming suit I'd ever had on. The svelte salesgirl patted her hair back and drawled, "You'll never find anything anywhere that looks half as good, Miss." But she'd seen our shoes, Mother's worn handbag. I don't think even the salesgirl expected us to buy the suit, but suddenly. . . .

"We'll take it," Mother said too loudly. Her cheeks were

Mother Plays Cupid

blazing red and her eyes were flashing. She dug the precious ten-dollar wedding bill out of her bag and handed it to the salesgirl. "I'll pay ten dollars down and charge the rest till the first of the month."

But Dad didn't approve at all of her charging things. He said if you couldn't pay cash for what you wanted, the honest thing was to go without till you could. The salesgirl asked doubtfully, "Do you have an account here?" My mother lifted her head. "No, but I soon will. Where do I go to start one?" One good thing about Dad's old-fashioned ideas, since he owed nothing, was that his credit was good.

I wore the green suit home on the streetcar, surreptitiously smoothing its soft folds every now and then with my proud hand. I told Mother, fiercely happy, "I never can pay you back for this, never."

"Every girl needs to feel beautiful at least once in her life," Mother said. "You'll never want *things* as much as you do right now, I reckon." Her eyes grew dreamy as she remembered, "When I was thirteen, Mother bought me a red dress to go to. . . ." She stopped abruptly, but I knew what she'd been about to say, "to go to a dance." Grandpaw and Grandmaw hadn't been as strict as a Methodist parson had to be; Mother had gone to dances when she was my age. Suddenly I knew this was why she'd bought me the suit; it was her way of making up to me for what she yearned to give me and couldn't.

Mother looked at me uneasily and said slowly, "I don't think there's any need to tell your father how much this suit cost. It'd just upset him. Oh, I don't mean for you to lie to him if he asks you, but there's no need to *volunteer* all you know."

"But if he asks me, what'll I say?"

"Just refer him to me," Mother said grimly. "Besides, I'm sure to get some more wedding fees before the first of the month. Then it's nobody's business but mine how much it cost."

This spoiled the fun of the new suit a little for I'd been planning to rush up to Dad's study, to pirouette, demand, "Notice anything?" Then he'd say, "Well, if it isn't my beautiful daughter! How did you ever get that way with such a homely Dad? You must take after your mother." It was an old joke between us, how beautiful I was and how homely he was, neither of which was true; but it was a comfortable family illusion. But fortunately Dad was too busy thinking of his sermon even to ask how much the new suit cost. When I said, "Mother bought it for me," all he said was, "Oh? It's very becoming. Was it worth being waked up for, Susie, at two A.M.?" So he thought the suit cost ten dollars; well, it did, plus. . . .

"Oh, yes," I managed. When I dared look at Mother, her face was flushed a bright pink but her lips were tightly closed, stubbornly silent. She would never have deceived Dad for herself, but her children had claims on her, too. As soon as she collected enough wedding fees, she'd tell Dad all about it.

But March didn't seem to be a month when a young man's fancy turned to love and marriage. Every time the front bell would ring, Mother would rush hopefully to open the door, but Mr. Hunter didn't send over a single "stray," for two weeks. When finally one couple did arrive, one of Lim's kittens, a sport who'd turned out to be completely black, got into the front parlor and ran up the bride's skirt to her shoulder. She had hysterics, yelling, "A black cat! Bad luck! Bad luck!" and refused to go on with the ceremony. So there was no wedding fee out of that. Mother began to grow cross and tense. Usually she was relaxed and smiling, but all of a sudden even Ike's slamming the back door as he always did made her angry; she scolded me for coming to the table with wind-

Mother Plays Cupid

tossed hair; and once when Dad ventured to joke that the crust of the apple pie was soggy, Mother burst into tears and ran up to her room. Dad stared after her, really worried.

"Your Mother needs a vacation," Dad said anxiously to Ike and me. "I wish I could afford to send her home to Texas for a month, but I don't know where I'd get the money." His face brightened as he figured, "I'll write your Aunt Gay to-day. Maybe she could come for a visit, instead. A few giggles would cheer Myrtie up."

Ike and I both loved our Aunt Gay, Mother's younger sister, partly because she told us stories about Texas and partly because she knew what presents we children cherished—an old .45 with no hammer for Ike, a Dickens book for me. But mostly we loved her because she was like her name, full of laughter, so outgrowing with happiness you had to be gay too. But I knew very well not even Aunt Gay could help Mother now; what she needed was a couple of weddings—or more—before the first of the month, so she wouldn't have to tell Dad she'd started a forbidden charge account and how much she'd paid for my green suit. But of course I could hardly tell Dad that.

But Mother was never one to sit back, to let fate defeat her without fighting back. Even since we children had been able to understand, she'd dinned into our ears that nothing was impossible; if you really wanted something badly enough to pay the price, there was always a way if you just kept trying to find it. When she sent us to bring her a spool of thread or a book, often we came back, whining, childlike, "I can't find it." "If it isn't there," she'd cry fiercely, "Then make it!" We'd usually go right back to find what we'd been looking for. It was this tenacity that made her try that desperate gamble with Minnie Hanes and Ernest Rutherford Sears.

I realize, looking back, the very moment the whole thing started at prayer meeting. Mother and I were sitting behind

Minnie and Ernest while Dad rambled on about there being small credit in loving your neighbor if you liked him anyway; it was the people who irritated us we should learn to love. Minnie and Ernest had been "going steady" for years. She was the skinny, dark-haired librarian who stamped books at our branch public library while he was large, pink-faced, well fed, the cashier at our local bank. What they saw in each other was beyond me but none of my business. They would have been married long ago except that Minnie had had an invalid mother whom she wouldn't let go to a nursing home, but who wouldn't live with them; she said it wasn't fair to turn a honeymoon into a hospital. But the mother had died six months ago and still the two hadn't married; perhaps they'd come to like the way they were, independent yet having each other's company to go places, as comfortable and used to each other as two gloves of a pair. Looking at them sitting there together my mother muttered under her breath, "a bank cashier."

I knew what she was thinking—a banker ought to be worth a five-dollar wedding fee! Maybe even ten! If she could just get Minnie Hanes and Ernest Rutherford Sears to the altar before the first of the month.... But how on earth did Mother think she was going to spur them into action? Then I remembered, "If you can't find anything, make it!" If anyone could find a way to make those two get married, my mother could.

The next day at breakfast Mother told Dad to save next Monday night to be at home because she planned to ask Minnie Hanes and Ernest Rutherford Sears for dinner. She'd phoned and they'd both said they could come. After that Mother was more like her old self; she sang as she polished the silver, got out the best tablecloth to see if it needed pressing. She even sang *"La Paloma,"* about the little gray dove, a sure

Mother Plays Cupid

sign she was happy, because this reminded her of being a girl in Texas. One morning I saw her standing for a long time, looking around our front parlor. It was a pleasant place to be married in now we'd got the new davenport and two chairs upholstered in green velvet. Also Aunt Laura had donated the oriental rug that was only a little worn, because the red, yellow, and green pattern went well with the new parsonage sofa. Mother had made fresh pale-green curtains herself and put pots of flowering begonias on the window sills for more color.

"It lacks something," Mother said looking around the parlor thoughtfully. "I know!" She ran upstairs, took the rose-colored shade from the lamp in her bedroom, put it on the lamp on the front parlor table, lighted the bulb, and stood back to look. Even in daylight, the rosy glow looked warmly romantic. "There," Mother said with satisfaction. She might be stubborn, my mother, but you couldn't beat her; when she started out to make a setting for romance she did it. All she lacked now was the bride and groom.

As if this wasn't enough excitement, there was an accident that Sunday in front of our church. The March night had turned icy and very cold. Dad shook hands with the departing congregation inside the vestibule instead of at the open door as he usually did, and while we were waiting for him to finish, a little old lady in black stood shivering next to the radiator in the vestibule. Mother went over to say "Good evening," and to see if she needed a ride home in this icy weather.

"Oh no, my son's coming for me," the little old lady who wore an expensive black fur coat and a pretty feather hat explained. "I'm Mrs. Sims. My son told me to wait where it was warm till he drove up to the door. Oh, what's that?" There was a terrible crash outside and when Dad ran out to see what had happened, a big Packard car had crashed into the maple tree in front of the church and the driver was lying across the steering wheel, unconscious. It was Mrs. Sims's son whose car had skidded on the ice; and by the time the ambulance had carried him away and the tow truck had collected what was left of the Packard, his poor little mother was a jelly of apprehension. "Would someone please call a taxi?" she quavered. "To take me to Brookline? My son's got the house key. I hope the maid won't be asleep."

"You're coming right home with us," my mother said warmly, putting her arm around the shivering old lady. "Lee will go to the hospital to see how your son is. Of course, you'll stay with us tonight at the parsonage." Mother made fresh coffee, kept up cheerful conversation until Dad phoned that the son was going to be all right but the doctor thought he'd better spend the night in the hospital. When little Mrs. Sims dissolved in relieved tears, Mother insisted upon lending her a nightgown about four sizes too big for her and tucking her into bed in her and Dad's room. Mother would sleep with me, and Dad on the study couch. The Simses must have had an ample income, for the next afternoon the son turned up in a new car, thanked us profusely, and drove his little expensive-looking mother away.

Mother drew a deep breath of relief as the Simses' new car purred off. "Thank goodness they won't be here tonight when Minnie Hanes and Ernest Rutherford Sears come," she sighed. "Children, you can eat supper with us but right afterward you make tracks upstairs to do your homework. Lee, after a little while, we'll go up to your study and leave those two alone. . . ."

"But you don't invite people to dinner and then walk out on 'em!" Dad protested, puzzled.

"You do what I say, hear?" There were two little spots of color burning in Mother's cheeks and you could see she'd like to shake Dad, but she didn't dare tell him what she was up to or why. She muttered as she took the coffeepot out into the

Mother Plays Cupid

kitchen and jerked it into the sink, "Sometimes men are so *slow.*"

Mother worked all day cooking a slam-bang-up dinner and I must say Ernest Rutherford did it justice. There was chicken fried slowly to a golden brown, mountains of snowy mashed potatoes, Mother's special little rolls, and salads made like butterflies. Mother made the wings out of slices of pineapple turned back side to, cut-up slices of stuffed olives to imitate nature's decorations, and the butterfly's body was a brown date. Even though Valentine's Day was long past, Mother made little heart-shaped pink-frosted cakes to go with the ice cream. If the happy couple didn't suspect that, whatever the date, spring was here and mating time, it wasn't Mother's fault.

"I haven't eaten a dinner like this since I was a boy in Ohio," Ernest Rutherford Sears chortled, digging into his fried chicken leg. He ate two helpings of everything and three heart cakes. But Minnie just pecked nervously at her food, I noticed, in a ladylike way. She kept looking at Ernest, at the vast quantities of food he was absorbing, almost as if he'd been someone talking out loud in her library. Was she wishing she could cook like Mother? I wondered. Or thinking her beloved shouldn't eat so much on account of the little corporation he was developing in front? Mother was beaming at both of them, urging, "Have another cake, they're so tiny." And wouldn't they like their coffee in the front parlor?

After dinner, we kids were shooed upstairs. Fortunately Mother didn't have to drag Dad away because a parishioner phoned that her husband was very sick, wanted to see Dad, so he lit out, promising to return as soon as he could. Mother must have made some excuse too because in a short while I heard her skirts rustle up the stairs, past my bedroom, and I knew that the long-awaited crucial moment had arrived—

Minnie and Ernest Rutherford Sears were in our front parlor alone under the light of the romantic pink lampshade.

How would he propose? I wondered, dreamily over the Cicero I was supposed to be translating for tomorrow. Down on his knees? No, presumably he'd done that long ago. He'd simply put his arms around her and—A loud scream from the front parlor sent my Latin book clattering to the floor. And then another scream—I flung open my door to see mother running down the stairs. I ran too. I got there just in time to see Ernest Rutherford Sears, his face very red, run out of the parlor, grab his hat from the hall rack, and rush out the front door, slamming it behind him so hard it sounded like a swear word.

"What did he *do?*" Mother was asking Minnie who was having hysterics in the front parlor. "For goodness sakes, Minnie, what *is* the matter?"

"He k-kissed me!" Minnie gasped. She stood there, her eyes wild, wiping her mouth over and over with the back of her hand. She cried, "He's no gentleman. He—he kissed me on the throat!"

"What did you expect, after waiting eight years?" my mother snapped. All her nice dinner, her rose-shaded lamp, her carefully laid plans gone for nothing, just because a little dried-up old maid was afraid to be kissed! Was afraid of living.... And yet, poor Miss Minnie. This was her last chance and now she'd always be alone. My mother sighed, went to put her arms around this sobbing little born spinster and offered, "How about a nice big cup of coffee?"

After Miss Minnie had gone, Mother went right to bed without waiting for Dad as she usually did; but next morning she looked as if she hadn't slept at all, so pale and drawn that Dad urged anxiously, "I wish you'd drop by Dr. Phillips' office today and get him to check you over."

Mother Plays Cupid

"I'm perfectly all right," Mother snapped. "I just have one of my headaches. I'll go up and lie down."

My own throat went dry as I stared after her, for if Mother got really sick it'd be my fault. If I hadn't wanted the green suit so badly. . . . After Dad had gone off to make a call, I crept up to Mother's darkened room where she lay on the bed, to make the supreme sacrifice. I offered, my voice trembling, "I'll send the suit back, if you want." Mother said, exasperated, "How can you send it back when you've worn it? It isn't your fault; it's mine. I should have told your father right off how much the suit cost. Now when the bill comes in, he'll know I've been deceiving him for weeks." She burst into tears and all I could think of to do was to smooth back her soft curly hair from her forehead; it felt silky like a little girl's and it came to me for the first time that Mother wasn't so terribly much older than I was.

On the morning of the first of the month when the bills usually arrived, Mother came down to breakfast looking ten years older, with her mouth a thin, determined slit. When we knelt for morning prayers as usual she put her hands over her face and prayed out loud.

"Oh, Lord," she said miserably, "I've prayed and prayed for help to make things right, but You didn't send it to me. I don't blame You at all. If You'll just give me strength to do what I have to, I'll never, never be so wicked again. Amen."

Dad shot her a worried glance as we got up from our knees but he didn't ask what her wickedness had been; that was between her and her Lord. Also he knew she would tell him anyway when she got ready, for Mother was normally as transparent as a piece of clear ice. No, he wouldn't force her confidence. Just then it happened, what Mother had been dreading. The mailman, who came early to our end of the street, dropped the letters through the slot in our front door, and the flutter to my frightened ears was like heavy stones dropping onto the polished floor. As Dad started to get up to pick up the mail, Mother spoke.

"Wait, Lee," she said. "There's something I have to tell you first." The two little red spots into her cheeks spread to a deep flush all down her neck as she told him about the green suit, how I'd wanted it to look like other girls, how she'd paid forty dollars for it, almost a week's salary. She'd known perfectly well she shouldn't have done it, she admitted, but that wasn't the worst she'd done: she'd told me not to tell how much the suit cost and that was just the same as teaching me to lie. Mother's voice trembled, faded away, and then grew desperately louder. She wanted to apologize right here and now, not only to Dad but to us children for being a wicked, lying, deceitful woman. Would we ever forgive her?

For a moment we all three sat stunned to silence. She made us feel terrible because we knew this wasn't true; our mother was everything fine and sweet and loving, only this once she'd been tempted, not for herself but for her child. When Ike and I both burst out into sympathetic tears, Dad took command of the situation. He went over and put his arm around Mother.

"Stop that caterwauling, you two!" Dad ordered. "There's nothing to feel badly about. Darling, you only acted like a mother!" He told Ike and me sternly, "If you two grow up to be half as fine as your mother is, you'll do all right." He kissed Mother and then ordered, "Now, let's all forget it." He walked out into the hall, picked up the letters, handed one to Mother. "It's for you, Sugar."

Mother opened her letter listlessly, announced, "It's from that little Mrs. Sims." Her eyes began to grow bigger as she read and her hands shook so that a blue slip of paper fell out of the letter onto the breakfast table. Mother read aloud, "This is just a little something for you to spend as you like, for

116

something you really want, for some frippery maybe. Don't you dare send this back. It's not payment for a night's lodging at all. The Lord sent you this with His love." Dad picked up the blue slip, stared at it as Ike demanded, "What is it, Dad?"

"It's a check for twenty-five dollars," Dad told him slowly.

Mother's eyes lifted to Dad were awed pools of light. "Oh Lee, do you think. . . . No, she must have mailed this *before* I prayed!"

Dad smiled down at her and his eyes were a gentle hand caressing his beloved as he said, " 'O ye of little faith. . . . Before ye call, I will answer.' "

Chapter Seven

SEX, BOYS, AND TERRIBLE HATS

ADOLESCENCE is at once a disease and a miracle of tender budding spring. It is a time of terrible uncertainty when the victim never knows ten minutes in advance whether he is to be man or child; it is a time of growth, swift and breathless, a time of beauty, laughter, and tears. The individual has not yet built him the hard shell into which his jellylike quivering self may retreat. Most certainly adolescence is the age of the herd instinct, when to be different from the hairdo or rumpled jeans of the gang can mean utter despair.

Ike and I were apart from the gang already, simply by being preacher's kids. In the safe cocoon of our early happy childhood, we had not missed the carefree mingling of boys and girls, the crowd who dropped by after school for a lemonade or to bang out "Alexander's Ragtime Band" on the piano. But after I got to high school, everything was different; boys had changed from dirty little pests who yelled "glass eyes!" at me, when I went by, to men who passed me notes in history class to find out the answers, who might some day conceivably even walk me home from school! But if by a miracle a boy ever did stroll along with my books, how, I worried, could I invite him in when the parsonage was already occupied? Like as not the choir would be practising "God Will Take Care of You" in the back parlor; and there'd be a couple of Ladies' Aiders making coffee in the kitchen; and perhaps even some poor Stumble Brother getting sobered up with coffee. The parsonage wasn't only my home; it was an institution.

118

Sex, Boys, and Terrible Hats

My worst problem was that as a good Methodist preacher's daughter I couldn't go to the high school dances. I couldn't dance, period. Yet I had rhythm in me; I knew I had. When the drums rolled and the saxophones called I felt the beat in my very bones. I had never danced but I knew I could. What was so wicked about it?

I begged Dad, "Can't I at least take ballet lessons with the other girls in the gym? Not even Brother Wentworth could object to gymnastics!" Brother Wentworth, a dried-up, devoted little man with a squeaky voice, was the Tuesday night class leader at our church who used to testify he knew from terrible experience (it must have been fifty years ago) that dancing was "a lure of the devil, just an excuse for hugging to music!" Dad, his eyes twinkling, agreed that the female form as displayed in bloomers and middy blouses wouldn't lure many to destruction. He didn't even object when our ballet class took part in the Spring Pageant at the high school. I was a "Raindrop" in a full gray dress with silver spangles. I wore a silver crown on my long flying hair as I danced, and I adored every single instant that I "showered."

"I simply cannot see why anyone objects to dancing!" I told Dad that night, flushed with success and applause.

Dad said slowly that I should have seen the early dance halls as he had in Dallas, Texas, with a bar at one end and the call girls. How would I like to have a strange man's arms around me? Have him breathing whisky in my face as we waltzed? I fought back a wild urge to say, "*How do I know? Maybe I'd like a strange man's arms around me!*" Did bars and dancing have to go together? Certainly not at our high school dances. Anyway what was the use of even discussing something that could never happen? Waltzing in a strange man's arms—me?

But if you could do none of the pleasant things which

brought boys and girls together naturally, how were you ever going to fall in love? Get married? Would anyone ever want to marry a girl who wore glasses, even if now they didn't have silver rims? I used to stand in front of my dressing-table mirror by the hour anxiously inspecting what Mother called my "crowning glory," my fine golden hair so hard to handle because it was so long and slippery. At least my complexion was clear. But who could tell how blue my eyes were behind my glasses? One day when I forgot to close my bedroom door, Mother saw me standing there with the tears rolling down my cheeks.

"Darling, whatever is the matter?" she asked, alarmed. "Are you sick?"

Sick of being me, I wanted to tell her; instead I begged, "Do I have to wear that awful big gray sailor Aunt Lizzie sent me, to church next Sunday? Couldn't I just wear my stocking cap?"

All the other girls in my Sunday school class wore berets this winter, cocked gaily on one side of their smooth heads, while I had to make a spectacle of myself in one of Aunt Lizzie's horrible concoctions—In a day when a trip to Europe was considered an event, my Aunt Lizzie, who owned the Dallas hat shop, went every other year to Paris to bring back her "models." The hats she really sold were, of course, modifications of these extreme styles; but the Paris models gave éclat to her establishment and when they had fulfilled their usefulness, they were thriftily shipped on to "my dear niece, Grace Sue." I knew as well as anyone that there was no parsonage money to waste on merely becoming hats, but this latest Parisian creation was the worst yet. It was a large gray cartwheel of gray felt out of which my thin face with its glasses peered with all the glamor of the headlights of a Model T Ford. The very thought of the whistles of the gang

Sex, Boys, and Terrible Hats

of boys who lurked by the Sunday school doors Sunday mornings made my blood run cold.

"Of course you'll wear the new hat," Mother decreed firmly. "It's a very distinguished, different hat."

"But—but—" Oh, what was the use? There simply didn't seem to be any communication between me and my parents any more; words didn't mean the same thing to us. I died a thousand deaths next Sunday as I slunk into a seat with my class, pretending not to hear the ribald comments of the older boys behind who scraped their seats clear into the aisle to avoid "that umbrella hat." After church, a gang of small boys walked home behind me mincing along, humming "Where did you get that hat?" loud enough for me to hear, but not any adults who might stop them. Once safely inside the parsonage door, I rushed up to my own room, flung the "distinguished" Paris hat under my bed and myself on top of the bedspread and cried myself dinnerless to sleep. I was positive at fifteen that I would die an old maid.

The trouble was, it wasn't merely *any* boy whom I wanted to walk home with me from the Dorchester church after service Sunday night. Theodore Schmidt—"Teddy, dear" I called him in my mind—had red curly hair my fingers ached to smooth down, big awkward shoulders, blue eyes, and such a high color you hardly noticed all the freckles on his face. Once when we'd been playing musical chairs at Epworth League, Teddy had squeezed my hand, so I figured that I had a chance with him. If only I wasn't the minister's daughter who sat conspicuously in the front pew! If only I could get rid of that awful hat! Next Sunday night, I decided, I'd sit in the very back pew; so maybe when the lights went out. . . . Maybe, just maybe, Teddy would get up enough courage to sit down beside me.

Dad's "Sunday Evening Sings to Warm Up the Heart" were

a great boon to teenagers. After the prayer and the first hymn, the choir would file down to the front pews, the big white screen would let down from the ceiling, the lights would go out except for the broad beam of the stereoptican lantern at the back of the church. As words and music flashed onto the screen, everyone would sing lustily, "Shall we gather at the river?" while the teenagers gathered closer and closer in the pews.

Ike at twelve was still too young to go in for this "gooey stuff" and he resented having to give up every Saturday afternoon to distributing around the neighborhood the advertising cards about the Sunday night sings. On one occasion when the call of the baseball bat got too loud for him, Ike parked his announcement cards in Dorr's barn till he finished his turn at the plate. When he went reluctantly back to collect his cards, they were no more.

"Your darn Warm Up the Hearts are gone!" Ike reported defiantly to Dad. "Dorr's goats ate them up!"

The Sunday night when I'd decided to try to lure Teddy, the fates were with me. I arrived late to find the church so crowded that the ushers had put an extra row of folding chairs across the back of the auditorium. I sank gratefully down on one of these just as the lights went out, took off my awful hat, kicked it under the seat in front of me, and when the organ began to boom, I lifted my clear soprano in the mating call.

"Day is dying in the west," I warbled,
Heaven is touching earth with rest."

"Watch and worship while the night
Sets her evening lamps alight,"

Sex, Boys, and Terrible Hats

an uncertain baritone chimed in. Someone was sitting down in the seat beside mine! The voice sounded familiar. Was it? Could it be? I turned my head, It was Teddy! "Hi," he whispered and I whispered back, "Hi."

> "Heaven and earth are full of thee,
> Heaven and earth are full of thee. . . ."

They were, indeed. Full of the nearness of Teddy. In the blessed dark his hand slid to mine, his fingers stroked my wrist. In fierce ecstacy I kicked my hat farther under the seat in front. I heard the words of the hymn no longer; they did not matter; nothing mattered. Even when the lights went on and Teddy drew away his hand, I didn't hear a word of Dad's sermon, for I was wondering, "Will he walk home with me?" If only we could slip out during the last hymn, saunter along hand in hand under the stars, with the spring maple leaves whispering over our heads. Sure enough, during the last hymn, Teddy whispered, "Let's get out of here, Susie Woozy." We almost made it to the door, then an usher rushed after us. "Grace Sue, you forgot your hat!" As he handed me the gray umbrella contraption, everyone turned to see what the disturbance was and then grinned at the minister's daughter sneaking out with her beau. The publicity was too much for poor Teddy. When I finally escaped outside the church door, he had fled into the lonely dark.

That agonized night, alone in my room, I wrote another poem. The first line read:

> "Tonight the heart of me died. . . ."

I never had a hat bought especially for me just because it was becoming until Ike and I went to stay with Aunt Laura that winter, because Mother was sick in bed after our new baby brother came. It wasn't Bildad's birth that had sickened Mother, but the abruptness of his death after only four days.

Ike and I had known for months that Bildad was coming to stay with us. Mother spent long hours making a gay, rose-sprigged ruffle for his basinette, edged with pink satin and sang *"La Paloma"* as she worked, so that we knew the new baby would be welcome. We all laughed over his name, Bildad—"Bill" because Grandpaw Rouse's second name was "William" and the last syllable, Dad said, was for him. Actually the new son was officially named for Dad but when the rosy round little mite was born in our front bedroom, Leopold Adolf Nies, Junior, seemed ridiculously pompous for one so small. Besides, Mother chuckled, Bildad was in the Bible—wasn't he a comforter of Job? Bildad was her comforter.

Ike and I were pleased but not enthusiastic about the new baby brother in the rose-sprigged basinette because he didn't seem good for much except to eat and howl, but still he was a kind of cute little nuisance. Mother kept his basinette in her room, would hardly let little Bildad out of her sight. Did she have a premonition? Four days later when the nurse was bathing the baby in the white porcelain tub in Mother's room so she could watch, right in front of her terrified unbelieving eyes, Bildad stiffened and died. Not even the doctor knew why; it might be the baby's heart wasn't strong, or perhaps something was wrong with his blood. The shock was too much for Mother; she crumpled against her pillow almost as still as Bildad and as white.

Ike and I lost our mother too that terrible morning. She seemed to take no more interest in either of us; when I took up her breakfast that I had painstakingly cooked on a tray, decorated with a rose from our garden, she didn't even say, "Thank you, Susie," but irritably, "Put it on the table. I'm not hungry." If Ike slammed a door, she would scream at him "Clumsy!" and the startled Ike would shrink into himself, frightened, for he'd never heard that hard angry tone before in his life.

"Your mother is sick. You must understand that, children," Dad explained, carefully. But why should even the shock of Bildad's going drive love for her other children out the parsonage window? Ike and I couldn't understand.

"She needn't take it out on us," Ike mumbled as we two kids crept out into our favorite haunt in the middle of Dorr's field. We lay there in the sun-warmed grass for a long time, but the coldness inside me refused to melt and even with Ike so near, I felt lost, alone.

Dad's calm matter-of-factness was the anchor to which we clung; he seemed to think Bildad's going was as natural as his being born. The parish was horrified because Ike and I, the baby's own brother and sister, did not go to his funeral held in our front parlor with Mother's bedroom door open upstairs so she could hear. But before Dad sent Ike and me to stay at a neighbor's that afternoon, he took us into the sun parlor where little Bildad still lay in his basinette. I kept my eyes lowered at first, for I didn't want to see Bildad dead. Strangely enough I'd never been to a funeral. Dad said there were other ways for children to learn about immortality than to look in an open coffin as Methodist ones mostly were, so I was sure "dead" meant something frightening. The nurse had been crying hysterically as she came down to the kitchen, blurted to Ike and me, "Your little brother turned blue, died right off!" But now, Dad spoke to Bildad as if he were still there.

"Heaven will be a wonderful place to grow up in, Son!"

But if he was going to grow up, he must be alive! I glanced, fearfully, at little Bildad. He wasn't blue at all; he looked small, soft, and very still but otherwise exactly the same as usual, lying in his pink-sprigged bed. And suddenly heaven was right there in the quiet room and death was nothing to be afraid of; it was only a baby asleep in a basinette.

Mother tried to have Dad's faith but for some reason hers was like a defective electric plug—she couldn't seem to make the connection with the power to carry her through, back to God's love. She lay there on her bed for long months, white, spent, a changeling from our happy mother who used to sing as she baked the golden cornbread for breakfast. Dad had to be both parents, housekeeper (though I helped after school), and preacher till finally Aunt Laura took pity on him, offered to have Ike and me for a long visit at her house.

"Aunt Laura" as both Ike and I called her, though she was actually no relative, was one of the loveliest women, both in body and spirit, I have ever known, for her beauty shone out from within her as a light illumines an alabaster box. Her eyes, gray, clear, and loving, expected you to be as nice as she thought you and you couldn't disappoint her; she carried herself like a queen, a gentle queen whose silver hair was her crown; and she understood all the yearning things an adolescent could not say. That winter when she took Ike and me home to stay at her house until Mother should recover was the happiest I remember. I was seventeen now, neither girl nor woman, conscious that I was far from pretty, except perhaps as Aunt Laura suggested gently "beautiful in your mind, Susie." She bought me the first hat I ever owned that was selected merely because it was becoming.

Aunt Laura took me into a Boston store reputed to be so expensive that Mother and I had never ventured inside, and turned me loose in the hat department.

Sex, Boys, and Terrible Hats

"You mean, I can have *any hat I want?*" I gasped, un-believing.

"Any that is suitable and becoming, dear," Aunt Laura agreed.

I looked around wildly at counter after counter of hats, at the shining mirrors, at the little tables where you sat down to try on your selection, at the waiting saleslady, chic and svelte in black. "Nothing from Paris," I told her firmly. "I just want...."

"How would this do?" The smiling saleslady interrupted to put upon my head the perfect hat. I remember every detail after nearly half a century; I shall never forget a ribbon. The hat was a brown cloth beret, soft as a kitten to the touch, with a perky shiny ribbon bow as its only trimming; the dark brown made my hair look spun-gold and when the jaunty beret was tipped over my left ear, my glasses hardly showed at all. I gulped, "This is my hat!" and burst into happy tears.

"There, there, darling, there's nothing to cry about," Aunt Laura soothed, handing me her sweet-smelling handkerchief. "Why on earth didn't I think of doing this before?"

Aunt Laura is looking after the adolescent angels now, but I shall love her till I die, for that becoming brown beret brought me my first real beau. Bill was a senior in high school while I was only a sophomore who wore my new hat to school because I couldn't bear to be separated from it except to sleep and eat. The hat did something to me, inside, so that my shining new self-respect looked out of my eyes, beguiling-ly. Bill noticed me after school, fell in step when he saw we were going home the same way, and after that, we walked home together to Aunt Laura's every afternoon.

Bill was not just anyone at our school; he played forward on our basketball team and was major in our Dorchester High School Cadets, and was in my trigonometry class. He with six other boys were entering Massachusetts Institute of Technology, but they had to have one more student before the school authorities would give them the trig class they needed; reluctantly I had agreed to be the extra math student if the boys would help me with my homework. Bill had been one of those who helped me with my problems, but he had never offered to carry my books or to work with me at home until that afternoon when I wore my new beret. It was a long, languorous half-mile hike, for children in those days were supposed to be able to walk instead of hopping into the car taxied by mother, around the block. It was late April, I remember, with the little leaves unfurling, the birds experimenting with their April songs, and my tight-held heart unfolded too, delicately, when he discovered, "Why, your eyes are blue!" I could have walked to Mars with Bill and never felt tired at all.

"I left some sandwiches in the icebox, children," Aunt Laura called down as she heard the back door bang behind us. She must have been watching at the window, leaped to help me, as she had with the beret. Mother was always so busy being a minister's wife she never had thought of me as another woman. "If you finish your homework in time," Aunt Laura planned, "why don't we all have a game of Flinch in the library?" After that Bill walked home with me nearly every afternoon, often stayed so late Aunt Laura invited him to dinner.

Flinch, a game played with numbers, was considered permissible, even for preacher's kids; I often wondered why the early Methodist fathers considered numbers fumigated, but not the King and Queen of Hearts. For weeks Bill and I played game after game with Aunt Laura, laughing at each other over the cards, as relaxed as an old married couple. *At last I had a home and beau of my own!*

Sex, Boys, and Terrible Hats

Bill looked marvelous (in my estimation) in his dark-blue cadet uniform; true, it fitted him only casually here and there but it shone with gold braid. *And I was the major's girl.* This honor assured me of a front seat in the balcony of the gymnasium where the girls watched the boys drill and drill, getting ready for the big parade where all the Boston high school cadets competed for honors. We girls made our friends huge boxes of fudge, wrote the boy's name on top of the candy boxes, and let them down over the balcony railing to the gym floor where the boys made a rush for the fudge. Imagine my awed joy at writing on my box the name of the commanding officer, *Major William West.* When he'd look up at the balcony to smile his thanks I'd nearly burst with pride and love.

Two months later, after Mother was better and Ike and I had moved back home to the parsonage, the blow fell that was to haunt my memory till even now my mouth goes dry, remembering my black despair. Bill told me one afternoon in June as we walked home together after drill parade that next week was to be the military ball. As commanding officer he would lead the grand march and I was to share his big moment. He bet there wouldn't be a prettier girl there! Would I tell him what color my dress would be so he could send me the right corsage?

Bill was asking me to a dance, me the Methodist minister's daughter! I went cold all over, stared up at him, running my tongue over my suddenly dry lips. He asked, startled, "For Pete's sake, what's the matter, Susie? Don't you *want* to go with me?"

"Bill, darling. Of course I do!" I gasped. "Only—you see—" How could I make him understand? Bill was an Episcopalian; he thought nothing of dancing, playing cards, going to the theater. Up to now, it hadn't mattered that I couldn't do any of these things. Oh I had to go! I simply had to! But I faltered, "I'm afraid. . . ."

"Afraid of what?" Bill put his arm around me so I could hardly think, let alone speak.

"You don't understand." I twisted myself away before he could kiss me and I would be lost entirely to common sense. "Methodists aren't supposed to dance. I'm afraid my folks won't let me go!"

Bill stared at me. "I thought you had a mind of your own! You went to the senior play at high school with me. If I wanted to go to a dance with anybody, I'd darn well go. Hang the parish! You're not their minister. You're *you!*"

We argued for an hour and when we finally separated, Bill was still shaking his head. "I can't see it Susie. If you really wanted to go, you would. Well, let me know. I'll have to have *somebody* to lead the grand march with!"

Ask another girl to take my place. I bet it would be that silken Sylvia Meadows. Bill had gone with her before he went with me and she'd always kept a sharp eye on him hopefully. If Bill took Sylvia to the military ball instead of me, I'd simply die. Dad and Mother *had* to let me go. *They had to!*

The three of us, Dad, Mother, and I, talked it over far into the night; at least they talked, and I mostly listened, the sickness growing inside me. "It would be just like waving a red flag of defiance, the minister's daughter leading the grand march," Dad pointed out. "The parish might even bring me up before the bishop!" "Let them," I muttered sullenly. "Tell him you told me not to go but I went anyway! He's not *my* boss!"

It was Mother who gave me the final blow. "What would you wear?" she asked. I stared at her, stricken. Because I'd never been to a formal party before, I had no long evening

130

dress; worse, I had no money to buy one. I simply couldn't go to the dance without my parents' help. I couldn't shame Bill by appearing in the short white organdy dress I wore at Epworth League parties. The struggle was over; I should have known it was settled before I said a word to my folks. *Oh Bill, Bill darling—I wish I was dead.*

"We'll make it up to you some way, dear," Mother promised anxiously, at my stricken look.

"If Bill's any kind of guy, he'll understand it's not your fault," Dad said heavily. "Wait, a minute, Sister. . . ."

But I'd rushed off, headlong, up to my room and slammed and locked my door. *They couldn't say a word against my Bill. It was their fault, not his. Oh Bill.* But he didn't even phone me that night as usual. I lay across my bed, straining my ears till nearly midnight for the phone bell, but it didn't ring. I didn't cry, just lay there, tense as the E string on my fiddle. There are some wounds too deep for tears.

I tried again to talk to Bill the next day at recess, to make him realize that I wanted to go to the dance more than I'd ever wanted anything in my life before; but I wouldn't let him say anything against my Dad. So we quarreled bitterly. He simply couldn't understand why the minister's family had to be bound by the parish's "fuddy-duddy" ideas. Wasn't I sixteen, old enough to make up my own mind what was right and what was wrong? Why didn't I just walk out the parsonage front door and come? Naturally I was too proud to tell him I didn't have any proper clothes. "But *why* is it wrong to dance?" Bill argued. "You danced in the spring ballet! Beautifully. I noticed. You had silver in your hair."

"No, it isn't wrong, I guess," I agreed wearily. "But it would hurt my Dad, might even lose him his job."

I longed for Bill to put his arms around me, to tell me it didn't matter, that things would be just the same between us.

I could feel his hot breath on my cheek, he was standing so close. But instead Bill said angrily, "What about me? What are people going to say when you aren't there? A nice way to end my senior year—my girl throws me down, flat!"

He stalked away. I couldn't cry right there in the school-yard; dry-eyed I let him go and then I turned, and, cutting classes, walked home alone for the first time in months. It was the longest, loneliest mile I ever walked, for at the end there was nothing. Bill wasn't mine any more; he was Sylvia Meadows'. And I myself had handed him back to her.

I saw Bill in trig class after that of course; I couldn't help it. We even spoke, smiled, but the words were meaningless. The balloon of my happiness had burst, but I had to hold up my chin, walk upon the flattened rubbery pieces as if they weren't there. I saw Bill and Sylvia laughing together in the corridor, knew that what I'd feared had happened. Would he send her sweetheart roses as he had me on the night of the senior play when I walked so proudly beside him to my seat, with the whole class envying me? Would he hold her hand under the folds of her skirt? *Dear Lord, I can't stand this.*

The night of the military ball I couldn't eat any supper and my folks made no comment when I left the table and went upstairs. As I lay in my dark bedroom, I didn't even bother to shut the door. What did it matter? What did anything matter? Lying so still was how I happened to hear Dad telephoning in a low voice behind his closed study door.

"Dr. Wriston? Hello, Henry. I've decided to sell my John Wesley *Journal.* I know how much you want a set, so I thought if I sold these cheaply. . . . Oh, you would? Fine. I'll deliver them tomorrow." I wondered dimly why on earth Dad should be selling his *Journal* when he adored reading it so, but I was so drenched in my own bitterness I didn't wonder long. I heard him phone again and then my bedroom door opened

Sex, Boys, and Terrible Hats

softly. Dad came in, sat down on the edge of my bed, and stroked the hair back from my wet cheek.

"Sister? I have tickets for Boston Symphony tonight! The Lord heard me—I mean, I was lucky because someone just turned them in. I—I thought perhaps—Oh my darling, will you go with me?"

Why not? Anything to get out of here, to stop seeing behind my blind eyelids Bill and Sylvia dancing together. "If you want me to," I muttered.

I didn't even bother to comb my hair; I just slammed on my brown beret and my coat, sleepwalked with Dad to the streetcar for Boston. The streetcar rattled and banged and there was a stern anxious look on Dad's face, but he didn't try to talk. When we passed the high school, the gymnasium windows were all lighted up and boys in uniforms and girls in long light dresses were going together up the steps. I began to tremble. "I wish, oh how I wish I could bear this for you, darling!" Dad's worried glance said; but he merely offered, "I forgot to show you tonight's program. Mrs. Brainerd loaned it to me." He pulled an orange-colored pamphlet from his pocket and thrust it into my shaking hand. "I've always wanted you to hear a good orchestra and Boston's is about the best."

They could have banged pans for all I cared but I was grateful for something to look at, to hide the tears in my eyes. I stumbled after Dad up the Symphony Hall steps, went down the aisle to almost the front orchestra seats in the great hall with its low-slung balconies backed by white statues in their niches. Sitting all around us were Bostonians whose families reserved the same seats year after year; they seemed to be mostly old ladies with black velvet ribbons holding up their sagging necks and I was young, young. What was I doing here when I ought to have been dancing in Bill's arms?

I caught back my desperate thoughts, realized that these seats must have cost plenty. Where had Dad found the money? Suddenly I remembered the low-voiced telephone call. The John Wesley *Journal—Dad had sold his beloved books to try to comfort me*. Looking up at his dear familiar bulk beside me, the bitterness began to seep out of my heart.

"You shouldn't have—" But my words were drowned out by the thunder of applause as the conductor strode out onto the stage, bowing right and left, and mounted the podium. "Dr. Karl Muck!" Dad whispered, awed. "Dr. Muck conducting the Fifth Symphony! Did you know Beethoven was almost stone-deaf when he. . . ."

"Sh!" An ancient Bostonian held together by a black velvet ribbon hissed and glared at us as the conductor tapped his baton; there was a moment of hushed expectant silence before the haunting majestic music swept over us in a flood of glory.

Do you remember the first time you heard Beethoven's Fifth, "Destiny Knocking at the Door"? I shall never cease to be grateful that I heard it first too young to analyze, just to feel. I felt in every shaking nerve the mighty call of the massed strings, the answer from the woodwind choir, from the clarinets, violas, cellos, horn calls, tympani, all saying over and over the mighty theme until the growing power of each added voice rose to such full splendor of triumphant sound it seemed to batter against the very gates of heaven. And of my heart. To me the mighty music said, "Lo, I stand at the door and knock. Lose your smallness in My greatness. . . ." For the first time since I was born, I lost my little self in beauty bigger than I was. When I looked up at my Dad, there were tears in his eyes, too. Suddenly I grew up enough to understand that there were two kinds of love—Bill's which could

134

snatch selfishly at happiness and Dad's which would never fail me, because it was me he loved, not himself. Smiling, I slid my cold hand into Dad's big warm one, and we drifted away together on the cry of the violins.

Chapter Eight

LADY WITH THE LONG BLUE VEIL

My Aunt Gay is a young woman pushing eighty. She has been an invalid since she was a girl but still loves life; she knows all about people, even how mean and little they can sometimes be, but she still likes them. Mostly you expect Texans to be big-boned, big-talking, and big-friendly. But my Aunt Gay is tiny with soft brown hair, soft hazel eyes; she has a soft-voiced Southern drawl, so, no matter what she says, the sharpness is frosted over. She has the smallest feet, size three, encased in heel-less leather slippers with bead patterns on the toes. Maybe the Texas in her shows up in that she loves bright things, a red ribbon in her hair, a plaid silk shirtwaist, a gay flower in her lapel. When she came to see us in Dorchester that winter I was sixteen, Aunt Gay used to sit on a round air-filled cushion on the floor, with a red ribbon in her soft brown hair, her child's feet in the bead-patterned slippers crossed in front of her, and when she smiled up at Ike and me a breath of fresh Texas prairie air swept through our staid New England parsonage.

Ike and I gathered (from listening in on telephone conversations) that Aunt Gay was to have another operation in a Boston hospital. Mother had explained to us that we must never ask Aunt Gay why she wasn't married; that long ago she'd been engaged to a boy in Fort Worth, but when she found out she couldn't have any children, she gave him back his ring. I've always thought he must have been crazy to take it back, because just being near my Aunt Gay would be happiness enough for anyone.

The best thing about her was that Ike and I could tell her anything but she never leaked a word to other grownups, not even when Ike told her about his running away when Dad licked him, then getting hungry and coming back home to supper. "Cowhands usually mosey along about time for chow," my Aunt Gay agreed. "Shows horse sense." And she understood just how I felt when I got turned down for the high school dramatic club because Sylvia Meadows, Bill's new girl, blackballed me. She must have; who else had reason to hate me? My Aunt Gay didn't try to soothe me with useless words; she just made a comforting sound in her throat, half sympathy and half chuckle.

"Well, that's one trouble crossed off," she said. "How about a good sing?" Something was wrong with her back so she couldn't sit on an ordinary hard chair, but you never felt sorry for her because she made a sort of game of rocking back and forth on her little air pillow and singing:

> Oh happy day that fixed my choice
> On thee my Saviour and my God;
> That bids my glowing heart rejoice
> And sings its raptures all abroad.
> Happy day, happy day. . . .

It was indeed a happy day when she arrived for her visit that spring at the Dorchester parsonage. She comforted Ike being punished for tying a schoolmate by her pigtails to the chairback by her mischievous remark that when our mother was young she had been even more of an imp than we kids were, that we came by our high spirits rightfully.

"When Myrtie was three, she was cute as a cricket but was she greedy!" My Aunt Gay's gray eyes twinkled sparks at Mother sitting there sedately mending socks out of the never-empty sewing basket, pretending disapproval but actually enjoying listening as much as we children did. "She'd sit up on the high piano stool, play and sing, "'Jesus wants me for a sunbeam.' Where's my candy?"

"Now, Gay, I was only a baby!" Mother protested, biting off her thread with strong white teeth.

My Aunt Gay chuckled, "Remember the time you learned a new grace in Sunday school? You sat down at lunch that day, folded your hands, looked straight across the table, and said loudly, 'God bless this fool. Amen.' Maw said, 'I was the only one there, so who could she mean but me?'"

Ike laughed so hard at this that his chair went over backward and Mother said primly, "No need to tell *all* you know, Gay."

Oh yes, there was need, my Aunt Gay said, smiling her little brown smile that started in her eyes, spread all over her face and then set her whole tiny body rocking with mirth on her air pillow. Children needed to know all about their parents, the bad as well as the good; the funny things, too, because each one of us is made up of bits and pieces of our ancestors. If we children knew our folks had had trouble being strong and wise, that this hadn't come easy to them either, we'd have more courage to go on trying to make ourselves into whole persons who could laugh at anything life could do to us.

I could see what she meant about the bits and pieces like the bright stones in a mosaic. Ike had a lot more of Grandpaw Rouse in him than just his name; he had Grandpaw's drive, tempered by our Mother's charm. Once he had made up his mind to do something, Ike never wavered from his goal; but he didn't force his will on other people as Grandpaw might

Lady with the Long Blue Veil

have done; he got what he wanted with so much grace that his opponent ended up by thinking he'd wanted what Ike did in the first place. He would never have crawled out a window, left the baffled cowboys to buy their own drinks; he would have persuaded them, Tom Sawyer-wise, that it would be more fun to ride down Main Street, shooting off their .44's at the moon in celebration. And with Ike leading, it would have been. I, on the other hand was more of a patchwork of Dad and my shy Grandmaw Rouse. I had the Nies nose—alas—and a grim sense of duty. I hated to be conspicuous but I'd do what I had to even if it made me sick to my stomach. Ike knew that sugar drew more flies than vinegar; all I knew was that testifying what I'd done wrong that week in front of all those people at Tuesday night prayer meeting (as I felt a PK must) gave me a puckered mouth. What need to parade my innermost sins when the Lord knew them already? Naturally Ike was a great deal more popular in the parish than I was.

One evening when Ike had gone to a party but I was home moping because I hadn't been invited, watching Mother sitting by the front parlor light at her eternal mending, Aunt Gay told me a startling story about the young girl in Fort Worth who up to now had been a stranger to me.

"Did I ever tell you," my Aunt Gay chuckled, "about the young man who came out of a saloon to ask your mother to dance with him? On a horse named Bonny?"

"Now, Gay!" my mother gasped but my Aunt Gay said it wouldn't hurt me to know that some people didn't have to worry over what the parish thought; they grew up laughing, carefree under a Southern sky; that they belonged to themselves and to no one else.

My mother laid down her mending and said she might as well tell that story herself if I had to know.

"Bonny was my brown mare when I was a girl," my mother

explained to me, her whole face beginning to sparkle so that she looked younger and younger, and the tight lines smoothed out of her face. "I rode her sidesaddle, of course. I didn't know she used to perform in a circus till one morning I was riding down the main street of Fort Worth—saloons were thicker there then than flies on a dead dog. Someone was playing a jew's-harp, inside at the bar, and Bonny began to waltz! I flipped her with my whip, but she wouldn't go on. When the tune changed, Bonny two-stepped! I was so surprised I could hardly stay in the saddle. A cowboy came out of the saloon, swept his wide hat into the dust and chuckled, 'Miss Myrtie, kin I have this next dance?' Was my face red!"

My sedate, blue-serge mother who never did anything more exciting than go to a missionary meeting, riding a waltzing circus horse down Main Street, and a man coming out of a saloon to ask her to dance! I stared at this glamorous woman I might never have known if my Aunt Gay hadn't worked Mother up to telling the story. Had Aunt Gay done this deliberately, trying to get my Mother's soft mouth to quirk up into a smile instead of being a straight, patient line? My Mother loved my Dad so much, I knew, that she'd have lived with him in a Hottentot's grass hut. She could even live here in a Puritan New England parsonage and like it.

"I bought Bonny with the first money I ever earned after I got back from taking the music course at Ohio Northern College," my Mother remembered, her darning lying forgotten in her lap. "I gave piano lessons and paid Maw ten dollars a week for board. I've always felt my music degree belonged to her, not me. Not many mothers work till they vomit just to keep you in college like Ma did for me."

Her voice broke but Aunt Gay said calmly, "You'd do the same for yours, if they needed it."

"She has!" I put in eagerly. "She bought me my green suit."

Lady with the Long Blue Veil

"Your Aunt Gay wouldn't be interested in that," Mother shut me up quickly. She sighed. "I reckon the reason Paw was so set on giving us girls an education was that he didn't get much schooling himself, what with being an orphan and going to war when he was sixteen."

Educating three girls had cost plenty, my Aunt Gay agreed. Paw had sent all of them to the best private school in Fort Worth; Myrtie had been the first to go on to college. Then the Big Freeze had come when Paw had had no more sheep or money for a spell. Maw Rouse had worried, "If Myrtie knew how tight money is she'd come straight home from that college in Ada, Ohio. Somehow we got to get the money to send to her same as usual, and say nothing. Don't worry, Isaac, I'll find me a job."

Neither of them had any degrees except in the college of hard knocks where you learned that no one was defeated until he admitted it. Susan Rouse got a job selling "inspirational" books from door to door. She did fine as long as she sold in the neighborhood where folks knew her, but when she tackled strangers. . . .

"Inspiration?" the housewife snapped. "Why should I pay good money for fool books?" Maw was so shriveled up by the angry tone, she couldn't tell the woman why; she just went back down the steps as fast as she could. It got so she hated even to ring a doorbell; it seemed to clang inside her frightened stomach, too. *Maybe,* she'd think hopefully *there's nobody home.* Once when an impatient woman slammed the door in the terrified Susan's face, she ran down behind the hedge and lost her breakfast. But she knew if she stopped ringing doorbells, she'd never start again, so she staggered up the steps to the next door—and sold a book!

"If they'd only told me!" my mother moaned, her own face going white just remembering the price of her college training.

"No music degree is worth that. Maw looked like a ghost when I got home that spring but when I asked her why she'd done it, she said, surprised, 'Why, honey, there wasn't anything else to do! We're a family!' "

I looked at my mother's bent curly head where the light made glints of gold, at the dear curve of her cheek and I knew there was iron in her also for those she loved.

"At heart you're still Texas, not Boston!" my Aunt Gay told my mother, "And you know it, Myrtie Rouse Nies."

I've often wondered what might have happened if Aunt Gay hadn't been there that New England spring to egg my mother on to take drastic action when the singer with the long blue veil tried to "vamp" my Dad.

A minister spends most of his day with women. They make up the majority of his Sunday congregation; he calls on them daytimes when their husbands are away at work; and he has to attend their meetings, often the only male in a coterie of fluttering, flattering females. He wouldn't be human if all this attention did not sometimes inflate his male ego. He may fight this spotlight complex on his knees, but he cannot escape it, for there he is, always high up in the pulpit Sundays or at the head table at every church supper. It takes a very humble, dedicated man to keep his sense of humor.

My Dad made practical arrangements to avoid emotional complications with too-intense ladies. Many women came to his study to complain about their husbands, about the wild oats their children were experimenting with, or merely because they were lonely and troubled, and to them he gave what he could of understanding and advice; but the most dangerous were the "ecclesiastical wives" (as Mother privately called them) for whom the church is their whole family and the minister as the head and symbol, a sort of scriptural husband, by proxy. They knitted Dad pansy-colored bedsocks,

Lady with the Long Blue Veil

brought over his favorite kind of pie, liked to talk to him in his study with the door shut. Dad had an arrangement with Mother that when she heard the study door shut, she'd wait twenty minutes, then knock and come in with a tray upon which were three friendly cups of coffee.

Miss Nash, the "singing nightingale," came to our house that spring afternoon while my Aunt Gay was still visiting us.

Each April Dad held a series of special meetings every night for two weeks, designed to "deepen the spiritual life of the church" and to give the parish a change from his own preaching. Usually he persuaded a missionary from China or Africa to tell us how we were all alike under our white, yellow, or brown skins, or Dad would exchange pulpits with one of his former theological school classmates who could preach his own barrel of sermons. There would also be special music, a singer, a violinist, or an organist who would make our usually staid keyboard wake up and shout. The meetings acted as a spring tonic for both pastor and parish, a sort of spiritual sulfur and molasses.

But this year Dad hadn't been able to find a friend with the right dates to "swop pulpits," so he'd been obliged to hire Miss Nash to help him; he'd seen only her picture in an advertising brochure but she was highly recommended in fine print. When the doorbell rang that afternoon she was supposed to arrive, Dad was out calling and I opened the door. The blonde young woman who stood there was full-blown and buxom in a tight-fitting, light-blue suit, but her fantastic headgear made me stare. A coquettish cap of sky-blue chiffon with a long veil of the same color trailing down behind came almost to her extremely high heels. All of her hair that showed was a brassy, impossible gold, but her voice was deep honey.

"This the home of the Reverend Nies?" she intoned. When I admitted that it was, looking beyond her at the bright red car where a man wearing a checked black and white suit and a cap cocked over one ear was sitting in the driver's seat, the blond visitor called, "Bring in my suitcase, Brother! This is the place."

As Brother deposited the suitcase at the door, my mother came up behind me, took one look, and gasped.

"You were expecting me? I'm Miss Nash," the vision in blue cooed.

"Oh," my mother breathed. "Oh yes. Come in." She stood staring, unable to take her eyes off the long bridal veil (only blue), as Miss Nash asked, impatiently, "Is my room upstairs?"

"Yes, indeed," my mother said. "It's all ready." Mother drew a deep breath, reached down for the suitcase which was brown ostrich leather, expensive and very heavy as she found as she led the way upstairs, explaining, "Susie is moving in on a cot with my sister and me so you can have her room."

I kicked at the white balustrade angrily. Why should even a singing nightingale upset the whole household? That meant Aunt Gay and Mother would have the big double bed where she and Dad usually slept and he'd have to spend the two weeks on his lumpy study couch. I watched Miss Nash go into my room, glance suspiciously at my bed with the brass knobs. "I hope the mattress is comfortable," Miss Nash yawned. She put her blue cap carefully on my bureau, flung herself down on my white bedspread without taking off her high-heeled shoes. When Mother explained that Dad was out calling, but would be home soon, Miss Nash yawned again. "Tell him to knock on my door when he comes in so we can pick out the hymns for tonight. I'll just spend a little time in meditation. Shut the door, will you?"

"Well!" my Aunt Gay snapped when Mother and I sleep-walked into our own room next door. "You going to let Lee and that blond have committee meetings up in her room, Myrtie?"

"You have no business listening, Gay," my mother retorted. But she dropped down on the big walnut bed with the wooden grapes on top, almost as if her legs were suddenly weak while I sat, ears cocked, on my cot by the window. "Lee's going to be terribly upset when he sees her," my mother defended Dad loyally. "She doesn't look a bit like her picture on the brochure." Mother brightened. "He'll probably ship her right back to the agency."

"I wouldn't count on that," my Aunt Gay warned grimly. "Ministers are men, too."

Mother sat right up on the bed, her eyes flashing, "Gay Rouse, if you're insinuating. . . ."

"I'm not insinuating anything," my Aunt Gay said. "But if I were you, I'd ship that phony bird-woman off to a hotel before Lee even sees her!"

"Oh, I couldn't do that. We promised to board and room her for the two weeks. It's a part of her pay," my mother explained. She lifted her head, listening to the purring sound coming through the thin wall between our rooms.

"Well, she didn't meditate long," my Aunt Gay noticed. "She was probably out late last night—singing hymns," she added hastily at the ire in my mother's eye.

"That's her *business*." Did mother say it just a little too loudly? I wondered. She tossed her head. She wasn't afraid of any brassy-haired female hoodwinking her Lee, she said firmly, just let her try. She flounced out of the room, went down to the kitchen. To start supper or to do a little meditating herself?

"Miss Nash had a boy friend," I told Aunt Gay. "They came in a red car."

145

"I wouldn't have been surprised if it had been a fire engine," my Aunt Gay snapped. "Mark my words, that woman's Trouble with a capital T. Go away, child. I want to think." I took one of Mother's rose-colored scarves out of her top bureau drawer, sneaked it off with me to the bathroom where I tied it around my head, letting the ends trail down behind. It made me look like an egg with a pink tail, not glamorous like Miss Nash.

My Aunt Gay was right. Dad didn't send Miss Nash packing; he seemed quite pleased to see her, long blue veil and all. I heard Mother hint to Dad when she was making up his couch in the study with clean sheets and blankets, wasn't that veil, well, a bit theatrical? Of course, it was, Dad said heartily; why should the devil have a corner on drama? A little beauty was important, even in church. "Beauty?" My mother stared at Dad, then went out, shutting the study door very quietly, came into our room to dust rice powder with a limp chamois on her shiny nose before she went down to serve supper. I noticed too that Mother wore her best Sunday dark-blue suit with the white blouse with ruffles at the neck and wrists when she started for service that night with Dad and his new nightingale.

My Aunt Gay wasn't well enough to sit through a long service but she asked me if it would keep me awake if she kept on the little bedside light till mother got home? I said it wouldn't. I squinted sleepily through my eyelashes when mother came in late, put on her long-sleeved white nightgown with the embroidery down the front.

"Everyone liked her. She has a really lovely soprano voice," my mother admitted, looking like a little girl in her white nightgown and short curly hair as she hopped into the big bed beside my Aunt Gay. "When she got up on the platform, swinging that long blue veil, clapping her hands softly and

146

singing—well, it got you. You should have seen the official board rush up afterward, to a man, to shake hands!"

"I'll bet," my Aunt Gay said, "I bet in three nights you'll have to put up a sign, MEN ONLY."

"Now, Gay," my mother giggled. "Her veil did sort of remind me of a cat's tail. I admit I don't like her. I don't even trust her. But I trust Lee." The little purring sound had begun already in the room next door. "I wonder if Lee can hear her from the study, meditating?" They both giggled then. It must be nice, I thought wistfully having a sister to laugh with. All Ike would say if I repeated this conversation would be, "Oh, slush!"

But to my vast surprise Ike at twelve fell under Miss Nash's spell, too. He rushed to pull out her chair at table before Dad could get there and he used up all his allowance to buy her a dozen chocolate peppermints. He didn't actually give them to her, just left them shyly on her dresser where she'd be sure to find them. They weren't there next morning when I looked so I suppose she ate them; I didn't. Ike even asked Dad if he could attend the special meetings but Dad said Ike had his homework to do; he could come Friday night. It made me hot all over, Ike's being so stupid. My "crowning beauty" was prettier than Miss Nash's; the gold was real.

"She's old enough to be your mother," I told Ike. "And her hair's black at the roots! I wouldn't go to hear her yowl if you paid me."

"Shut up," Ike snapped and slammed out of the room.

Miss Nash soon had everyone from short to long pants buffaloed, my Aunt Gay agreed, when I told her how silly Ike was acting. Maybe we'd have to do something about it. But what? Boarding and rooming Miss Nash was practically a full-time job for Mother. The singer always had breakfast in bed because the night meeting "took so much out of her"; it never seemed to occur to her that Mother had been up after midnight too, had had to get up early to get us kids off to school, to feed Dad and Aunt Gay, and then had to carry up Miss Nash's heavy tray, so Dad wouldn't. Miss Nash came down, gracious, rosy, and rested for lunch. Afterward she and Dad would settle down at the front parlor table to sort out the "decision cards" from last night, to decide who should get a prompt call from the minister. There were more men attending these special meetings than any he'd ever held before, Dad told the family proudly.

"Do they know you're only going to be here two weeks?" my Aunt Gay asked Miss Nash pointedly, from the front parlor doorway.

That had nothing to do with it, my Dad protested hastily; Miss Nash sang not as a person, merely as an instrument for worship, like the organ. Miss Nash said, "Amen," and my Aunt Gay sniffed. The spirit blows where it listeth, my Dad explained sternly, and who were we to question? Naturally a few of the cardsigners would drop by the wayside later; that was to be expected. By this time Miss Nash was so exhausted counting cards, she asked Dad if he'd mind taking her out in the Ford for a breath of pure air? Dad said he'd be glad to.

"Can I go too?" Ike begged, rushing in from the back parlor where he'd been watching Miss Nash's white hands sort cards.

"Not this time, Darling," Miss Nash murmured, but she flirted her long lashes at him and patted his hand so that Ike blushed deep red. The dope was too far gone to realize that he'd been turned down; he went up to her room to sniff at her perfume bottle. "It smells so strong, it's a wonder he isn't gassed," I told my Aunt Gay jealously, for Ike had been my partner ever since first grade, right up till I'd gone to high school. "Does he have to go gooping after a rag, a bone, and a hank of blue veil?"

Lady with the Long Blue Veil

"Yes," my Aunt Gay sighed. "Ike's having growing pains." She hesitated, said slowly. "Sometimes I think your father's not much older. I only hope your mother does something, before it's too late, to help him see that even the milk of human kindness can curdle."

When Miss Nash came home from her ride with Dad, rested and hungry enough, as she said gaily, "to eat fried bear," my mother said stiffly that we were having lamb stew.

Things went on this way at the Dorchester parsonage for ten days with the atmosphere getting more and more tense and the attendance at the special church meetings going up by leaps and bounds. There was no doubt at all that Dad's nightingale was a great success. The night after her picture appeared in the local weekly paper, smiling and draped in her long veil, the church was so crowded they had to turn people away.

"You home so soon?" I gasped when Mother came back into the front hall when it was barely half-past eight.

"It took me so long to wash the dishes, when I got there, there wasn't a seat," my mother explained, not looking at me as she went upstairs. I didn't remind her of what we both knew perfectly well, that one of the ushers would have opened Dad's church study door beyond the platform and put a chair there for her. This was the first time I remembered that Mother hadn't waited through a service to walk home afterward with Dad. What would he say?

He didn't say anything. He and Miss Nash woke me up coming in at midnight, laughing and hungry. They must have had a cosy snack out in the kitchen, because I heard the icebox door slam. Mother must have heard it too, but she didn't get up to go down to help: she just turned over and over, restlessly in the big bed. I wondered if my Aunt Gay was awake too but she didn't let on if she was. Maybe she figured

149

talking wouldn't do any good or maybe she was just plain disgusted with my mother for being an ostrich. I considered going downstairs myself, pretending I was hungry, but the thought of Miss Nash patting my hand and calling me 'Dahling,' made me sick to my stomach.

The climax was triggered next Monday afternoon when Dad told Miss Nash, down in the front hall, that the meetings had been so successful he was thinking of holding them over for another week. He and Miss Nash had been out in the car all afternoon making calls on people who'd signed the decision cards. I was doing my Latin up in our bedroom with the door open, where Mother and Aunt Gay were lying down on the big bed, pretending to nap. We couldn't help hearing what those two were saying downstairs.

"Sheila, the Lord has greatly blessed your efforts," my Dad said. Since when had he called her by her first name? "Would you consider staying on for another week? I'm very grateful to you."

"Are you really, Lee?" Sheila's perfume coming upstairs was loud as her brass hair, exciting, pungent. Little shivers ran over me, knowing how blue her eyes were looking up under her long sky-blue veil. Over on the big bed Mother rolled over, hid her face in the pillow, but her small fist was clenched on the white spread. "Of course, I'll stay, Lee. If you want me." Sheila coaxed, "Let's relax, sit on the couch. I'm exhausted."

"Relax?" Did Dad sound scared? But kind of pleased, too, I thought. He stammered, "I'm sorry. I—I've just remembered —I have to call at the hospital." The front door slammed on his craven retreat, the Ford roared outside, and Miss Nash's high heels tapped angrily up the stairs into her bedroom and her door shut, hard. My Aunt Gay sat up in bed, glared down at my mother.

"No use pretending you're asleep!" my Aunt Gay snapped.

Lady with the Long Blue Veil

"Myrtie Rouse, not even a preacher's wife has to be a worm. *Are you going to let her get away with it?*"

"No!" My mother rolled over, sat up, her brown curls standing up every which way and her eyes blazing. "No, I'm not!"

She marched right by me as if I wasn't there, burst into the next room without knocking and shut the door. My Aunt Gay and I couldn't understand the words, but we could hear their raised voices, a banging as if bureau drawers were being opened hastily and closed; then my mother went downstairs and we could hear her phoning for a taxi.

"Whew!" my Aunt Gay let out her breath, and I didn't know I was holding my own till it came out a great sigh. "She's done it, Susie!" my Aunt Gay whispered. "But what will your Dad say?"

I couldn't imagine; the special meetings were very near his heart and Miss Nash *was* the meetings. Mother didn't come back upstairs after the taxi came and went; she was waiting for Dad in the front hall when he came home from his suddenly recollected hospital call.

"Your nightingale is sick, Lee," Mother said, so low my Aunt Gay and I had to strain to hear. "She had to leave right off. You'd better phone the organist to get someone to sing tonight."

"Sick?" My Dad roared. "What's the matter with her? She was all right half an hour ago. She can't just walk out on me like this!"

"She has walked out!" My mother's voice rose, too. "I—I sent her. It was either her or me. Would you rather I left, Lee?"

"Myrtie Nies!" Dad gasped, shocked. "What's got into you?"

In the long agonized silence that followed, my heart thudded sickeningly. *She didn't mean it. She wouldn't really walk out on Dad—on all of us. Not Mother. Or would she? After all, she was Texas, not Boston.*

151

"Miss Nash! Miss Nash, I brought you some ice cream," Ike's shrill boy's pipe coming in the back door broke the brittle stillness, as his feet in their heavy boots thundered up the uncarpeted back stairs. He rushed into her room, then out again, hurried next door to where Aunt Gay and I were. "Where is she?" Ike had run so fast to get here with his favorite chocolate for his favorite girl that his tie was under one ear, and one long lock of hair hung down on his sweaty forehead. He wailed, "She's gone! Even her suitcase is gone. She didn't even tell me good-by!"

"She didn't know herself she was leaving till the very last minute," my Aunt Gay soothed, "or she'd have told you, Honey." A young boy's love was pure, faithful, redeeming, cleansing—it must stay that way.

"Ike," Dad called from downstairs, "She didn't say good-by to me either, Son!" His voice shook as he told my Mother, "I reckon you were right. She was sick. I'll phone the organist right away. Kiss me, Sugar—if you can."

She could. And we were a family again. My Aunt Gay began to rock back and forth on her pillow and to sing under her breath, "Oh, happy day. . . ." But her eyes were full of tears.

Chapter Nine

IKE SOWS HIS WILD OAT

ENTERING a new parish was rather like detecting a path through an uncharted mine field; not only the church was unknown, the parsonage, the people, but each one had an area of violent likes and dislikes which the new preacher and his family had to explore cautiously to avoid an explosion. Once when Dad found two members of the same official board who hadn't spoken to each other directly for twenty years, he called both of them into his study, ordered, "Let us pray, Brothers!" and kept them on their knees till they spoke not only to God but to each other. One organist turned out to be such an ardent pacifist he wouldn't even play "Onward, Christian Soldiers." We PK's learned never to comment adversely on any *objet d'art* displayed by the new parsonage committee; the "Yard of Pansies" or "Stag at Bay" usually had been donated by the beaming committee member's Aunt Jennie. "If you can't say something nice, *keep still!*" Mother cautioned. But when we moved from Boston to Trinity Church, Worcester, when Ike was in high school and I just entering college, the committee seemed as interested in fixing up the parsonage for us as their own homes.

"I feel as if I'd come to my own place," Dad beamed.

Trinity, one of the largest churches in New England Methodism, was a big, ugly, red-brick building in the throbbing center of the city, with traffic and streetcars screaming by on two sides; inside, the church was spacious, friendly, dimly lighted, but humming with activity. When we first came, fifteen hundred members crowded the church nave and big overhanging balcony for three services every Sunday, but after Dad had spent almost every waking moment for a year calling upon the neighborhood families, the membership roll had risen to two thousand. There was hardly an hour, day or night, when some group wasn't meeting, eating, or praying at Trinity, and as often as he could, Dad would drop by with his cheerful smile, his eager suggestions, although he never was the Big Boss.

"What I like about him, he isn't too proud to listen to what anyone else thinks," one enthusiastic parishioner told Mother. "He's common, like the rest of us."

The inevitable result of Dad's incessant church activities was, however, that he was seldom at home any more when we kids were—that Ike lost his Dad when he needed him most. Not that Dad could have told his adolescent son much; Ike, nearing sixteen, was a vast amorphous cloud of feeling. He didn't even understand, himself, what he wanted.

"It always seems such a pity," Dad said wistfully, "that we parents find it so difficult to hand on to our children the small gleanings of wisdom we have made. We can leave them houses, books, stocks, and bonds—but not peace of mind. Each generation has to dig that out for itself." He sighed, smiled ruefully, added, "There must be some sense to this or the Lord wouldn't let it go on. Perhaps falling down and getting up again is the only way a boy can develop spiritual and mental muscles."

Certainly Ike was different from the amenable, jolly little

Ike Sows His Wild Oat

boy who used to play scrub hockey by the hour in our Dorchester back yard, who had hung onto Dad's coattails to learn to skate "single-runner." Now he was going to high school, had discovered girls, he was practically never at home. You could hardly blame him, for the Trinity parsonage was very different from the cheerful sunny colonial house where we had played and squabbled as youngsters.

The wealthiest member of the Trinity committee admired the Victorian, so that the new parsonage was a big, gloomy house, crowded in close to the neighbors so you had to grope your way about the first floor rooms, avoiding the heavy lurking furniture. The house was painted an ugly brown, with windows of colored glass in the front door—blue, green, purple —which set Ike's teeth on edge.

"We might as well live in a funeral home!" he grumbled. "I'm getting out of here!"

"Where to?" Mother demanded anxiously.

"Just out." The parsonage door slammed behind Ike exiting moodily from gloom and authority.

Ike didn't even ask Dad if he could go that winter to the high school dances, he just went. He told me later half-defiantly, half-proudly, what had happened. "At first I only watched everybody dancing round and round, laughing, in each other's arms, and I thought 'What the heck! They can't hang me, if I am the preacher's kid!' So I got up, bowed in front of Else Peters. 'I don't know how to waltz but it looks like fun,' I told her. 'Will you show me, Else?' So she did, and it *was* fun."

I knew there'd be fireworks over what Ike had done even if Else was the red-haired popular daughter of John Peters, a member of our church's official board. Dad called Ike into his study and they yelled at each other for about ten minutes before Ike came out, thundered downstairs, and then I could

hear his footsteps pounding off outside down the brick sidewalk. When he didn't come home for dinner that night,
Mother was sure he'd been run over, but Dad growled, "Don't
worry. Nothing will ever happen to that kid. He'll always land
on his feet." Ike landed at the Peterses where he helped
Else with her Latin. Else must have laid down the law to her
father (she was an only child and he worshiped her) for the
next time the high school had a dance, she called Ike up
herself, asked him to drive her there in their car. Things had
certainly changed in the three years since I was sixteen, I
snapped to Mother, but she said, some things never changed;
a man set on doing what he wanted to could get away with
it; but a woman had to do what everyone thought was right
or be labeled a pariah. It wasn't fair either that a woman had
to bear the babies while the man merely paced the waiting
room floor, and thought he was the one sweating blood; it
was just so and you might as well face it.

But Mother didn't approve at all of the way the girls in the
parish ran after Ike. The phone rang constantly at mealtimes,
with girls inviting him to go on picnics, to the movies, for
a birch beer or it was Else needing help with her homework. "*Amo, amas, . . . amamus*—that's all she wants to study!"
I snorted and Ike grinned, "So what?" I envied him his gay
lighthearted ways. Actually I thought Else's heavy braids of
red hair and great gray eyes were lovely, and I admired the
way she went after her man. Mother sniffed that *she'd* never
had to call up a boy for a date when she was young; no lady
would think of doing such a thing; she'd rather cut out her
tongue.

"Nobody's a lady now, Mom," Ike told her, bending down
to kiss Mother's soft cheek that smelled of violet talcum
powder, "They're just girls. Good night. See you tomorrow
morning."

Ike Sows His Wild Oat

Why did Ike, who was a boy and therefore didn't need it, have to inherit Mother's charm? Her eyes with the invitation to laughter in them? The door slammed behind Ike going whistling off down the street. But I knew in my envious heart that either you had the "come-hither look" or you hadn't; and if you had, your phone kept ringing.

Mother's own eyes looking across the supper table at me were soft, sorry. She said, "The day will come, Sister, when someone will find you beautiful. Just pray, 'O Lord, let my beauty be within me.'" But what good was praying when a man to take me to the movies was what I wanted? I could only be grateful that the strict Methodists found innocuous the shadow figures moving across the screen while real people on a real stage still indicated what dear old Brother Wentworth called sternly, "the trail of the serpent!"

It was after midnight when Ike came home and crept up to his room. Only then did Mother's anxious light shining out the window next to mine go off. Ike couldn't possibly have been at Else's that late—or could he? Dad was even later getting home but Mother didn't worry about him. What upset her was that Ike was no longer a crystal glass she could see through.

"Oh, the lad'll be all right," Chris Reisner assured her, Dad, and me that Sunday evening he came to dinner before he was guest preacher at one of Dad's special Sunday night services at Trinity. "They all go through the tadpole stage." Dr. Christian Reisner, a theological school classmate of Dad's, big, jovial, with a nose almost as generous as his heart, was one preacher who did not believe in hiding his church's light under a New York City bushel. Chris did everything in a big way including conducting the Lord's business in the largest city on earth; he had once even hired a brass band to attract worshipers from the teaming city street, explaining,

"The Lord can use any kind of an instrument to speak His will!" Chris comforted Dad now, "I wouldn't give much for a boy who didn't have enough gumption to sow a wild oat, Lee." Dad grumbled that Ike might at least be on time for dinner when they had company, and a big meeting afterward at the church. With Chris advertised on posters, a full choir, and a violinist, Trinity would have every seat jammed, standing room only, most likely. Chris suggested chuckling slyly, "Perhaps all Ike needs is to get away from Ma and Pa?"

"Here he comes," Mother shushed, fearfully, for it made Ike awfully mad if he thought we were talking about him. But he seemed to take to Chris right off. They joked and talked all through dinner, Chris telling about the listener who'd gone to sleep down in the front pew till Chris roared, "Fire!" and the sleeper woke up, yelled, "Where? Where?" Chris roared back, "In hell, Brother!" Ike thought this terribly funny and after Dad and Chris had gone off to service (Ike said he had to help Else, with her French it was, this time) Ike told me Chris wasn't like a preacher at all, just a regular guy. Why he even lived on Broadway. Imagine a parsonage on the Great White Way!

I said stiffly that I liked Dad's quiet brand of religion better than the shouting kind.

"You would," Ike snorted. We didn't seem to agree about anything these days. "You even like Bach. You and the organist. All those scales running up and down the keyboard. Sounds like a kid practicing. Give me a real tune like 'Brighten the corner where you are.'"

"Barbershop stuff," I sniffed, for I'd gone classical in a big way that winter, even earned the ticket money by baby-sitting to go to Boston Symphony every week.

Mother soothed as she cleared the table, "Bach's chorales were the popular religious songs of his day, you might say. He

158

wrote them chiefly for his village choir to sing. Simple words for simple people, to comfort them in their daily living." She began to sing, low but clear in her silver-flute soprano:

> Break forth, oh beauteous heavenly light,
> And usher in the morning. . . .

Ike pushed back his chair rudely, grabbed up his French books to go out again. "Give me a little life. It's dead as yesterday's newspaper around here."

Dad and Mother thought long and hard about Chris's remark that maybe Ike needed to get away from Pa and Ma, so when Ike was offered a scholarship at Wilbraham Academy, the Methodist boy's preparatory school which was far enough away so that Ike couldn't live at home, date every evening, they accepted gratefully. Ike said philosophically that Wilbraham wasn't far from New York either, on the train. At Mother's startled look he added hastily that maybe he'd save his allowance, go down to hear Chris Reisner preach some day. "New York!" Mother gasped. It sounded like China to her, but Dad told Ike grimly, "*Doctor* Reisner to you, young man. But it might not be such a bad idea. Chris might knock some sense into you." When Dad and Ike glared at each other, I decided it was a good thing Ike was going away. I'd miss him but not this squabbling at every meal.

Before Ike went, Dad as always when one of us was going away from home, asked us all to kneel to ask the Lord's blessing "while we are absent, one from the other." Ike scowled, muttered something about "kid stuff" but finally he knelt down by his chair, embarrassed and rebellious, while Dad prayed:

"Oh Lord, this Thy child is going out into new paths, to

learn new ways. Please, be with him and with us who are left behind, so that we may all be one in Thee. Amen."

Then we sang, even Ike, for we'd sung so often together that we were almost one voice even if Ike's boyish treble had deepened now to baritone. It had begun to change, I remembered, right after he'd fallen in love with that brass-haired Miss Nash, with her sky-blue veil. Now Dad sang tenor, Mother soprano, I alto, and Ike growled around the lower notes:

> Be not dismayed what'ere betide. . . .
> Beneath His wings of love abide. . . .
> God will take care of you,
> Through every day, o'er all the way,
> He will take care of you. . . .

After Ike had gone, rattling off with Dad in the old Ford, the words of the hymn kept running comfortably in my head; it was the first time Ike and I had been separated for any length of time and already I was lonesome for him though he'd barely left. There would always be an empty place inside me only he could fill. Would he change at Wilbraham? Become a stranger whose mind would no longer talk to mine without words? "Be not dismayed what'ere betide. . . ." Maybe they're not great music but the old hymns can still make my throat tighten nostalgically. Whenever I'm in deep trouble, wondering which way to turn, the familiar assurances come flooding back to me, "Through every day, o'er all the way. . . ."

That fall I went away from the Worcester parsonage too, for I was a sophomore at Boston University; but for some time Ike and I came home weekends, swapped notes about our respective schools. There were boys in the dorm from all over, not only from nearly every state but from China, South America,

Ike Sows His Wild Oat

Siam, Ike enthused. The only joker was—no girls. Ike spent nearly every waking moment of those Worcester weekends with Else; the family hardly saw him, awake that is, except at the breakfast table. He borrowed the Ford Saturday nights to take a carload of friends to the movies; we'd hear them go by the house, laughing and calling back and forth to each other. Dad would look at me uneasily, but he took the streetcar that ran only a block from the parsonage down to the church so Ike could have the car.

"Why don't you ask your sister to go, too?" Dad snapped one evening and Ike said, surprised, sure she could come, plenty of room. This was purely a figure of speech. There were nine kids in the car which made the old jalopy groan in its tortured springs; Else sat in front with Ike with his arm openly around her while he steered with one hand, I saw uneasily. The other girl in the front seat sat in her boy friend's lap, while, in back, I shrank over into one corner to give room to the other two sardine couples. Ike never took his foot off the gas; we roared past the church, down through the center of town, and were just turning into the movie parking lot when a man reeled out of the bar next door, staggered off the sidewalk directly in front of our car. Ike slammed on the brakes but it was too late. A coldness ran down my spine when we poured out in a frightened flood, saw the man lying there, flat in the street in front of the Ford.

"Hey, what's going on here?" the Irish policeman's voice demanded as he came running up from directing traffic at the corner. "Glory be to Saint Peter, it's old Sam! Is he dead?" He bent over the old man, dressed in shabby pants, an old faded Mackinaw open at the throat, his white hair wild. Old Sam was still breathing stentoriously. "Who was driving the Ford?"

"I was," Ike admitted miserably. His face was white, frightened. "He—he stepped right out in front of me! I didn't mean to hurt him."

"They never do," the cop grated. "Stay here, all of you."

We stayed, miserably, not daring to do anything else, so scared we didn't even talk while the ambulance roared up. If the old man really died. . . . No matter who was to blame, Ike would be in deep trouble. The cop took out his notebook; when he saw Ike's name on his driving license, the cop's red face lifted. "Ain't you the son of Father Nies? Up at Trinity?"

"Yes," Ike admitted.

"Headlines in the newspaper tomorrow," the cop grunted. So now Dad was going to be punished for this, too. What would the official board say? *Minister's son kills pedestrian!* I shivered as the cop asked, "How many were in the front seat?"

"Two!" Else cried. "Ike and me." She knew, as we all did, the law said there should be only two riders on the front seat. But when the cop eyed the gang of us with a sarcastic, "Oh, yeah? Where were the rest of you? Under the hood?" Ike said defiantly, but clearly, "Four of us on the front seat. And four—five in back."

The cop snapped his book shut. "O.K. You can go now. But you'll hear from this, young man, no matter who your Pa is."

We didn't go to the movies; we went back home to phone the hospital to find out how Old Sam was. Dad was waiting for Ike and me when we came into the front hall. He had on his old gray and black plaid bathrobe over his nightshirt and his hair was standing up every which way as it did when he was furiously angry.

"It wasn't Ike's fault!" I rushed in first. "The drunk stepped off the sidewalk right in front of us!"

Ike's face twisted. He asked Dad, "Is—is he dead?"

"No thanks to you he isn't," Dad snapped. I'd never seen him this way; it just seemed as if he and Ike didn't even like

Ike Sows His Wild Oat

each other any more, were no longer of the same blood and sinew. "No. He was just so drunk he fell down, I guess. Anyway they can't find a bruise on his body. The car didn't hit him. You wriggled out of this scrape, Ike, but perhaps you won't next time. You know better than to overcrowd the car that way."

But he himself had asked Ike to add me to the gang! I opened my mouth to say so but shut it again as Ike slammed the car key down onto the hall table in front of Dad. "Take your key," Ike said, his voice breaking into a childish squeak. "I won't ever drive your old Ford again!" He rushed up to his room, shut the door, and, next morning, even though it was Sunday, Ike didn't go to church; he took the early train back to Wilbraham.

I was having to study hard to make the grade at college, so I didn't come home for a weekend for several months, though the train trip took only an hour from Boston, so I didn't know Ike hadn't been there either until Mother phoned me one Saturday night, half-frantic. "Susie, can you come home? I—I need you. *Ike's run away from school!* Your Dad's furious but he can't leave to look for Ike till after Sunday morning service tomorrow. Luckily we're having a union meeting with the Baptist Church Sunday night so Dad can go by noon."

"Where is Ike?" I gasped.

"He went to New York with another boy to spend last night at a friend's house." Mother reported. "They didn't come back this morning as they were supposed to, so now the headmaster has phoned Dad that they're expelled!" Her voice ended in a sob.

"I'll take the next train," I promised.

If Ike was expelled from Wilbraham, I worried, Dad, all of us were disgraced! The whole New England Conference of the Methodist Church would know. What was wrong, with that boy, anyway, that all of a sudden he was surly, unreasonable? Had Dad been too hard on him? All the way from Boston to Worcester, the train wheels clacked the silly old taunting refrain:

> Preacher's kids and cackling hens
> Seldom come to any good ends.

Ike was just growing too big for the eggshell I decided; he had to peck his way out, to find his own horizons.

When Dad picked me up in the Dodge at the station that Saturday noon I didn't have to ask if Ike had been heard from; the set, white mask on Dad's face spoke plainly enough. He said he was going to work on tomorrow's sermon, shut his study door, but Mother and I, sitting together next door in her bedroom, knew Dad was praying. Finally his agonized voice rose, so it came even through the study wall, confessing, "Lord, I'm the one to blame. I put my job ahead of my boy. But it was *Your* work. There's nothing I can do for Ike now except to ask You, a Father too, 'Give thine angels charge over him, to keep him in all his ways.'" As we listened, Mother's eyes lost their wildness. No matter how they might argue, Dad and Ike loved each other. Surely, his basic security would keep Ike safe wherever he was.

But, Mother worried next day when Dad came home from Sunday morning service, ready to leave, how could he find Ike in a city as big as New York?

"I don't know," Dad said frankly. He wouldn't even stop to eat dinner; he'd buy a sandwich on the train, he promised impatiently. "I thought I'd ask Chris Reisner's advice, find out if he thinks I should go to the police." Mother's hands knotted convulsively. "If anyone knows New York, Chris ought to. He's lived and preached there for years."

Ike Sows His Wild Oat

As Dad's train drew out, it began to rain, a chill silent weeping from the sky. I wished I had gone with him; it'd be easier than waiting at home with Mother for the parsonage phone to ring. I drove the Ford back home so slowly I should have been arrested for obstructing traffic; I didn't want to get back to that house with the mortician's colored windows, the house that was no longer a shared happy home. I looked at Mother's set, drawn face and I knew what she was saying inside, "Oh Ike, how could you do this to us? How could you? Ike, I do love you. Please, please come home."

It was nearly midnight that Sunday night when Dad phoned. Neither Mother nor I had been asleep and we both leaped for the receiver. I won. I gasped, "Did you—Is he? . . ."

"Yes, I found him," Dad said. "He's O.K. I'll be back to tell you everything tomorrow. Tell your Mother not to worry. Good-by."

"I'll be back. . . ." Then Ike wasn't coming home, too? But he'd been expelled from school. Where was Ike going? Telling so little was worse, almost, than nothing for you imagined so many things. When I told Mother, she swayed, caught hold of the hall balustrade, as if she were faint. "Thank You, Lord," my mother whispered. But we didn't really know anything, I fretted. Where had Ike been? Has he done something terrible? Is he in jail? In the hospital?

"It doesn't matter," my mother said, "so long as he's alive and safe. Come to bed, Susie."

I cut classes that Monday to meet Dad at the Worcester station because Mother was too upset to drive in traffic and we couldn't have anyone in the Worcester church know what was wrong. Perhaps Ike would come home, after all; but when Dad got off the train he was alone. "Wait till we get home to your Mother," Dad said. "I can't go all over this twice." Mother took one look at Dad's face, tired but with the color back in it, burst into tears and flung her arms around Dad's neck. He patted her shoulder and we all three went into his study and sat down.

"Now, Sugar," he soothed. "Our boy's all right, He's got the right stuff in him. He isn't a boy any more; he's a man—almost."

"Where is he?" Mother insisted.

"Back at school," Dad told her. "After we told the headmaster the whole story—I didn't gloss over my sin in spending too much time at the church and too little time with Ike, I can tell you—he gave the boys another chance to make good. If they don't, out they go. But I have a hunch this weekend has taught them more than a year in class."

Then Dad told us what had happened. Ike and his friend from school had gone down to New York to see a show. They'd signed up at school to visit a classmate who lived on Riverside Drive, to go back to Wilbraham next morning for Saturday classes. Actually the classmate and his family were out of town for the weekend, so Ike and his friend were footloose in a wide-open big city for the first time in their lives, with over ten dollars apiece to spend! However, their money shrank alarmingly. After they'd bought dinner and musical comedy tickets, they didn't have enough left to go to a hotel or for their train fare back to Wilbraham next morning, so the boys decided to spend the night out on a bench in Washington Square. But a cop shook them awake, so they took a late bus up to Central Park; it was a warm night for fall, not unpleasant under a tree, and the boys were very tired. They didn't discover that both their wallets were gone till they woke up next morning and went to a hot-dog stand to buy breakfast.

They were too scared to call home or the school, even if they had had fifty cents between them which they didn't. New York with no cash in your pocket is no musical comedy and their stomachs were getting pretty empty. They walked up to

Ike Sows His Wild Oat

116th Street and Riverside Drive, but their classmate and his family were still away. They tramped the streets, looking wistfully in restaurant windows, taking long drinks of water at the public fountains to "fill up the void." By dinnertime Saturday night they were famished, dead beat, but determined not to go back to the school to be expelled in disgrace as they surely would be. They decided the only thing to do was to find a job, but to do this in a strange city when you're only sixteen, penniless, was about as easy as dipping up the East River with a teaspoon. Finally, unable to keep their eyes open any longer, they fell asleep on another bench on Riverside Drive, but another cop turned them out at midnight, so they sleepwalked some more, going east toward upper Broadway. The boys hadn't had anything to eat for thirty-six hours and they were desperate.

Broadway.... When Ike looked at the sign up over his head that early Sunday morning he was so starving dizzy the letters seemed to jiggle up and down, but the name was familiar. "I have a friend who runs a Methodist church around here," Ike remembered. "He lives on Broadway! The church must be around here somewhere, too. We can ask that cop over there. I guess maybe Chris—Dr. Reisner—would lend us money to eat. They won't give you the bum's rush, anyway, out of a church."

When the boys found Chris's church, it was so early no one was there, but the big front door was open. They simply lay down on the red cushions of a back pew and went sound asleep. Chris discovered them there when he went alone to the church to pray for the morning service, as he always did. As he went down the aisle, Chris saw a muddy shoe hanging down from the pew, looked over, expecting a Broadway bum— instead there was Ike, his friend's son!

Ike looked so disreputable, with his dirty face, tumbled

hair, and rumpled clothes, that at first, Chris told Dad later, he didn't recognize him until Ike grinned, "Chris! I mean Dr. Reisner!" The preacher didn't have time before service to find out why the boys were lurking in his church in this condition. He merely gave Ike a bill and his home address, 2626 Broadway, told the boys to take a taxi there, raid the icebox and go to bed. "But take a bath first, both of you!" Chris stipulated. "My wife and family are away for the weekend."

The boys didn't wake up till almost time for evening service. Sheepish, and more than a little scared, they told Chris their story, asked him to lend them money to go back to school or perhaps it'd be better to go home? Chris said he wasn't sure they should be trusted with cash after what had happened. They'd better come to evening service, and afterward he'd buy them a ticket and put them on the train himself.

"Why didn't he have Ike phone home?" Mother demanded indignantly of Dad. "At least Chris could have stopped me worrying!"

"Ike had had enough of hanging onto his Mother's apron strings," Dad pointed out.

"Oh," my mother said, her eyes blinking away the tears. But it had to be faced; Ike wasn't her baby any more.

"That was where I found them—sitting in the back of Chris's church," Dad explained. "I had telephoned the parsonage but with family away and boys dead asleep, I got no answer. But I knew Chris would be preaching that night so I went to his church. It's a huge place, with vested choir of—oh, I don't know how many voices, fifty to a hundred, I'd say. Chris had an actor from a musical comedy up in the pulpit with him to say a few words, so the place was jam-packed. Some quibblers say that Chris makes a circus performance out of his service, but I'm here to tell you that whole big church was so full of worship, even worried and upset as I was, I could feel peace

Ike Sows His Wild Oat

there. The congregation and choir were singing as I came in, in a mighty wave of sound that lifted you up.

"There's a place on the pulpit steps, Sir," the usher told me. "We let folks sit there when the rest of the seats are full."

"But I stopped dead in the aisle," Dad said, "for I saw Ike and his friend standing there, holding hymn books but not singing, and if I ever saw two sorry-looking, worried kids! But Ike looked fine to me. I leaned over, took hold of his hymn book too, and Ike cried, 'Dad!' I put my arm over his shoulders. I guess they're used to drama in that church, for no one paid us very much attention as Ike and I with the other boy tagging along behind went out down the aisle, all three of us with the tears rolling down our cheeks. The big congregation just went on singing. 'God will take care of you. . . .'"

"Oh Lee!" my mother gasped. "Oh Lee!"

Dad grinned down at her and patted her hand. "So I wrote a 'thank you' note for Chris, left it with an usher, and took those two kids to the nearest restaurant. They were practically bottomless. We caught a train back to the school, got there before 'lights out' and the headmaster was so glad the boys were safe, he said they both would have to be suspended, of course, but they could go to classes, take a make-up exam later. If they passed, they could stay. The headmaster's a good egg, with a boy of his own."

Dad yawned, stretched out on his lumpy study couch, closed his eyes as if he were dead beat too, in body, mind, and spirit. Queer, how nobody ever speaks about how much it took out of the Prodigal Son's father, worrying and waiting for his son to "come to himself." But my mother couldn't let Dad rest yet.

"Didn't Ike even say he was *sorry?*" she demanded, her eyes deeply hurt. "That he'd worried us so?"

"When I left he said, 'Pop, we're having a big football game

169

up here next Saturday,'" Dad reported without opening his tired eyes. " 'You too busy to drive up?' "

"But next Saturday night's the big Men's Club banquet at the church!" my mother remembered. "They're planning on fifteen hundred plates . . . turkey supper, with all the other churches in the district invited!"

"I won't be here," my Dad announced drowsily. "After the game, Ike and I are going to the movies."

My mother stared down at Dad, then a faint smile twisted her lips and she bent down to kiss him. He was sound asleep before mother and I had tiptoed out of the study. It's exhausting being the pastor of a big church with two thousand members; but first of all, my Dad had discovered, you're a father.

Chapter Ten

MY PRIVATE WAR OF INDEPENDENCE

I DIDN'T find out till I got to college that you absorb a philosophy for living in a parsonage without even knowing it, by osmosis. Ike and I had discovered early that some of the things our Sunday school teachers taught us were not the same as Dad's realistic, unorthodox views. He held that just because you believed in the goodness of the Lord, in a heaven where you'd go on growing wiser and happier century after rolling century needn't make you a feckless visionary.

"You can't build a faith without facts any more than a skyscraper without steel," Dad told us kids. "Facts are just as real —and dangerous—as the red-hot rivets a welder's helper tosses to him. Truth can burn you badly unless you handle it right."

He was lying on the couch, exhausted from his preaching, while I had my nose in a book that Sunday noon, waiting for Mother to call us to dinner. Was that heavenly smell from the oven only meat loaf? No, I figured, it was just after pay day; perhaps a nice, juicy, rare roast?

"Even a child—especially a child—can understand religion," Dad mused aloud. "It's theology that can mix you up. You have to get down to the red-hot truth."

"What red-hot truth?" Ike demanded, leaning his head back against Dad's big shoulder.

"Jesus Christ."

I drew a quick breath. This was not a name spoken lightly in our household. You talked familiarly about "The Lord," invited Him "our guest to be," but when you spoke aloud the name of the Son of God, you held your head a little higher, because were not you also "a child of the King"?

"Pain, suffering, and bitter tears come to everyone. There's no use pretending otherwise," Dad explained. "But if you know Jesus Christ as your personal Saviour, he can lead you through. No one can defeat you except you yourself by refusing the help that is offered."

I did not then understand the terrible power Dad was entrusting to our childish hands; it took four years of college and a near-failure at the end for me to find my way back to the red-hot rivets of faith and prayer which held together my own Dad's life structure. Everyone has to fight his own war of independence, win or lose.

Ike's and my going to college was a natural extension of our browsing among Dad's books. We merely moved on to a bigger library. "I can't leave you money. An education is all the inheritance I can give you," Dad explained. "Still, you won't have to pay any inheritance tax on algebra and philosophy books."

But sometimes I wonder—is college worth all the sacrifice a preacher makes so his children may form the *habit* of learning?

I didn't know until after I was graduated that, to pay my college bills, Dad borrowed to the hilt on his life insurance, and wore his blue serge suits till they were so shiny and threadbare the pulpit committee tactfully bought him a black silk gown to cover his shabbiness when he preached; that for me he'd cheerfully bought cheap shoes in the bargain basement, then soaked them in the bathtub to take out the squeaks. When the money he could borrow ran out, he and Mother

My Private War of Independence

ate oatmeal mush for three weeks to pay for my college diploma, and to save the five dollars to buy my small gold Phi Beta Kappa key.

Dad and Mother wanted Ike and me to be like the other college students, carefree and happy; and we were, God forgive us, we were. We never even questioned the hard-won checks they sent us.

I went to Boston University because it gave us preachers' kids scholarship help and I lived at the YWCA because there were then no women's dormitories for the College of Liberal Arts.

Most of my high moments during my four years, as I look back through the binoculars of the years, were nonacademic, extracurricular. Classes I frequently found dry bones, not worth exhuming, couched in words unnecessarily pedantic. As preacher's kids we were used to having at our modest dinner-table conversations with bishops, philosophers, even scientists of note who ate with delight our Mother's homemade rolls, light as Texas tumbleweed, and who took Ike's and my childish questions seriously. They even answered in words we could understand!

I shall never forget coming in the door of my first college class in religious education, hesitating in the doorway when I saw forty theologues already seated there, eighty men's eyes staring at me, the only girl. The professor was orating, "Gentlemen, the theory that ontogeny recapitulates phylogeny has yet to be exploded." Good grief, I panicked, as I crept to a vacant seat, he might as well be talking Hindustani; this was no place for me! But my seatmate, leaning over, whispered comfortingly, "He just means kids are little savages in Sunday school!" "Why doesn't he say so, then?" I muttered.

The real scholars on the faculty, however, found it much easier to communicate with us lesser mortals, The Oxford,

Sorbonne, Göttigen degree holders disdained our American thumping of scholastic drums; they even associated with us students after classes so that something of their tolerant world-mindedness rubbed off on us.

I told my Dad, half-defiantly, "I learn more German singing student drinking songs while we thump down our pewter mugs on the wooden table in Professor' Perrine's garden, weekends at the Deutscher Verein, than I do in class, translating Goethe's *Faust!*" I saw Dad's eyes widen, and added unwillingly, "Oh, it's only lemonade!"

Dad came down to Boston from Worcester every Monday morning to attend the Clerical Club. (Monday is the minister's "day off" or should be.) The Wesleyan Building where they met was almost across the street from the college, so Dad and I frequently lunched together, then he came back with me to class. I wished heartily that Dad hadn't worn his long-tailed preacher's coat when he came to visit my class in Shakespearean drama. I didn't take my regular seat up front, but slumped down at the back as if we were both visitors, for I was a little uneasy about the state our professor might be in when he arrived—and Dad was never one to hide his feelings. If he felt like snorting his disapproval out loud, he would. I didn't even answer the roll when my name was called; much better to take a cut than to be conspicuous.

The professor, a raw-boned Scot with a lanky body and brilliant mind, had, as I'd feared, refreshed himself with more than food at his own lunch. His face was flushed, his eyes glittered, and he held onto the lectern in front of him as if it were a ship tossing at sea; but he gave a rollicking, masterly, unforgettable characterization of Falstaff that almost lifted you out of your seat to cheer. He *was* Falstaff, big, bawdy, riotously funny. In one leap we were transported from 1916 Boston back to the days of the great Elizabeth. The professor was marvel-

174

ous, breathtaking; but I couldn't help casting anxious glances out of the corner of my eye at Dad sitting there in his long-tailed preacher's coat. Would he realize what had pepped up the professor?

"A magnificent act," Dad murmured as he and I strolled out together after class. "Pity it all had to come out of a bottle!"

Dad also took the part of Professor Dallas Lore Sharp against his own daughter, which seemed to me, at first, the basest treachery.

Dallas Lore Sharp, the little professor of English composition, with the keen gray eyes behind his steel-rimmed spectacles, the acid-sharp mind, and the black Windsor tie which he always yanked at when excited, became for me the most hated man in the faculty. For early in my freshman year he punctured the balloon that I knew how to write. Having had poems, articles, and stories published since I was seven, at eighteen I was smugly serene. Freshman Comp. met in the big amphitheater with its soaring rows of seats and down front was the dissecting table where the Harvard Medical Students from whom we'd inherited the building used to cut up smelly cadavers. Here Professor Sharp ripped the heart out of my first theme also. "Nauseating!" he howled. "Who wrote this—this jello?"

"I did!" Stung to fury, I rose up from my top seat in the big amphitheater, glared right back at Sharp. "That story has already been printed and an editor paid me good money for it."

"The more fool he." Sharp marked a large F on my theme, tossed it aside as if it should actually go into the wastepaper basket. F meant complete failure, I knew, sinking back into my seat, shaking with anger and embarrassment. I'd flunked English for the first time in my life! I wished I could sink down to the basement but I had to go on sitting there while the rest in the amphitheater grinned.

I was so upset, I went home to Worcester on the train that weekend, to accept the healing sympathy of my family. Mother said warmly Sharp must be crazy; everyone knew I was a fine writer. But to my surprise Dad didn't apply any soothing poultice to my wounded literary pride.

"Sharp's own books sell widely," he pointed out.

"What does he write about?" I raged, walking up and down the study floor. "About what he sees in his own backyard in Hingham! About bees, bugs, birds—and. . . ."

"Bugs are interesting," Dad said mildly. "An ant's world is a microcosm."

"I'm not interested in microcosms!" I shouted. "There's a cockroach that lives under my radiator at the YW—I suppose I should write about that!"

"You might do worse." Dad was laughing at me. I had flunked college English, and this was all he cared. "I don't think I'll stay over Sunday, after all," I snapped, outraged. "I have a Latin paper to write." I waited for Dad to urge me to stay but he didn't, though Mother gave me the cake she'd baked for dessert to take back with me. I ate most of it on the train and then walked the empty, crowded streets of Boston for hours; there is no place so lonely as a big city when everyone has a friend to talk to except you. But even my roommate was away over this weekend; she'd gone to Dartmouth to moon with her fiancé. I had no fiancé, no talent to write apparently, and now no family.

This was the beginning of my war of independence. I didn't go home again that semester and I ducked Dad's Monday invitations for lunch till he stopped asking me. I would live as I liked, I decided defiantly, write as I liked. The joker was that I had to pass freshman English somehow. Professor Sharp flunked every theme I turned in, though occasionally there would be a red pencil note, "This paragraph is better. Not so much pink frosting." I felt even more truculent when Dad sent me an article clipped from a magazine about an author who never sold a line till he went to the hospital for an appendectomy. Then he got a thousand dollars for writing about "My Big Stomach-Ache." I'd never fall that low, I told myself savagely; the purpose of literature was to uplift, not to bare one's anatomy for people to laugh at! Surely a minister should know that.

One night as I sat moodily up in my narrow room, waiting for genius to burn, sniffing the YW atmosphere which is like nothing else on earth, a compound of soap, disinfectant, gardenia talcum powder, and kindness to lonely females, my pet cockroach peered out again from under his radiator, darted for the crumbs I'd brought up for him from my supper tray in the cafeteria. I was getting rather fond of him. He was a funny little bug, at that, swarming greedily all over his supper, then nibbling daintily almost like a child whose mother had warned, "Now, watch your manners."

"My pal, Cocky. . . ." The words chuckled in my mind as I seized my pen, began to write how night after night, the cockroach and I shared my room and board, studied companionably, he under his warm radiator and I at my desk. His world was the floor, the crack in the liver-colored wall; mine was the desk, the window out of which my thoughts flew. The cockroach and I were more than friends; we were fellow insects in a vast universe of which we saw only our own narrow cracks.

Suddenly I realized that this was exactly what Dad and Professor Sharp had been trying to make me see! *The red-rivet facts of the real world about me*. I caught my breath, impulsively added a footnote to my theme. "Dear Friend

177

Sharp, I have hated you for six months but tonight I see what you mean—cockroaches *are* people! Cocky and I thank you. GSN."

"My dear child," Sharp wrote back by return mail, "If you hadn't been worth saving, I wouldn't have pursued you. I know now how Livingston felt when discovered by Stanley in darkest Africa." In my heart I knew that I owed my first theme to be marked A to my Dad's laughter, but I didn't tell him what had happened. It would have meant surrender and I was still fighting my own battle.

From now on I would be a realist; I'd write facts, grubby down-to-earth realism about people fighting, stealing, shooting each other. I might even get a job as a reporter! Of all the newspapers I should have picked to pursue my grimy career, the last one should have been the *Christian Science Monitor,* but the college employment bureau told me they were looking for a BU correspondent, so I went there to apply for a job.

The city room was huge, urgent with teletype machines, typewriters, and telephones. The city editor was busy. As he asked for my credentials, he kept scrawling hieroglyphics with a thick black pencil on the papers on his desk. Finally he asked absently, "Are you a Scientist?"

"No," I snapped. "Are you a Methodist?"

He really looked at me then. He chuckled, then he laughed aloud, laughed and laughed till he had to wipe his eyes. "You'll do. You're hired, young lady. Write up the Klatsch Collegium for us, will you? A couple of sticks."

Would I! I had no idea what a stick was but I rushed around gathering up names. My story was as factual as the telephone book and about as interesting; "The Boston University Klatsch Collegium, the outstanding social event of the college year, will be held next Saturday evening in the College of Liberal Arts. Among those present in the receiving line will be. . . ."

My Private War of Independence

The faculty names took up about an inch and the names of the student committee another; the story I cut out for my "clip sheet"—I was paid twenty-five cents an inch, as I recall—was short but I wore it out, reading and rereading. Wasn't I on the staff of one of the world's great newspapers?

I went so "whole-hog" in my turnover of ideals that I contracted a severe case of theological measles. I was even sure enough of myself now to lunch with Dad on Mondays when I told him over a tomato salad sandwich and a cup of black coffee that I no longer believed in miracles or in prayer which was merely man talking hopefully to himself. God might have wound up the springs originally, I conceded, but after He'd started up the machine, it was up to us to attend to the repairs. What place had a religious miracle in a scientific world?

"The same place a scientific miracle has," Dad said mildly. It was disappointing that he wasn't shocked at the cornhusks his Prodigal Daughter was rustling so proudly. "Miracles are mostly facts that we don't know enough yet to explain. Can you imagine what John Wesley would have thought of radio— a voice talking out of a box? Witchcraft, indeed!"

"But you can *prove* a chemical formula or a law of physics," I argued.

"By experiment," Dad agreed. "The power of God can be proved in the same way. You've seen it change lives right in our own front parlor, Susie."

"But you can *see* the law of gravity work. Newton watched the apple fall!"

"Ask your physics professor to show you an atom."

"Well, maybe you can't see it with your naked eye," I conceded. "Or even with a microscope. But you know it's there by the way it acts. . . . Oh!" For I'd suddenly remembered the man throwing away his gin bottle, the paper executive to whom Dad had given his second-best dark-blue suit, who'd

179

gotten his sales manager's job back. What did that prove, if anything?

"We know by the way a man acts, whether or not he's God-guided." Dad's very blue eyes smiled into mine but there were shadows there too of remembered pain. "I don't ask you to swallow my beliefs, Sister. But someday you may need to try an experiment in prayer yourself. Sometime, somewhere, you're sure to need help desperately; and when you do, remember this scientific formula. 'Dear Lord, give me strength to do Thy will. And a quiet heart. For Jesus' sake. Amen.'"

"All the shibboleths," I thought impatiently. But as I stared across the lunch table at my Dad I saw that his face was thinner, whiter than it used to be, and he looked tired. Stubborn and backward in his Puritan creed as he might be, I loved him. I murmured, "Yes, I'll remember."

When my picture came out in the newspaper saying underneath that Esther Nazarian and I were writing and staging Boston University's first musical comedy, *The Coy Co-ed* (how a name does date you!) I waited for a scorching letter from Dad, saying I'd let him down, that I was no stage-struck daughter of his—but no word came from Worcester. Of course, parishes were more tolerant now; most Methodists went to the movies—but a musical comedy! I was sure some old fuddy-duddies were giving Dad a bad time because his own daughter was writing lyrics, even dancing in the student ballet, but still no word of reproof came; only when I sent Mother and Dad a couple of tickets for the opening night, there was no answer, either.

But Ike's reply to my invitation was prompt and to the point. "Thank heaven, the pictures in the paper don't look a bit like you! Did you or Esther ever even *see* Broadway? (He needn't think he was so smart. Broadway hadn't turned out too

My Private War of Independence

well for him!) No, thanks, I won't come down. My face is red enough as it is."

So I made my musical comedy debut without my family. I told myself fiercely, after scanning the overflow audience through the hole in the red velvet curtain, that I didn't mind; but my throat was dry with something besides stage fright when the curtain rolled up and the footlights blazed in my eyes. Being a rebel is a lonesome feeling.

That summer for the first time I did not go to Maine with the family; I landed a job as counselor at a summer camp in Northfield, Massachusetts. I got my board and tent and the cash I made hardly paid for candy bars and stamps but at least I was on my own. I was myself, free as the mountain air above Little Round Top where we had our "Sunset Sings," while the western sky blazed crimson. This fall when I went back I'd be a college senior; Ike would be a senior too at Wilbraham Academy. I was startled to find he was taller than I was when he came down to Boston for the weekend. He wore his clothes differently, in a lordly yet careless fashion, with his necktie tied just so, but a lock of brown hair falling down on his forehead. He usually came with a friend, picked up another girl so the four of us went out on the town. (It never occurred to either Ike or me that our war of independence couldn't have gone on a week if Dad hadn't continued quietly paying our bills.) On one of these big evenings I danced my first two-step with a Siamese gentleman.

"Chula," as Ike called him because the rest of his name was too long to pronounce, had an apparently bottomless pocketbook. Ike explained to me that Chula had some sort of connection with the royal palace because he was under the supervision of the Crown Prince of Siam who was studying at Harvard. Perhaps Chula was the son of a minor wife or even

181

of a favorite concubine! This made Chula even more exciting, I agreed enthusiastically.

"Susie, what about the Brunswick roof next Saturday night?" Chula phoned me. "Is good orchestra, yes?"

"Splendid. Pick me up at eight at the Y," I agreed. I'd never heard the Brunswick orchestra but I wasn't going to let on. "Has Ike a girl?"

Chula giggled. "Ike has harem. This girl's named Mae."

A murmur of surprise ran around the nearby tables as the four of us sat down at our table that evening, Ike with his red-headed girl in a fluffy green gown. I wore blue because it made my eyes the same color, to charm Chula who to me was fascinatingly exotic, heaven-sent for a girl determined to prove she was "different." He had a flat ivory face, almond eyes, a short chunky body, and his black hair was attached to the very top of his skull rather like that of the Japanese doll I used to keep on my bedroom shelf because it was too delicate to play with. When the orchestra began playing a dance tune, Chula and I got up. A girl at the next table gasped audibly, "Why, she's going to dance with that Chinaman!"

Chula's arm stiffened against my back but his inscrutable Oriental face remained blank of expression as we swung out onto the dance floor. He danced the waltz and the two-step very well. Floating around in his arms I grinned to myself, "Quite a change from being a 'Raindrop' in the Dorchester High gym!" As the orchestra's rhythm quickened, Chula murmured in my ear, "Shall we try two-step? That's the music for it. I not berry good."

I had watched the two-step danced many times, but I'd never tried it myself. I said recklessly, "I'm not very good either. Let's go!"

We were getting along fine, doing as well as anyone else anyway, when suddenly there was a small commotion at the

My Private War of Independence

door of the roof garden—and Chula stopped dead on the dance floor. He couldn't go white with his yellow skin, but he was staring as if petrified at a large party of men and girls seating themselves around a reserved table. "Is Prince!" Chula gasped. "Is Prince of Siam, from Harvard College!"

Before I could stop him, he had rushed over to the royal table, was salaaming deeply while everyone watched, startled. I stood there, red-faced, uncertain, alone on the ballroom floor, till Ike came to the rescue and took my arm. We stared at Chula bobbing frantically up and down, babbling incomprehensible things in his outlandish language.

"Talk English!" the Prince snapped to Chula, getting up to come over where Ike and I stood, uncertainly. "Are these your friends?"

"Mees Susie Nies," Chula introduced us unhappily. Had not his Prince found him acting most unseemly in crazy American dance? "Meester Ike Nies, from my school." Ike held out his hand cordially to the Prince, but Chula moaned, "No, no, Ike! Just bow!"

But already the Prince had taken Ike's hand, held it limply, dropped it. "When we are in Athens of America, we become Athenians," he reproved Chula coldly. He shook hands with me, too, spoke briefly, politely, in faultless English, then went back to his own table. But he ignored the frightened Chula completely from then on and Chula never asked me on a date again. I had made him "lose face."

I didn't go home for the midyear vacation either that senior year; I wasn't sure how much Dad knew about my Bunny Hugging, theater-going, and other un-Methodist actions in this spring of my independence, 1917. I stayed with a classmate in Belmont instead. But Dad's check for my last tuition was waiting for me at the YWCA when I got back there, together with a brief note saying that Mother and he were pleased with my marks which the college had just sent them. They were proud of me. I wondered how proud they'd have been if they'd seen Chula, Ike, and me on the Brunswick roof?

The following Monday after we registered I almost literally bumped into Dad in front of the Wesleyan Building in Copley Square. "Susie!" he beamed, rushing to throw an arm across my shoulders. "Did you have a nice vacation? You look gay as a cricket in that red coat!"

"Oh, I just picked it up last week at Stearns," I told him. "I'm glad you like it. I charged it to you. Hope you don't mind?"

He hesitated only momentarily. I thought it was because he hated charge accounts so. "That's all right. I expect you needed a new coat for your senior year."

Dad looked rather shabby himself. His blue serge coat was shiny at the seams, and there were spots on his vest. I hated myself for noticing so I said brightly, "How about taking me to lunch?"

"Oh, I'm on a diet," Dad chuckled. "I don't eat lunch any more. I'm just here because I have to read a paper for the Clericals. How about coming home to Worcester some week-end soon? We hardly ever see you."

"Pretty soon," I promised.

But I didn't go. I had no idea that Dad wasn't eating lunch because he couldn't afford to, that his own new suit had gone into my tuition check. Is all youth kitten-blind or was it only I?

Two weeks before the final examinations that June, I had the flu, stayed in my narrow YW cot, unable to read a text-book, but when I went back to college, the dean sent word that I must take the final examinations with the rest; I couldn't be granted any extra time to study. My classroom work had been satisfactory that semester, he insisted, and this should carry me through. I was frantic but the dean wouldn't budge from

My Private War of Independence

his decision. My first exam was in French. I went into the big hot stuffy room so upset, unsure of myself, that when I sat down at the desk, opened the blue book, saw the first long list of irregular verbs to conjugate, I couldn't recall ever seeing one of those words before. But this was ridiculous! I'd studied French for four years now. But my mind was as blank as new blotting paper. I knew those verbs and knew that I did, but my hand simply refused to make connection with my brain.

"What'll I do?" I panicked, beginning to sweat so that my clenched palms were wet. If I rushed with my screwy tale to the monitor sitting high up there on the platform, he'd think it merely another unprepared student's alibi. He wouldn't believe me and I'd flunk the whole final exam. For half an hour I sat there agonizing, not writing a word, staring up at the hand on the big clock on the wall going inexorably round and round, ending my college career in flat failure. I *had* to begin to write soon; but I couldn't. The ticking of the remorseless clock grew louder and louder in my frightened ears till it spoke in remembered words. "Sometime, Susie, you're sure to need help desperately—and when you do. . . ." But how could I come crybabying now to the Lord? Prayer, Dad had insisted, was a red-hot rivet fact. All I had to do was to hurl my red-hot fears at the Lord, hope He would catch them. I dropped my face onto my shaking hands, asked desperately, "Dear Lord, give me a quiet heart if You can." The mist was clearing already! I ended humbly, "For Jesus' sake. Amen."

My panic was gone; I could think again. I snatched my pen, reopened my blue book, and like a scroll unwinding, the verbs began to write themselves under my flying fingers. Call it "the breakdown of an emotional block" or "an answer to prayer"— what did I care? It worked, oh yes, it worked, this miracle of a quiet heart.

It was this examination which (as the dean knew) helped to decide my eligibility for the honorary scholarship society of Phi Beta Kappa. The possibility of graduating "summa cum laude" had never entered my mind; no one was more startled than I when my roommate came running across the dance floor at Senior Prom. By this time all our class who were sure of graduating had put on our best evening clothes and highest hearts in a frantic merry-go-round of relief. I couldn't imagine what ailed my roommate when she grabbed my arm, stopped the whirl of my waltzing.

"You made Phi Bete, Susie!" she gasped. "The list has just been posted!" As I stared, stock-still on the dance floor, unbelieving, she rushed on, "It isn't fair, you know. I'm just as smart as you are! I study and study but you're the one who hauls down the golden key. How did you wangle it?"

"I don't know...." I thought back over the four years. What had I gained? A smattering of books and languages; a knowledge that older civilizations were not insentient dust but had been engaged, as we Americans, in the pursuit of happiness; an understanding that people and cockroaches wanted much the same things—food, a mate, a safe crack into which to crawl when danger lurked. But all of these odds and ends of knowledge were chaotic, incoherent, made no pattern without the wisdom of the quiet heart which my Dad had given me.

"Excuse me?" I brushed aside my dancing partner. "I have to phone home. Right now."

Chapter Eleven

SHOULD I MARRY A MINISTER?

"No MORE parsonage spotlight for me. I'll never marry a minister!" I told my mother firmly as we washed the dinner dishes in the Somerville parsonage where she and Dad had moved from Worcester. "He-dishes," she called the pots and pans with distaste, leaving them for me to scrub while the delicate dainty china was naturally, "she."

I stopped to eye with satisfaction my new dark-blue tweed suit in the kitchen mirror; even covered with an apron, the suit did all the right things for me, made my hair more golden; and the new hairdo that "little" hairdresser in the shop in Boston had "created" made my glasses hardly noticeable. Earning your own money had its compensations, even if Boston University didn't exactly overpay its Associate Director of Publicity. In 1917 when the boys in our class had graduated from college into the Army or Navy, we girls had puttered with "war work," not making airplane parts, but handing out doughnuts, inspiring the troops with "It's a long, long trail a-winding" on a hot ukelele. Women were still homebodies, not crack shots or sailors in uniform. Now by 1921 the boys had trailed back home, many to take graduate studies, and I was helping Professor Taylor wheedle stories about the university into the newspapers. There were side benefits also; it was a bad Saturday night when some student didn't invite me to dinner—after all, Boston University now had some twelve thousand students, half of them men—and Sundays I could always count on a meal at home, if my cash ran short.

"What's wrong with ministers?" Mother asked. She looked almost as young as when Ike and I were kids in Dorchester, merely a little plumper here and there. How could I look so blonde and cool while Mother had all those luscious curves and a tall son about to graduate from Ohio Wesleyan University? "Your father and I. . . ."

"Are two ants in the sugar bowl," I chuckled. "I know, darling. But you and Dad fell in love when you were six and he built you a tree-house. I could marry Ham easily" (he was a red-haired, six-foot theologue I'd been dating for six months now) "but I refuse to run a free, all-day, all-night lunchcart. You and Dad hardly ever have a meal alone! You haven't even had on that blue chiffon negligee I gave you for Christmas."

Mother sighed, "It's rather diaphanous for anyone but your father. But the parish are neighborly. Why, that time I had flu, we were inundated with pies, cakes, a roast chicken your father could just warm in the oven. . . ."

"I guess I'm the hermit type. When I'm sick, I want to enjoy ill health alone. I hate 'the communion of the saints.'"

"Why, Susie!" Mother gasped, waving an appalled dish towel.

I banged the last pan down under the sink, explaining it wasn't the saints themselves I objected to but their X-ray eyes. I loathed testifying at prayer meeting. Every Wednesday night, when I was younger, I used to get sick to my stomach knowing I'd have to stand up, speak in public. It wasn't the Lord I didn't want to let down, I confessed, it was Dad. Besides, who wanted to listen to Brother Wentworth squeak, "Amen, Sister!"

"Brother Wentworth was a dear old soul!" Mother protested. I agreed but a fifty-year-old bachelor, even a saint,

Should I Marry a Minister?

was not terribly inspiring company for a ten-year-old girl; I preferred to choose my friends rather than to have them thrust at me. Why should my husband or I be routed out at midnight because 'Enry 'Iggins, drunk again, was beating Sister 'Iggins? No parsonage or minister for me.

Mother's eyes twinkled. "Didn't you and Ham go to a tea last week at BUST? To the senior reception? And had a chapel date at Robinson Memorial. . . ."

"Covering all the news at Boston University School of Theology is *my job!*", hotly.

Hamilton Stewart was a brilliant boy with football shoulders who'd won the DSM in the war just ended (whoever dreamed then that we'd come to list world wars, to call this the First?), who'd wandered over Europe, China, and India before he'd decided that the only likely job for an ex-soldier was to preach peace. "Ham just happened to be there so you went out to lunch at the Parker House, after chapel?" You couldn't deceive Mother; she had an instinct when it came to men. She knew that if I ever did marry a minister, he'd be Ham—if he asked me, which he hadn't as yet.

They were hard-hitting realists, these senior theologues, older than most students, who'd learned that bullets never settled anything permanently, that the real battles were fought between ideas, ideals. Ham said, his gray eyes and red hair aflame with passionate earnestness, "Until we know that India's lowest untouchable is our brother, there will be only uneasy breathing spells while we cast bigger and more terrible guns." He and other perennially hungry students from 72 Mt. Vernon Street used to drop by my apartment frequently to raid my icebox and to "shoot the breeze." The eighty-year-old Boston spinster with whom I shared the rooms on Hemenway Street always went to bed promptly at nine P.M. Every night she'd put on her white cambric nightgown

189

whose ruffles showed at neck and wrists below her dark dressing gown, braid her long hair into a pigtail, gather up toothbrush and soap box, and parade past the open living room door to the bathroom, announcing loudly, "Nine o'clock! Bedtime!" After their first startled vision, my friends would call back, "Sweet dreams!" and settle deeper into their comfortable armchairs, arguing to the obbligato of my dear old chaperone's ladylike snores.

"Up late last night, Grace?" Professor Taylor would twinkle when I came, yawning, into the publicity office next morning. "One of your theologues blow you to a show at the Old Howard?"

The Old Howard was a Boston burlesque show almost as famous as Bunker Hill Monument. Like most Bostonians, I'd never visited either landmark, but Professor Taylor had; the newspaper cartoonists used to love to picture the learned professor, a Greek scholar who quoted Euripides and Aristophanes by the yard, as peering through delighted spectacles at the chorus girls. He had a long white beard, very little other hair on his head and a twinkle in his eye. As the head of the classical drama department, Professor Taylor explained, he was "observing human drama." This wise old gentleman had explained the facts of university life to me when I first came to work with him.

"Each dean in the eleven departments will be jealous of any newspaper space you get for the other ten. Several of them will hate you for printing anything. I think we'd better start a 'slat list.'"

" 'Slat list'?" I puzzled as the professor drew a sheet of yellow quiz paper toward him, reached for a thick black pencil.

He explained that he'd once heard a newsboy in front of the Old Howard tell another boy who was horning in on his territory, "If you don't get out of here, I'll knock your slats

Should I Marry a Minister?

in!" We could achieve dramatic catharsis by listing those people whose slats we publicity people would like to knock in. Dean X who'd phoned us yesterday that we'd better keep our hands off his department, that he knew more newspaper editors than any fuddy-duddy professor or half-feathered girl would head the slat list. Professor Taylor solemnly wrote down, "Dean X," handed me the quiz paper for safekeeping. "Well, we'll see what happens to *him!*"

Only a week later the telephone at my apartment woke me at two A.M. "A college boy went up the fire escape to a party in the girls' dormitory!" Dean X's despairing voice blew me almost out of bed. "The fool janitor thought he was a thief, called the police! The boy got away but he left his derby hat behind. You've got to do something, quick, to keep this out of the newspapers!"

With the story on the police blotter, I assured the frantic dean, there was nothing anyone could do but sit tight, tell the exact truth but no more, and wait for the hurricane to blow over. Next morning one Boston newspaper was topped by a derby hat hanging on a question mark with big black head-lines underneath: WHO OWNS THE DERBY? THE WOMAN ALWAYS PAYS. The shaken dean ordered that no one in the building was hereafter to speak to a policeman or a newspaper reporter except to Professor Taylor or me.

Ham laughed so loudly when I told him about the girl, the dean, and the derby that people turned around on the side-walks of Boylston Street to look at us. "You're wasted in an office, Susie," Ham told me. "A preacher's wife could use a slat list. Come on down to the Esplanade while I tell you about the church that's been offered me when I graduate next June."

The Esplanade was the dimly-lighted walk for lovers along the Charles River, but I wasn't ready yet to go there with

Ham. I reminded him, "You're chairman of the reception for first-year men at School tonight!"

"Oh, that," Ham muttered. "They can get along fine without us. I left plenty of cookies and weak fruit punch."

"I'm going anyway," I told him firmly. "I have a story to phone into the *Herald*."

The very next night I met my Englishman at the Hotel Vendome where his cousins, Henry and Angela, had invited us young people to dinner because they figured both of us could use a good meal. The Englishman's name was (of all things) *Vivian*, but Cousin Henry explained jovially that V's fraternity brothers at Dartmouth had called him "Jock."

"Dartmouth?" I asked as Jock bowed to me, clicking his heels. He was dark-haired, erect, rosy-cheeked and he bent so low over my hand I wondered if he were going to kiss it? No, that would be French, continental. . . . "Why not Oxford? Cambridge?"

"My mother was American before she married my father," Jock explained. Being torn between two countries did have its drawbacks. "Because I was an alien, I couldn't hold a commission when I fought in the U.S. Army."

"A GI named *Vivian?*" I gasped. "They must have kidded the pants off you!"

"Good chaps. Most of them came from South or East Boston. We got along fine after the first few weeks."

There must be more to this man than rosy cheeks and clicking heels. As we sat down beside each other at the hotel table lavish with silver, crystal, and rich food, mildly interested, I asked Jock where his home was, exactly?

"The island of Jersey," he told me, proudly. "Off the coast of France." So my instinct had been right! "It's only about four hours by sea from St. Malo."

"Cows," I said brightly. "Jersey and Guernsey. . . ." A howl

Should I Marry a Minister?

of anguish interrupted me. Guernseys were not to be mentioned in the same breath as Jerseys; didn't I know that their cream content was only. . . . I had small interest in measuring cream, but Jock went right on pouring out the advantages of Jersey as if someone had turned on a spiggot—how the cabbages grew on stalks twelve feet high to be made into handsome walking sticks, how the plump immaculate pig who lived in the yard of the stone house where V. was born was scrubbed to its pink skin as frequently as the children in the family. It was rather a relief when dinner was over, though I found out later that Jersey was the only subject upon which Jock was voluble; on any other theme than his tight wonderful little island he was apt to hesitate, even to blush before he found the right words. But Jersey was the "Open Sesame" to his heart and tongue.

Jock took me home after dinner. It was such a lovely evening that we walked up Commonwealth Avenue under the tall trees with the street lamps winking at us through the autumn leaves. I asked, "What are you doing now in Boston?"

"Cambridge," he corrected. "Getting my master's in business administration at Harvard. I felt I needed to brush up a bit after the Army and Cousin Henry insisted upon sending me there—my grandfather and his father were brothers. The business school's so new we have classes in a basement but the faculty's top-hole."

He murmured, his face close to mine, "Will you go to the Harvard game with me next Saturday? We're playing Princeton. I could fetch you about one, say?"

Who said the English were slow? I hesitated. I had a half-date with Ham to study at the Public Library but football in the Cambridge Bowl, and this boy was so different, intriguing. "All right. I'd like to go. Call me." I fled upstairs to my room, a queer light happiness inside me which I didn't try to analyze. I'd drop Ham a note so he couldn't argue.

That first afternoon Jock and I spent at the Harvard stadium was one of those lucent, blue-sky New England days too perfect to seem real. The crisp October air intoxicated, effervescent as youth itself. We yelled ourselves hoarse with the rest of the vast crowd, but when the Harvard team neared the goal line, Jock yelled, "Well played!" instead of "Kill 'em! Touchdown!" But he was as exuberant as all the rest as we surged across the crowded field to the goalposts when we Harvardians won. To celebrate, we went to that homely wonderful restaurant up over Fanueil Hall Market, where the steaks are thick enough for even hungry students' bottomless stomachs. Generations of Harvard men had celebrated victory here and the comfortable plump waitresses looked mature enough to have served both father and son. We sat, twenty of us, strangers yet familiar, along a white boardinghouse table with no frills but good food; when Bostonians discover a good thing, they see no need to change or to gild it.

"This is rather like an English pub," Jock beamed. "At least, it has the same feeling, good fellowship and a joint of rare roast beef."

We ate so heartily we decided to walk back home along the Esplanade beside the Charles River where the stars were reflected twice, once in the dark dreaming water, again in our eyes. It had been a perfect day to hold in your memory, to cherish. There was indeed something about this gentle English boy, Jock, that spoke to me in my own language. Was it because he had sometimes been lonely, too?

That winter I dated Jock and Ham alternately trying to make up my mind as, I dare say, they were searching their own. An ecstatic letter from Ike at Ohio Wesleyan finally made me decide to take both boys out to meet Dad and

Should I Marry a Minister?

Mother, to see how they fitted into our family. Ike had fallen in love with " 'a daughter of the gods, divinely tall,' whose name is Lillian." She was wonderful; they could hardly wait till he graduated in June, got a job, to be married. The letter slid from my hand to the bedroom floor as I stared out the window at the red banners of sunset over the parkway trees. *Ike married, gone.* . . . He'd been a part of me for so long; now the bright invisible cord which had bound us together as PK's would be broken. I *wanted* him to have a family of his own, but still—life's soap-bubble had burst wetly in my face. I'd better make up my own mind whether I wanted to marry a minister, a "Johnny Bull," or to travel alone. I knew by now I could write well enough to feed myself; I could imagine a travel article beginning, "Once as I mounted my rickshaw in Singapore. . . ." Well, it didn't hurt to dream.

Mother's feelings had been hurt because I preferred my own apartment in town to one of the several empty bedrooms in the Somerville parsonage. Why spend good money when you could have board and room free? I took Ham home with me one Sunday morning to the shabby parsonage sandwiched in between two other houses. Dad asked Ham to read the Scriptures at morning service when the little church was filled to capacity; at Sunday school Ham took over a class of lively boys and then did hearty justice to the Southern fried chicken and raised biscuits Mother had provided for dinner.

"You boys at 72 still have to eat out as I did, don't you?" Dad said, noticing with approval the amount of chicken Ham was stowing away. "I earned my meals waiting table at a restaurant down on Charles Street."

"My Dad owns a furniture factory in Michigan," Ham confessed, apologetically. So that's how he could travel the world after he got out of the Army! Ham would never have to scrimp along no matter how small his preacher's salary, mother's quick glance assured me across the table. It was obvious Dad and Mother both liked Ham, that he fitted with them as neatly as the missing piece in a jigsaw puzzle. But it was I who'd have to live with him in the parsonage where there'd be small time even to read about far-off Singapore. . . .

On our way back to town on the streetcar, Ham asked me to marry him, in his loud cheerful voice, with the motorman staring at us in his little mirror and the fat lady behind us all delighted ears. Ham ran his finger down inside the clasp of my brown glove as he spoke so that my palm quivered as he rushed on that the church in New Jersey where he was going in June had a pleasant parsonage. He was going down there to preach next Sunday and he'd like me to go with him, to meet the parishioners.

"Audition me too?"

Ham beamed at me. "The president of the Ladies' Aid is a tartar, but you can handle her, Susie. You're a PK; you know the ropes."

So that's what Ham wanted, someone to handle the Ladies' Aid, to plan pleasant programs for the missionary society. . . . Doubtless our son would be president of the Junior Epworth League! He took for granted that we loved each other. But even though they'd been married years and years my Dad was always asking my mother, "Darling, did I ever happen to mention to you that I love you?" Right in front of us kids, as if he were proud of it. "O. K., Susie?" Ham begged.

I jerked back my gloved hand. "I'll be no one's assistant minister!"

Ham stared at me, the angry red rising in his face till it flamed like his hair. "You knew what my job was!"

"Fares, please!" As Ham and I glared at each other, the conductor held out the silver-plated coin-holder. Ham brushed it aside, sprang up to yank the cord to stop the car and rushed

Should I Marry a Minister?

for the door. I had to pay both fares, go home alone to my apartment. Served me right for dating a red-headed, smug-sure preacher, I told myself, furious; it had been a narrow escape. I was glad, glad to be free of Ham. Bursting into tears, I flung myself across my bed.

Jock's first visit to my parsonage home was hardly less un-nerving. He would like, he said, "a few moments' quiet talk" with my Dad. Did that mean he wanted to ask Dad for my hand? But that was as outdated as those tall collars that used to prop up a man's chin. Why did I have such peculiar suitors?

That Sunday happened to be one of those parsonage days that try the soul. The phone rang six times during dinner and finally Dad had to leave his dessert, rush off in Jehu (his car so called because it "driveth furiously") for the hospital with-out his quiet talk with Jock. The organist rehearsing with the tenor in our front parlor had a fight over the proper tempo for the night's solo, "I came to the garden alone while the dew was still on the roses. . . ." Mother soothed both musicians, brewed them a cup of coffee. A nervous couple arrived to be married, and had to be entertained till Dad got back. The wedding party had barely gone down the front steps when a tornado of teenagers rushed into the front parlor to plan an Epworth League picnic, stayed so long they had to be fed cocoa with marshmallows, buns and hotdogs which mother kept in the icebox for such emergencies. Jock asked, wild-eyed, "Is it always like this? Why don't we go back to your apartment?"

As we settled down in the blessed quiet, Jock said surpris-ingly, "I wish I had my roots deep in a friendly home like yours. The way your Dad looks at your Mother—I love you, Susie."

When his lips met mine, they were not English or American; they were warm as the sun on a yellow cliff at Newagen. I said dreamily, "Darling, let's be married up in Maine. There's a pine grove back of our shack there where you can hear the sea. Dad can marry us. Only the family and as many friends as like us enough to make the long journey. . . ."

"Wonderful," Jock agreed hungrily against my lips, for he hated a commotion even worse than I did.

I should have known no PK could be married outside a church! Mother wailed, what did Jock and I mean, sneaking off to be married under a pine tree? What would Dad's parish think if they were not all invited? We'd have to be careful which girls we asked to be bridesmaids to avoid hard feelings. Useless to wail, "But I don't want any bridesmaids!" Then Jock's family tuned in. Cousin Henry had died recently leaving Cousin Angela a great deal of money, so she considered herself the Voice of the Family. Jock and I would never be happy together, she insisted, our backgrounds were too different. Why didn't I marry that nice red-headed theologue who was always hanging around? Jock would be "driving his pigs to a bad market." When Jock stiffened in angry protest, Cousin Angela added, "As a relative, you could expect some of Henry's money when I go. But not if you persist in this idiotic alliance!"

"Thank heaven, she isn't *my* blood relative," Jock sputtered to me later. "Cousin Henry was. And don't think you're doing me out of anything. Cousin Angela changes her mind about her fool money every other day. I don't want it anyway; I want you."

I murmured against his cheek, "Why can't they just leave us alone?" Whose business was it if we wanted to say "I do" under a pine tree? To walk off together along the shore, our only wedding attendants the Maine sea and the sky? Why was Jock's English background so insuperably different from my American parsonage?

198

Should I Marry a Minister?

"Underneath, we value the same things, but the surface is quite different," Jock admitted, honestly. "Why don't you go to England this summer to visit Mother? See for yourself? She lives in a fairy-tale cottage in a place called Molehill on the Green. Go to Horsham to see Christ's Hospital, too, where I went to school. Then you'll know me, inside out."

As I walked up the gangplank of the great ship which was to take me to Southampton, Jock slipped a small black leather case into my hand. "A letter of credit," he smiled. "For you to pick out your own diamond. They're much cheaper in Amsterdam. And they set stones beautifully in Belgium."

"Spend *your* money?" I gasped. "Oh, I couldn't. You might change your mind."

Jock smiled away my protest. "I'm sure. Have a happy holiday, Sweet."

It was like him to want me to be sure, too, to wait patiently, to give me all he had. The letter of credit was for $400. Did he have enough left in the savings bank to eat properly? I worried as I waved frantically to the three of them standing there on the dock, Jock beaming, Dad smiling too and waving, Mother waving and weeping as if this were my funeral. Why had I ever started on this fantastic expedition? There was a bon-voyage letter from Ham waiting for me in my stateroom. He wrote that he knew he'd acted like a schoolboy in a tantrum, but if I could forgive him, he'd like to see me when I got home. He loved me and he didn't care if I ever went to Ladies' Aid or not, so long as I was there at the parsonage when he got home. Thoughtfully, I put Ham's letter into my purse along with Jock's letter of credit.

London reminded me of a comfortable elderly relation with an ugly mole on her chin but with a big motherly breast to lean against. I felt at home at once with Jock's English cousins who not only showed me the usual—Westminster, the Palace

Guards changing, the Beefeaters, and the friendly Bobbies with sticks but no guns—but one cousin, secretary of a century-old Safe Deposit Company, took me to his office where there were no typewriters but he wrote all his own letters in a fine Spencerian hand! The teashop where he invited me to lunch had several reserved tables still set up with half-played games of dominoes which "brokers, businessmen, regular patrons will come back to finish with their tea," the cousin explained. No ulcers here; yet, I pondered, the Old Lady of Threadneedle Street could still give Wall Street a run for its money. Did our frantic American pace get us ahead any faster? It was different from the English certainly; and this was the leisurely way Jock had been brought up. Dominoes, heel-clicking, Vivian. Was this really what I wanted instead of the familiar parsonage Ham would give me?

Jock's mother turned out to be more British than those who were native-born. She was dark, handsome as he was, quiet-spoken, friendly but infinitely remote from the half-frightened Yankee parson's daughter. She neither approved nor disapproved of our marrying; it was Jock's and my own business. I sleepwalked after her into her Hansel and Gretel thatched cottage where a tiny fire burned feebly in the vast arched fireplace of the front room. You went down two steps to the red-tiled kitchen and up a ladder to the bedrooms above where you went to sleep to the chirping of birds in the thatch, for it stayed daylight here long after it should have been night. The cottage was so frigid compared with the furnace-heated New England parsonage I was used so that on rainy days I spent most of my time inside the big fireplace huddling over its small basket of coals.

"Central heating dries the blood," Jock's mother assured me. "You should wear woollies and exercise more, Susie."

She was kindness itself, but by the end of a week the Eng-

Should I Marry a Minister?

lish quiet got so on my nerves that I wanted to shout, to rush out to buy an American flag, to wave it wildly in Piccadilly! To add to my restlessness, another letter arrived from Ham which Mother had forwarded from Somerville, wanting to meet my ship when I landed back home if I'd tell him the landing date. At least I should listen to what he had to say before I married Jock, Ham insisted desperately. I knew how Mother felt; she needn't have forwarded the letter at all. I also knew by now what Cousin Angela had meant about Jock's and my backgrounds being so different. When I visited Christ's Hospital, the little schoolboys in their quaint long dark-blue coats and monk's collars had seemed more like miniature old men than our roughneck American youngsters. I was also coming to suspect that no well-brought-up English girl would think of spending a man's hard-earned money for a diamond when their engagement was not yet even formally announced. Had Jock been merely testing me subtly?

Impulsively I cabled home: HAVE DECIDED NOT TO BUY RING. There, at least that was settled! It never even occurred to me that Jock might interpret this to mean I no longer wanted to marry him. So I went happily on my scheduled way to Holland, then to Belgium where his frantic pursuing cables never quite caught up with me. But in spite of all my sight-seeing I wasn't happy; uncertainty hung over me in a dark cloud. Loneliness for home? For Jock? For Ham? I simply didn't know. Was the parsonage really the place where I would go on being happy? Could handsome Jock go on loving homely me after the first bloom of romance wore off? Restless, I wandered alone into the huge Brussels cathedral.

The vast nave was dim but candles in small red cups were lighted at a side chapel altar where several women with shawls tied over their heads were kneeling; hesitantly I knelt also. Would a stranger be welcome? An old lady with a brown wrinkled face, kneeling beside me, suddenly thrust her open missal into my hand. The unfamiliar prayer book was in Latin, but I could read the French translation well enough to make out the meaning: "I love the beauty of Thy house and the place where Thy glory dwells. . . ."

"The place where Thy glory dwells." The word echoed and reechoed in my ears, an organ diapason swelling; the vast cathedral, the little old lady, the candles were all telling me, "You are welcome; there are no strangers in the Lord's house." Jock and I had been drawn together too because we valued the same things—quietness, loyalty, gentle faith in our common Lord and in each other. Ham loved these too but he was "practical" enough to select a wife conveniently trained to his work. All Jock wanted was me, Susie Nies. What if Ham was a minister and Jock a banker? What mattered lay deeper than how you earned your living, than even what language you spoke or how beautiful you were to look at. Jock and I both knelt before the same things. "I'm sure," his deep English voice said again. "Have a happy holiday, Sweet."

I handed the missal back to the old lady with murmured thanks, went out of the beauty of God's house into the street, with peace and sureness in my heart. As I passed a jeweler's mullioned window, a sparkle caught my eye; I stopped. The diamond lay there on a piece of black velvet flashing up at me in the sunlight, "Here I am! Come in!" Mesmerized I went into the shop, asked to see the ring in the window. It fitted my finger exactly, as if it had been designed for me, its band of platinum so slender as to be almost invisible so that the diamond glittered solitary upon my shaking finger. When I hesitated, the jeweler assured me that the whole Belgian government would stand back of my diamond, insure that it was unblemished!

"I'll wear it," I said slowly, out of my dream.

Should I Marry a Minister?

Poor Jock, not sure if he was still engaged or not, was anxiously pacing the pier at Quebec when my ship docked, but it was not until I saw his tense face at the gangplank that I realized anything was wrong. Without even waiting to speak to me, he yanked off my glove, stared at the diamond winking up at him.

"You bought it!" he gasped. "Oh, my dear." He swept me off my feet, kissed me thoroughly in a very un-English way, while the black porter holding my bags grinned. Jock blushed, set me back down, ordering, "Taxi for the Chateau Frontenac!" Safe together on the back seat he held my hand tightly, explaining with the anxious perspiration still on his forehead, "I thought you'd changed your mind! Don't ever go away again, Sweet. Don't leave me!"

"No," I promised. "Never again."

He laid my hand with its flashing promise against his warm cheek, murmuring, "Let's thank the good Lord for bringing you safely back to me. Ask Him to make our home His, too." Our prayer was neither Methodist nor Church of England, but wholly catholic, universal, and silent. We had a formal church wedding later in Robinson Memorial Chapel, complete with organ music, bridesmaids, two ministers to tie the knot securely, but I've always felt that Jock and I were truly married that morning in the taxi when we prayed wordlessly, hand in hand.

Chapter Twelve

CASTLES IN SPAIN

QUEER, isn't it, how our sense of values changes with the years? The bright-colored rattle gives place to the baseball, the Scout knife with five blades to the jalopy, to secure cash in the bank, and finally to a quiet place in the sun. When Jock and I were first married, our great ambition was to make enough money between us so we could retire from business at forty, go together around the world. When Jock was offered the big increase in salary to go to Detroit, it looked, we exulted, as if we were really on our way!

"Why are you and Jock going out to the Middle West?" Dad asked me that bright October morning as we rattled along in his big ancient jalopy, Jehu that "driveth furiously." We were on our way up to the little country church in the hills where Dad was to preach that Sunday. "Just for more money?"

"Well," I stammered, taken aback at his sharp query, "I suppose so. But he'd be crazy to turn down a raise such as he's been offered. A young man has to have some ambition."

"We all have our castle in Spain," Dad agreed. "I'm glad you could come home to say 'good-by' before you leave."

But it hadn't been easy to get even a word alone with Dad, he was so busy now he was superintendent of the Springfield District of the Methodist Church with some sixty churches to visit; he merely slept at the district parsonage, often getting home from a fourth quarterly conference long after midnight.

Castles in Spain

So I was driving him up to his preaching appointment in order to have a quiet talk. Frost had set in already and the hills were fantastically beautiful with autumn foliage, gold, crimson, and yellow. I waved my hand at the open car window. "If an artist could get *that* down on canvas, he could ask any price he wanted."

Dad shot me a keen glance from his eyes still as blue as the sky over that far crimson hill. He said quietly, "He'd be paid whether he sold his picture or not, if he could paint like that."

"You think a young man shouldn't even try to make a million?" I flared.

"Ambition is a grand mare if she doesn't run away with you. Very few people are strong enough to handle great wealth and still keep their equilibrium." He grinned. "Maybe that's why the Lord never trusted me with very much cash. Hey, stop, quick!"

I jammed on Jehu's brakes so hard he protested in every squeak and rattle, but we weren't about to run into someone on the narrow country road as I had feared; Dad just wanted to get out to look at the view. We stood for a moment, silent, drinking in beauty. As far as the eye could reach was breathtaking color, the gold of maples, the bright red of sumac, the deeper red of the oak trees. The rich wine-colored sacrament of color flowed down the sloping hills into the deep chalice of the valley below us, where stood the little white church, its slender tower rising. The sun was a golden trumpet shouting, higher than human ears could hear, "Glory to God in the Highest!" Christmas in October.

"The Lord didn't bother with a brush when He painted that!" Dad cried. "He dipped both hands in glory and flung it against those far hills! Fill your eyes and your heart, Sister, against a rainy day. Where your beauty is, there will your heart be, also."

Dad was right about Detroit: Jock and I went there to drain it dry, but instead it drained us. An army of young Harvard Law and Business School graduates had invaded Michigan to make their fortunes. As the city grew to a million inhabitants almost overnight so did these young dreams of wealth. It was impossible not to be infected with the virus of easy money. Jock and I bought our first car, a modest Essex, though most of our friends' cars were much larger. We told ourselves smugly that we were too New England to spend all we made; we'd save instead, invest our spare cash. Perhaps even before we were forty we'd find our castle in Spain, in Paris, in the wonderful island of Jersey with its cleanly pigs and fat cattle; or maybe we'd land in Timbuctoo. . . . Who knew or cared? Lucky, lucky us.

It was excitingly true those first few years that whatever Jock or I touched ballooned into success. His salary went higher and higher. We bought stock in the company he worked for, not only with savings from his salary but with all I earned writing for magazines. I took frequent trips to New York to see the editors. Always at the hotel where I stayed would be waiting a huge welcoming bouquet of roses from Jock with a card that said, "Good luck, my Sweet." A warm happy feeling to know you did not walk alone.

I was hurrying down Fifth Avenue to an editor's office one sleety February day—bad weather is more horrible in New York than any place, no room for an umbrella on the crowded sidewalks, while the tall cliffs of buildings drop cataracts down the back of your neck, wet bits of dirty newspaper blow against your clean nylons—when I noticed in the American Express window a picture of spring incarnate, dripping hot sunshine. A young girl in a white lace mantilla was standing on a high yellow cliff, staring out at a peacock-colored sea, while above her foamed fragile white almond blossoms, so warmly fragrant you could almost smell them. On an impulse I went inside to ask the clerk at the desk where this pictured heaven was.

"Majorca, an island off the coast of Spain." The clerk added wistfully, "Great place to be, this kind of weather. Especially with the peseta down, forty to a dollar. I have an artist friend who swears she lives high there on ten dollars a month! Sell you a ticket, lady?"

"Not today, thank you," I smiled. I had no faintest idea that less than a month later Jock and I would be on shipboard, bound for this fairy-tale island where poor people lived like princes—so long as their cash held out to eat.

The only lack in our handsome Detroit apartment was that Jock and I had no children. I felt this the more keenly after I went to Cleveland to help Lillian care for her and Ike's first baby, Perry Lee, named for both grandfathers. After I got home to Detroit I went to the doctor to be assured again that there was no reason why Jock and I couldn't have children, except perhaps nervous strain. If we'd both take life a little easier, relax? But surely one must provide for his middle and old age while he was still young, I countered. I even took on another job which was to have far-reaching consequences.

Mrs. E., the chairman of the fund for endowing the Methodist colleges for women in the Orient, was soft-voiced, silver-haired, and the whole world of girls was her family. She wanted programs and a pageant to interest donors to Ewa College in Korea, Isabella Thoburn in India, Yenching in China, and a college in Japan, which she insisted upon paying me to prepare. "Writing is your business and after all I can afford it," she pointed out. But she soon became more friend than employer, for her mind and heart were young as mine.

And then the clock struck midnight, for Jock and me as well as most 1929 Cinderella investors. Overnight the New

York stock Market and the Michigan banks changed to frightened mice; not only were all our paper savings in the company Jock worked for wiped out, but his job also. Years of hard work, of Cinderella scrimping had left us without even the pumpkin to make into a nourishing pie! And Jock was ill; the shock had sickened his overworked body. We sat stunned, jobless, in our expensive Detroit apartment wondering how we could break the lease, if we could sell the oriental rugs.

"You need a six months' vacation," the doctor had assured Jock briskly and he'd retorted bitterly, "Using what for cash?"

"We, the smart, busy New England ants!" I thought, looking uneasily at Jock's white, drawn face. Retire at forty indeed; we were retired right now, but with no money except. . . . "We still have that $500 government bond," I reminded him. I looked at the cold rain slanting against our apartment windows. Where had I seen a picture of sun and almond blossoms recently? "Let's spend every last cent of it! We'll go to that island where you can live so cheaply—to Majorca!" I reached for Jock's fever-hot hand. "Then we can come home, each of us can get a job. I might even write some travel articles there."

"But—but it isn't safe!" Jock protested. "It's grasshopper-crazy. . . ."

"Getting your health back isn't crazy. We'll borrow some more from friends, pay them back when we come back, well. We can both get jobs then."

Three weeks later we had stored our furniture and were on the great ship ploughing the rough furrow of the March sea toward the lovely rock in the Mediterranean. "Lots of people have run away to Majorca," I rattled away to Jock as we stood together on deck; I was trying to sound gay but achieved only a shrill worried pipe; he looked so white and ill. "Julius Caesar got his slingers from there to conquer Britain. Sure, I've been reading a book; why not? Chopin lived there with George

Castles in Spain

Sand, in a monastery, no less. Imagine a light o' love who brought all her children along! Did you know young King Jaime was seven feet tall. . . ."

But Jock hadn't heard a word! he was shivering. "I think I'll go below," he chattered. "I'm frozen." I was cold too, deep in the frightened marrow of my bones. Were we grasshopper-fools to spend our last cent, to go in debt, even, looking for health? For our castle in Spain? "Where your beauty is," Dad had promised, "there will your heart be, also."

One incident at Barcelona where we changed to a smaller boat to take us out to Majorca reminded me of Dad's values. We explained to the American Express courier who met us that Jock was ill, that we had very little money, so would he please find us a cheap good restaurant for dinner? "I'll take you where I eat myself," he offered. Over the dinner table he and Jock discovered they had fought the same battles in France during the war, but on opposing sides! For the courier was German-born. They swapped battles happily, "Do you remember at Chateau Thierry?" until our island boat was about to sail, when Jock reached into his pocket for the inevitable tip.

"No, no!" The courier pushed the money back at Jock, handed me a large basket of luscious Spanish oranges, and bowed low. "For mine enemy who is now my friend," he beamed. "Welcome to Spain!" It was the first time in our experience that anyone had refused an American tip; he had even tipped us!

Jock and I, unable to sleep for excitement, were up at sunrise the next morning, to see our ship dock in Palma. The crescent-shaped harbor was misty lavender; the dreaming white and yellow houses were a rosary of beads, strung along the hills, leading our eyes up to where the great cathedral stood so high on its hill above the city it seemed to float, as

Jock said, "like a holy bishop on his cloud." We drove to the Grand Hotel. But the racket under our hotel window was deafening. Each clamoring church bell was answered by the crowing of roosters, the clucking of hens, and the grunts of the big black pigs pastured on the roof of the thrifty householder below us, for lack of a back yard. Add to this the uninhibited shrieks of the taxi horns of most of the secondhand cars from the U.S.A., arguing in the streets. . . .

"Did we come here for rest?" I yelled to Jock over the din. "Let's get out of here!"

Next morning we rode the toy train, tooting gaily in and out of tunnels, to the white village of Soller at the foot of Puig Major, the highest mountain in Majorca. We hired a car to drive us out to the Puerto and peace. The quiet stone terrace by the sea where Jock and I ate our dinner was fragrant with orange blossoms growing on the surrounding hills and the only sound was the contented humming of a sun-browned fisherman, seated on his three-legged stool beyond us on the beach, mending his nets. Nothing, it seemed, had disturbed these placid waters since the triremes of Julius Caesar sheltered here.

I yawned to Jock. "The only other guests here in the hotel are the Allens, those three Irish Quakers the proprietor introduced us to, and they ring no bells when they pray—I hope. Want to go to bed early?"

"No rush," he yawned back. "Let's just sit here for a week."

The magic of Majorca had begun its healing. For days we happily did nothing except eat, sleep, walk for the first time in years instead of hopping into the car to go around the corner to the grocery store. So many things were pleasantly lacking at Puerto Soller—no phone, no committee meetings, no evening rush of homebound commuters breathing garlic and tobacco down the back of our necks.

Castles in Spain

"If I ever again get to rushing around, aimless as a water-bug, drown me, will you?" I begged Jock sleepily one morning as we sat on top of a yellow cliff looking down 400 feet below to the incredible peacock-blue of the sea.

"Don't talk," he begged, stretched out relaxed as the sun-warmed earth. Before us lay the immense blue-green carpet of the sea; behind us the almond trees were a mass of fragile white, drifting down the hill to the gray-green olive trees. Paler colors than Dad's autumn-glory-splashed New England hills, but beauty to treasure in the heart forever. Because new trees were taxed, the thrifty Majorcans had grafted new shoots onto these tortured trunks, some of which were a thousand years old. Yet every year, I thought drowsily, came this miracle of new leaves, rustling, life, life, *life!*

"You know something?" Jock's hand slid over mine. "This is the first time since we've been married we've had time to get acquainted! We've been moles, burrowing blindly for security in a world where it no longer exists, if it ever did. We've spread ourselves out so thin, we've been no use to anyone, not even to the one we love best." He sighed, drew his hand away. "Money may not be as important as health, but if we keep on spending two dollars a day apiece at the hotel, we can't stay very long. What say, we look for a very small castle, to rent?"

The very next morning we found our modest castle in Spain. The hotel proprietor's cousin had a nearby *casa* for rent; he loaned us a key about a foot long to unlock the front door. The tangled yellow road unwound up the very steep hill into the hot morning, but as we climbed, a polite little breeze fresh from its bath in the Mediterranean wiped itself dry on the olive leaves and went before us, humming up the road. The cousin's low orange building was too small to boast so large a key; its iron shutters were closed against the sun, but when we went into the kitchen Jock gave a joyous shout.

"Look at the plumbing! It's a brook!"

A laughing little stream ran down from the hill above us, came in a hole in our sink and out another hole in the kitchen floor! And when we flung open the shutters, there was a wonderful view of Puig Major. "A brook in our house and a mountain in our back yard!" I walked laughing into Jock's arms and he kissed me. "Darling," he said, "welcome home!"

The weeks of content slid by, bringing color to Jock's cheeks, brightness to his eyes, a new spring to his steps. It was a merry game to shop every morning down in the village market in the square while the dew was still on the vegetables brought down on donkeys from the farms. Such goliaths of fruits and vegetables, lemons as big as small grapefruit, oranges with leaves left on the stem to prove how fresh they were, native dates and figs and crisp almonds! Huge baskets held rainbow-colored fish whose names we did not know but which cost almost nothing and tasted ambrosial. More stalls were heaped with berets, rope-soled shoes, sheepskins, and household wares; and whether or not we bought at her stall, each friendly proprietor would greet us politely, *"Buenos días, Señor, Señora!"* We learned to call back, *"Tenga!"* the lovely island subjunctive which means, freely translated, "May you have and hold these beautiful days forever."

The Allens, our Irish Quaker friends of whom we had grown very fond, talked Jock and me into making a pilgrimage with them on horseback as the ancient pilgrims went, up to the monastery and school for choirboys on the very top of Puig Major. There in the chapel was the famous Black Virgin of Lluch.

"Nobody seems to know why she's black, except she's very old," Julia Allen explained her guidebook gleanings. "A shepherd found her under a bush and knew by the bright light shining around him that she must be very holy. But the guide-books says the statue may even date back to the Romans!"

"Methodists and Quakers on a pilgrimage to see a Roman Catholic Virgin who may have been a pagan statue!" I chuckled. "I only hope I can stay on my donkey. I never rode horseback before."

The village square seemed to be full of milling animals and donkey boys that morning we set out and the native saddles turned out to be wooden, covered with very thin, very dirty sheepskins; you mounted by leaping several feet into the air, landing by gosh and by gorry between two woven panniers which you gripped convulsively—if you were I. The Sollerites leaned out their windows, laughing and calling as we started off amid shouts of "*Arri*" from our guide and donkey boys. Julia's donkey didn't want to "*Arri*," but brayed rebelliously, with her going up and down on his back till she gasped, "He's an accordian! I'm all of a jelly, just!"

Thus our little procession started up the yellow path that climbs through the terraces up the mountain, then edges precariously along the cliff, with a thousand-foot drop on the off side. After one look down, I shut my eyes, until we stopped on a safe plateau. The scene far below was worth risking a look; the tiny houses of Soller were scattered white toys along the green floor of the valley; beyond, the yellow road unraveled to the shore, edged by the peacock-blue sea. "Hey, stop that, you!" Julia yelled as her donkey tried to push mine off the edge of the cliff. We both screamed together for the guide, but when he came rushing up, it was Julia and me he scolded, not the beasts.

"There is nothing to fear! Are we not pilgrims for Lluch?" he demanded, shaking his long mustaches reprovingly. "The Black Virgin looks out for her own!"

I wondered if she minded that Jock and I were Methodists

but decided not to ask. When finally at dusk our little pilgrimage arrived in the stone-paved monastery courtyard on top of Puig Major, my legs were so numb I had to be lifted from my wooden saddle. Evensong was being sung in the chapel, so, limping painfully, the assorted pilgrims followed the high silver chant of little boys' voices to the open chapel door.

Rembrandt might have painted the scene within, the dark velvet shadows in the chapel corners, the blaze of light as forty choirboys carrying lighted candles came, singing, down the aisle, followed by the cowled monks. The unearthly glow on the young faces, the ring of candles burning at the altar drew your eye upward—to the Black Virgin! I caught my breath at the sculptured clarity of her dark face for she was indeed beautiful with the patina of time and of many prayers. What did it matter who she was? Or from whence she had come? She stood for worship, for man reaching out for an unseen God. In the winking of the candles she seemed to smile. As the choirboys' voices soared, silver and sweet, I dropped to my Methodist knees on the cold stone of the chapel floor; painfully Jock and the three Quakers knelt also. For this was a holy place. Here in a strange monastery on a mountaintop in Spain I found once again the dear Lord of my American parsonage and we talked together in the cool of the evening.

But after we'd paid for the trip to Lluch, Jock and I found our cash was running very low. We'd been grasshoppers, indeed; we should have saved out enough for the boat trip home at least, not have depended hopefully upon my selling an article. It might still sell of course, but editors were often very slow in making a decision and mail to Spain took time. Meanwhile we had to eat. We hated to borrow more money from our friends, our family, to admit how reckless we had been. Still, I figured, ruefully, Jock mustn't get sick again with worry. We had to do something to get some cash and soon.

Castles in Spain

Then one morning Jock came back from the post with a letter he dropped into my lap.

"From Detroit," he said. "Now, whom do you think. . . ."

I tore open the envelope. "It's from Mrs. E.! You remember, the friend I wrote the Chinese and Japanese college programs for." She wrote:

> I've been thinking of you all day, my dear, with a queer sense of urgency. How is your husband? When are you coming home? Soon, I hope, for I still need your help with the colleges. I thought you might be able to use a small salary payment in advance. . . .

The enclosed blue slip fluttered from my nerveless fingers and fell to the floor whence Jock picked it up, gasped. The check was for five hundred dollars! Enough to pay our fare home third-class, to keep us till Jock had a job. This wasn't the first time the Lord had answered my need in a strange way; Mother's face had been as radiant as Jock's when she took from her envelope the check that paid for my longed-for green suit. "The Lord sent this with his love. . . ."

"Wealth isn't just money in the bank," I admitted to Jock, wiping my wet eyes. "It's things you can't buy but are freely given—loyal friends; Ike smiling at his baby son; the lovely big oranges the German soldier tipped us; the choirboys singing at Lluch."

Jock murmured practically, fingering the check, "I doubt if the steamship company would have settled for oranges." He came to put his arm around me, to lean his tanned healthy cheek against my hair. "But we're rich, all right. We can work and we have each other." He kissed me, jubilantly. "*Buenos días*, my wealthy *Señora!*"

"*Tenga!*" May we have and hold these beautiful days forever.

215

Chapter Thirteen

SONS AND DAUGHTERS OF THE MORNING

Ike now had two children, Perry Lee, a handsome grave little boy who thought through whatever he had to say before he spoke; and bright-haired little Sue, who called Perry "Worry" because she couldn't as yet manage her P's. When young Sue had been born, Ike had been so delighted that he'd wired us her weight in ounces "because every little bit of her is precious."

Dad and Mother had driven out to Cleveland to visit the grandchildren, but actually Perry and Sue were only two in Dad's large family, for he adopted every child in his parish. He always kept a large paper bag of candy in the sagging pocket of his dark-blue suit when he made his parish calls, so that all the small fry on the street ran for him, homing bees to honey, when Jehu rattled to a stop in front of a house.

Once at morning service, when Dad was preaching, a two-year-old escaped her mother, ran up the aisle to her friend; he merely reached down, gathered her starched white little skirts into his arms, and went right on preaching while she twisted a lock of his blond hair contentedly. "Of such," Dad ended, "are the kingdom of heaven." He sat the little girl down, smiled at her, gave her small rear end a pat to send her back to her mother.

Jock's and my great sorrow was that we had no family.

Sons and Daughters of the Morning

Ever since I was a small girl playing with dolls, I had known what my first son's name would be—*Richard*. Ike used to tease me, "You could call the kid *Junior,* I guess. You could hardly wish 'Vivian' onto a defenseless boy battling his way through an American public school and as for *Vivian Leopold Isaac*—heaven help the poor kid!"

After the Detroit fiasco and our Spanish holiday, Jock and I had both gone to work in New York City, he in Wall Street and I at my magazine stories. Looking back at eleven child-less years, Jock and I were discussing the possibility of adopt-ing a small son so seriously that when I went to Manhattan to buy a new davenport I told the salesman hopefully, "I'd like a covering tough enough to take a small boy and his dog climbing all over it." I could hardly believe it when I dis-covered that my very own *Richard Nies* was actually on his way! The Majorcan sunshine must have encouraged him.

With debts to repay, we had as yet no bank savings nor had we been living in New York long enough to acquire a family physician. Where were we going to find an obstetrician skilled enough to trust with our long-awaited baby? A doctor who at the same time would charge fees we could afford? Jock hadn't attended Harvard Business School for nothing.

"Why don't you do a little research, Susie?" he suggested. "If we were going to buy a car, we'd look at all the different models, compare engines, horsepower, paint jobs. New York must be full of good obstetricians. Maybe," he grinned, "we can pay the doc on the installment plan, a dollar down and so much a week!" Jock's face sobered. "But be sure to pick a competent man. After all these years we can't take any chances."

On the theory that I'd at least take a look at the Packard doctors even if I did have to buy the utilitarian Ford, I went first to Park Avenue. The impressive office of the chief of staff of a large women's hospital was paved with black and white marble so that my heels made a nervous clicking as I walked up to the vast mahogany desk where a stiffly starched white-capped nurse finally condescended to notice me. I asked timidly for an appointment with the doctor; also could I inquire about his fees? She snapped "Doctor's minimum fee is a thousand dollars!"

But Jock's yearly salary was only a little over four thousand dollars! I gulped, "Perhaps, 'Doctor' would be willing to recommend some other younger, less expensive but experienced obstetrician?"

"I'll get him to send you in the name of someone who'll do your job for less," the nurse agreed. We settled for that and I went back home to await the letter of advice about "my job." But when the letter arrived a week later, it consisted of only two typewritten lines:

> I am enclosing the names of two competent men. Dr. Smith [let us call him] will deliver you for $200. Dr. Jones's [also fictitious] charges are $300.
>
> Sincerely yours.

"Doctor" had actually condescended to sign his own name!

"Not a word about the younger doctor's medical background!" I stormed to Jock. "Are they fresh out of medical school or specialists like him? *Anybody's* baby is important! I just can't believe many doctors are like this. I'm going right back there to find one who's a human being, not a cash register or social climber!"

(I could hear Mother saying urgently, "If you can't find something, make it!" Was it possible there was still "no room at the inn" for a little boy?)

That wide avenue that calls itself a park because it boasts

Sons and Daughters of the Morning

a dingy strip of iron-fenced green down the middle had Cadillacs and Rolls Royces parked by the wide sidewalks, and doormen sprouting gold braid to open the ornate lobby doors. These were mere window dressing; however, I figured that obstetricians wouldn't be here unless they were successful and a woman perilously near forty, having her first baby, needed experienced care. The baby must have the best chance I could give him.

Of the ten doctors I visited on my research tour, seven saw me, but their prices were too Packard from my Ford income. Two doctors sent out word to their secretaries to take down "the data"; but unless I met the doctor himself, how could I tell if I could trust him as I would our family doctor at home? To be at rest mentally was surely as important as medicine out of a bottle. So I crossed off these doctors, too.

Late one afternoon, tired, heavy-footed, I turned into the office of the tenth doctor who was probably the busiest man on my list. The office was empty but the lamps were still lighted so I sank wearily into a big green velvet chair, which made me remember the parsonage sofa Mrs. Newte had lied about. A big man in a rumpled suit, whose lined face wrinkled into a smile as he came in, said pleasantly, "My nurse is gone. What can I do for you?"

At the kindness of his voice, I burst into tired tears. "I don't know. But I'm having a baby."

"Why, come in, child," he urged. "Sit over there in the comfortable chair by my desk. Let's talk this over." I should have known that the most famous physician would be the simplest, the kindest. When I poured out the story of my research on doctors up and down Park Avenue, the big man leaned back his head, shouted with laughter, patted my shoulder. "I'll take care of you for whatever you can afford to pay," he agreed. "But you'll have to go into the ward in my hospital."

"How many are there in a ward?" I asked nervously.

"Twelve. But they get as good care as the private room patients. Better, I sometimes think."

"I'm sure they do if you look after them," I told him gratefully.

We moved into a house in New Jersey in order to have room for the new baby. Young Richard was probably the first baby in our neighborhood to pay his own medical expenses before he was born. I wrote an article about the difficulties of having a baby in a strange city, and the first editor I sent it to mailed me a check by return post. The *Reader's Digest* picked up the article, and encouraged, I wrote more about the problems of young married people. Before the months were gone there was an adequate sum in the bank labeled, "Richard Nies Fletcher, Grace N. Fletcher, trustee," for I never admitted for an instant he might not be a boy.

Dad and Mother suggested that since New York was so humid, why didn't I come to them in cool Newagen? Dad had another reason for wanting to see me that August; when Rick was waiting to be born was also the summer when Dad was waiting to die. Not that he ever mentioned this; I had no inkling how close was the door to immortality. I did notice, however, the luminous quality of Dad's face; how his skin seemed so transparent his smile was an inner flame shining "—behind glass; how slow and careful was his step on the cottage veranda." Dad and I sat there day after day, remembering the parsonage years behind us, or just watching the ever-changing sea, the moth-white sails fluttering in the wind as the ships inched by on their way to the harbor. Actually these scenes had little reality; my whole mind and body were focused on our child-to-be's comforting kicks, the sureness he was alive. When Dad teased me about my miracle baby, I retorted that if he'd waited nearly twelve years, he'd be excited, too!

"Do you think he'll like being President of the United States?" I grinned companionably one morning when Dad and I were soaking up sun so near the hush of the sea on the cliff that the cottage veranda might have been the prow of a ship sailing nowhere—and everywhere. "Dad, what would you like your grandson to be when he grows up? What makes a man happy?"

"I've always thought creative people had the most fun," Dad said slowly. "Because they live at will in the past, the present, and the future. For them there is no time, only eternal truth, as they see it."

"You mean, write a poem? Or a symphony like Beethoven's Fifth?"

"Not necessarily. You can create in a material way, too. A washing machine for busy mothers." He hesitated, glanced at me sharply, ended in a voice so low I almost couldn't hear, "To create something—someone—who will carry on after you're gone satisfies a deep human hunger."

"Preaching does this for you?" I interrupted impatiently.

"Being a pastor does," he corrected. "A Sunday sermon is merely a crutch to help people walk on Monday. It breaks my heart when I come down from the pulpit and someone says, 'What a masterpiece that sermon was! It should be printed!' But when a man wrings my hand, promises, 'I'm going to try to find out God's plan for my life,' then I know what I've said has been a success. It will go on."

"Theology will never save the world! Some of these pompous, know-it-all young men I used to have in my district, green out of theology school, worry me. They know all the gadgets, how to teach the boys to tie square knots for Scouts, how to put a dotted line on the church calendar where a newcomer can sign his name 'if a call is desired.' Of course a call is desired if the minister's on the job! I sometimes wonder if they keep a card catalogue of sins!"

I stared, open-mouthed, at Dad; it was so seldom he criticized "his boys." Dad was no saint. That he had a paralyzing vocabulary of invective collected as a boy delivering telegrams in the saloons of early Dallas, Texas, Ike and I had discovered by accident one day when we were doing our homework behind the closed back-parlor parsonage door in Dorchester. A big Irish policeman had brought into our front parlor for identification a man who'd been caught trying to sell a fourteen-year-old Chinese girl, one of our Sunday school children, to an old man. When Dad had finished his blistering tongue-lashing of this salesman of human flesh, the policeman took the cringing, sobbing man away. Dad, appalled by his own fury, went up to his study, shut the door, prayed there all night for forgiveness. Yet his own frailty had made him understand that of others, had given him insight into the problems of ditch-diggers and debutantes, of college presidents and simple fishermen. Knowing their weakness in himself he could help each to find his humble path back to God.

There was one more question I wanted to ask Dad as we sat there together on the Newagen veranda, listening to the summer sea hush down below, but I found it hard to put into words. I stammered, "I can't help worrying over what would happen to the baby if—well, I mean, women *do* die in childbirth. . . ."

"Bildad would be very glad to see either of you, I expect," Dad said calmly, but I shivered. I hadn't even considered anything happening to the baby! Bildad had been gone nearly twenty years now but Dad still spoke as if he'd left our Dorchester parsonage for heaven only yesterday.

"We come in the door of birth and we go out the twin door

Sons and Daughters of the Morning

of death," Dad said, stretching lazily in his deck chair in the hot sun. "Neither door is frightening because Jesus Christ has gone through both of them before us."

Dad got to his feet, went to the veranda railing, his lifted face luminous with reflected light as he stared up at a white cloud, a frosted window in the blue roof of the sky you could see through but dimly. "What a glorious day that will be when we go through the last great door, with the trumpets shouting, 'Hallelujah!'" Tears were running down his cheeks but he was radiant, yearning, his voice a prayer. "When we cry, 'My Lord and my God. . . .'"

He was not afraid of anything in this world or the next, and this was my heritage too and my son's. I went to Dad, slid my hand into his and for long moments we watched while the sun above the shining blue of the sea lost itself in the white-drifted sky and I knew at last what it meant, "the glory of the Lord was in the cloud."

From then on I was not afraid. The baby was a boy as I'd expected. But it did turn out fortunate that young Richard had his own bank account, for he was premature, an eight-month's incubator baby, who weighed only four pounds at birth, and things went wrong with me, so we needed more cash for additional medical attention. We also managed a private room where Jock's sister, a nurse who came over from England, took us both under her competent care.

Ike wired from Cleveland his usual gay shout:

> Dear Richard: We are overjoyed at your safe arrival. We think you might have given more thought to the matter of weight, but let that pass. The many in-laws and outlaws, who have been worried about you and your mother, can now relax. Many happy birthdays.
>
> Aunt Lillian and Uncle Ike

To greet the new grandson, Dad and Mother drove down to New York City from Townsend in faithful old Jehu. They had returned to the shrewd New England country people whom they loved, to the same pulpit where Dad had preached his first sermon on the meaning of prayer, as had been his ambition. "I married your Mother there and you were born there," Dad explained. "Youth never comes back, but among those lovely hills is a grand place to remember. I'd like to stay there till my Coronation Day. These hill people live so close to the good earth and the sky."

Dad was chuckling that day as he came into the hospital room to visit young Rick and me.

"A farmer at prayer meeting last night preached a better sermon on immortality than I ever did," Dad beamed, while Mother rushed off to the nursery to see the baby. "He said, 'Folks, you know how it is with a honeybee.' All the other farmers and their wives pricked up their ears, yes, they knew. 'He comes a buzzin' around and you dodge, scart you'll git stung. You git stung, anyways, but when you pick the bee's stinger out o' your hand, you ain't scart any more. You can reach up, play with that old buzzer! That honey bee's name is "death." But Jesus Christ's pulled out his stinger for us!'"

But as Dad chuckled, suddenly he swayed and his face went white. He dropped into a chair as if his legs had given away. "You're sick!" Frightened, I rang for the nurse, but Dad sat there, gasping for breath till the nurse brought the doctor who gave Dad something to drink that made him feel better. He insisted he was fine now; he'd just lie down on that couch by the window for a few moments. After he lay there for a while, his color came back, his eyes were blue as ever; he was himself again by the time Mother came in with the baby on a pillow because not even his proud grandmother was allowed to handle so tiny a boy.

Sons and Daughters of the Morning

"Isn't he homely?" I asked fondly. But his long body would some day make him a tall man and his fingers were strong, artistic. Would he be a concert violinist, maybe? An artist? When his tiny hand closed convulsively around my own finger it squeezed my heart, too. "He just isn't quite finished."

"He's beautiful!" Mother cried indignantly.

Rick opened his blue eyes and the fuzz on his well-shaped head was golden as Dad's. Or would he be a minister, perhaps, too? Dad didn't even sway as he got up, cupped the baby's tiny head in his big warm hand. "Hello, little feller! You know your old Grandad?" he crooned gently to little Rick. "Lord love you as I do, lad. You make a hundred and twenty-four, exactly."

Mother smiled as I asked, puzzled, "A hundred and twenty-four what?"

"Sons and daughters of the morning," Dad chuckled. "Keepers of the star." What did he mean?

"Show her your notebook, darling," Mother suggested as the nurse came in to take the tiny baby away to his own overheated nursery.

Dad pulled a worn red notebook from his vest pocket, handed it over to me. As I turned the pages the names written in his fine careful hand were familiar, boys and girls who had gone out from Dad's different parishes over the past forty years to work in various parts of the world. Dad didn't say that he'd helped to send them there but Mother remarked rather wryly that the tithe from their small income at Townsend hardly spread over so many; and Dad retorted he could spare more now he no longer had to help Ike and me financially. There was that boy from Trinity who was doing such startling things in rural education among the Apache tribe out West. The girl from Dorchester had set up such successful secondary schools in the Phillipines that the government was copying her methods. That laundry boy from the Chinese Sunday school at Framingham had turned his whole village to Christ when he went home on a visit to Canton, China. Then there was Dad's girl who was teaching Bible in Japan; and the three boys (out of the one hundred and two from Trinity who'd gone to the World War) who hadn't come home to Worcester from France. . . . How many was that?

"You mean, they were killed there?" I asked, running my tongue over my dry lips. Would anyone but Dad count his big family in two worlds?

Dad nodded, matter-of-factly. "I pray for them all every night." He took back his well-thumbed little red notebook, slid it into his vest pocket, confessing with a chuckle, "Sometimes when I'm too sleepy, I just say, 'O Lord, bless 'em all!' " He glanced at me and then at Mother. "Well, Sugar, we'd better be moseying along!"

"I must say good-by to little Richard," Mother pleaded.

As the door closed behind her, the determined light went out of Dad's face; he slumped down onto the couch gratefully again. The room was getting dark so I snapped on the bedside lamp on my table, but Dad's face was in shadow as he murmured wearily, "I'm glad I met young Rick once, here with you, so I'll recognize him later on."

Then, at long last, I knew. With a great effort he'd been able to keep his weakness from Mother because in his aging she would grow old too and that must never be; she must stay his Myrtie, his young, dear love. Young Rick, Dad knew, would never know his Grandad but it didn't matter; they would find each other again on the other side of the great door with the trumpets blowing, "Hallelujah!"

"What are you sniffling about, Susie?" Dad asked.

"Not a thing on earth and you know it!" If he could talk in riddles—bless him—so could I. "The light hurts my eyes." I snapped it off and we sat there together, Dad and I. "Rick's lucky—not every boy has a ready-made family so big it takes two worlds to hold them!"

"Sons of the morning?" Dad murmured. "Surely, you remember the Lord's glorious promise to him who overcometh? 'And I will give him the morning star.'"

Chapter Fourteen

HOW BEAUTIFUL UPON THE MOUNTAIN

"CHILDREN certainly don't owe us anything; they're such fun,"
I told Ike proudly when he came on from Cleveland to New
Jersey to inspect his new nephew. Now he'd grown a pound
a week, Rick was a husky handsome boy you could toss to
ceiling while he chuckled with laughter. "Queer, isn't it, how
three people can love each other more than two?"

"Until Perry was born, I never really understood the Trinity," Ike agreed. His eyes twinkled, "But in our house there's
only one boss. You should hear young Susie yell when she
wants something bad! She gets red 'way down her neck."

"She inherits it," I chuckled. "You used to get red too when
you 'preached' at us from your back-stairs pulpit, when you
were four, maybe five, and we laughed at something you said.
You used to wheedle Dad, Mother, and me into the back hall
while you climbed up high enough to yell at us, 'God is love.'
'Jesus wept.' 'Now, Brother Nies, will you kindly take up the
collection?' And hand Dad a tin pie plate."

"I needed those pennies for an ice cream cone," Ike grinned.
"At least my sermons were short. Maybe I should have been
a preacher at that, instead of selling life insurance. One thing's
certain; the preaching isn't all in words. Remember how cheap
we felt about Teeta? When Dad pointed out that we were
the dimwits, not she?"

How Beautiful upon the Mountain

"Teeta" had been our family nickname for a parishioner in Worcester who made her living scrubbing other people's floors because she had strong hands but not a very strong mind, but who never missed a prayer meeting. Because she had an impediment in her speech, you had to listen carefully to understand what she said. One night she beamed to the congregation in the vestry, including a bunch of us high-schoolers. "Lookit." She thrust out into the aisle an enormous shiny-new bright-red shoe on her large foot, explaining joyfully, "My head ain't so good, but my feet work hard for me all day, so I give 'em a treat!" When a giggle rippled down our line of young people, Dad threw us a stern glance.

"They're lovely red shoes," Dad beamed back at Teeta whose face was hurt, bewildered. "There's a song about them." He walked down from the platform, seated himself at the vestry piano, ran his fingers lightly over the keys, flung back his bright head and began to sing, " 'How beautiful upon the mountain are the feet of him who bringeth good tidings, who publisheth peace.' "

"Kindness, to Dad, is one of the sacraments," I told Ike. "Kids that age don't mean to be cruel; we were just afraid of being thought different."

"We had to show off," Ike said thoughtfully. "When I was sixteen, I decided to be a Buddhist like Chula."

I laughed. "And Dad asked if you wanted to borrow the prayer wheel the missionary from Korea brought him home."

"Susie, whatever became of Dad's first sermon on prayer?" Ike asked. "The one he gave us to read that Sunday you came home from college and told Dad he was too old to understand our modern point of view?"

"I think I still have his sermon notes here in my desk somewhere." I fumbled through the overcrowded pigeonholes, drew out two yellowed sheets of cheap paper filled with awk-

229

ward typing, where letters, even whole words, had been x-ed out. On one corner was written in Dad's fine hand in ink, "Townsend, May, 1893."

"Before he was even married. Dad was just a boy himself!" I marveled. Together, with me leaning over Ike's shoulder, we read again with new interest now that we ourselves had children of our own, Dad's young thoughts about the meaning of prayer.

PRAYER—WHAT IT IS AND IS NOT

Many people's prayers are very wicked; they use God as a convenience. When the weather is fair, they don't need Him; but when a tornado hits they cry mightily for help. This is the baby-bottle stage of prayer. One evening when I was five, I hurt my knee, went to my mother to be comforted. My father teased, "Aren't you pretty big, Lee, to be sitting in a lady's lap?" I looked at him, snuggling closer. "No," I sobbed. "I'm a man in the morning; I'm a boy in the afternoon; but at night *I want my mother*." When trouble comes in the night, we're all babies, crying out for our Mother-God; but too often panic results, not prayer.

2) Many so-called prayers are merely superstitions. The same people who won't walk on cracks or look at the moon over their left shoulders, try to make a trade with God. "If You'll do this for me, I'll do that for You." This is a purely heathen concept; you might as well whirl the Buddhist prayer wheel I have in my study, let prayer rags blow in the empty wind. Such primitive prayers, based on fear, put God on a level with the fetiches of the witch doctor.

3) Some use prayer to get material advantage, to avoid working for what they want. A pretty girl in our church in Dallas told the Lord in open prayer meeting that she wanted three dozen oranges—and got them because a boy in the congregation wanted to walk home with her in the dark. Such prayers are an insult, not only to God, but to intelligence. Are you any more God's child than the man whose job you covet?

4) Some try to pray without faith. "It's all right to pray for your daily bread," they complain, "But I notice you have to hustle for it." But who gives strength for the hustling? Ask any infantile paralysis victim about the miracle of just walking, breathing.

5) Others try to tell God how to run the universe. (Many preachers are guilty of this; they are not only impious but boring.) If we can't run our own small lives, how can we advise Him about the other fellow? About the Bantus, French, or Japanese? We know so little—not even how to make a butterfly out of a worm or the chemistry to "born" a blade of grass. All these things are negative.

Then
WHAT IS PRAYER?
IT IS COMMUNION WITH GOD. EVERY REAL PRAYER STARTS WITH GOD.

Prayer is when what we want and what God wants are one and the same. Then only do we reach up to touch the hand of God, our Father.

"To touch the Hand of God. . . ." My awed eyes were raised to Ike's who said slowly, "If you don't mind, Susie, I'd like to take this home with me. Some day I may have to answer Perry's questions." As he folded up the yellowed pages and put them carefully into his inner coat pocket I asked Ike, curious, "Do you make Perry go to Sunday school and church the way we had to?"

"He goes to kindergarten. I teach a class of older boys right next door. He seems to like it, so far."

"Jock and I have a sort of—well, not exactly a problem," I confessed to Ike. "Of course, Rick's just a baby yet, but—frankly, Jock misses his own church. Oh, I know, he's been a good Methodist, gone with me for nearly fourteen years; he's taught Sunday school, been on the official board, but now he has a son, it's different. When we pass by the gray-stone Episcopal Church downtown in Englewood with all the ivy and tradition growing over it, Jock looks wistful: but he says, as long as Dad and Mother are alive, he won't hurt their feelings by changing churches."

"Ask Dad frankly how he feels about it," Ike advised.

After he had driven off in his big car, I sat down on our front veranda beside Rick asleep in his carriage, blessedly quiet for once. Being expected to go to every church service as parsonage children hadn't soured Ike and me, merely given us deep roots. In each new place where Jock and I had lived, the church had brought us new friends with similar interests. Our first caller in our walk-up Brooklyn apartment when we married had been the young persuasive church-school superintendent who wouldn't leave until he'd signed me up to teach a class of girls and Jock to play basketball in the parish-house gym; we'd become such close friends he was now young Rick's godfather. When we'd moved to Detroit, Jock and I had run the Junior Methodist Church, with youngsters who had their own chapel service, official board, their own choir with their ridiculously small black robes and piping voices, as young as Ike on his back-stairs pulpit. Wherever we went, the church had been home to us. But should you go to church because you were lonely? Was it habit that had drawn us or a real desire to worship?

Here in Englewood Methodist Church I had a Sunday school class of girls, too. But I wasn't doing too well with them.

"This business of trying to interest thirteen-and fourteen-year-olds in the Old Testament is getting me down," I told Jock irritably when I came home that next Sunday. "They can't even *read* the King James version. It might be Greek they were translating this morning. I suppose I should change to a more modern version but there's such majesty in those old words, a heritage of thunder and glory!"

"Why don't you let the girls make their own translation?" Jock asked quietly.

I shuddered. "The Bible in modern slang? 'O.K., Moses!' Never!"

But the very next Sunday I was driven by despair to trying out Jock's suggestion. The girls giggled, squirmed, and yawned over the drama of Esther who had risked her life for her people. The prettiest girl even openly got out her lipstick from her brown leather vanity case, made up her cherry-red lips carefully in the mirror. Well, if boys were all that interested them. . . .

"Do you realize this is a *love* story?" I demanded. "How would you like to act it out? Translate the story of Esther into your own words? Each of you pick out a character you'd like to be. Then we'll write the play ourselves, find costumes, act it out on the stage up front there."

Great excitement woke up the class. The prettiest girl with the cherry lips was chosen as Esther; King Ahasuerus had to be the tallest; Vashti, the beautiful rebellious queen, was snapped up eagerly, but nobody wanted to be Cousin Mordecai or Haman who got hanged. I explained that the best actors always grabbed for the parts of the hero and the villain, so two more girls agreed to join the cast. Then, without urging, each amateur playwright eagerly grabbed her Bible to find out what had really happened; it was amazing how fast they could read when they got excited.

The first act of *Esther, the Brave Queen,* as written in teenage vernacular, made next Sunday's session vivid, to say the least.

"Vashti, take off that veil!" King Ahasuerus roared while the Queen replied haughtily, "Who says so?" The chorus of Persian husbands huddled together muttering, "Queen's talking back? Pretty soon all our wives'll be doing it, too. Then where will we be?" Not exactly the King James version. But Esther had become a girl who might have gone to Englewood High. The girls dug eagerly into histories and encyclopedias to find out how she dressed, why the Persians and Jews hated each other, what all the fight at court was about anyway. The class was thrilled when the superintendent asked them to give their final performance of their homemade drama in costume, before the whole church school and the invited parents.

The dress rehearsal was a riot of laughter, tears, and bruised feelings. King Ahasuerus, resplendent in bloomers down around her ankles and a long silk jacket loaned by a pregnant relative, assured Queen Esther, "Just say what you want, girl. Up to the half of my kingdom. But what does that Jew, Mordecai, want hanging around my gates?"

At this, Mordecai, who was wearing a long white nightgown with a red portiere thrown over one shoulder, burst into tears. "I don't want to be Mordecai!" she wailed. "I don't want to be a Jew!"

"But," I began, startled, "What about Esther? She was. . . ." But King Ahasuerus, bursting in, finished for me.

"Why, you dumb bunny," the furious King sputtered, "*Jesus was a Jew, too.* You ought to be proud!"

How Beautiful upon the Mountain

Esther, the Brave Queen was a great success if it did run for only one Sunday morning. But the performance started the girls wondering—what was a modern Jew like? Next week the whole class attended worship at a nearby synagogue in Manhattan where they were thrilled by the cantor's singing and were startled to hear the same benediction the superintendent used to dismiss their own Sunday school; "The Lord bless thee and keep thee; the Lord make his face to shine upon thee and give thee peace. . . ." As we all went back down the synagogue steps, Mordecai put her discovery into words:

"Why," she said proudly, "we Methodists are part Jewish, too!"

Still the problem of which creed Rick was to be brought up in, Jock's or mine, remained unsolved. As I fed Rick prune juice, ran peas through a sieve into a green mess over which he smacked his lips, then smeared it into his hair as fair as Dad's, I wondered. Would Dad really mind if Rick did not go to the Methodist church? The next time Dad came to visit us, I'd ask him tactfully; no, I couldn't wait that long; I'd write to Townsend.

> My dear child (Dad wrote back)
>
> Why should I mind when my own mother was born a Roman Catholic, my father a Lutheran, then both became Methodists?
>
> Each church fulfills its special function and this changes with the years. John Wesley never really broke away from the established church; he merely brought it a new spirit. Tell Jock he has my blessing.

But I didn't show Jock Dad's letter yet; I merely suggested that next Sunday we play hookey from our classes, go to eleven o'clock service at the gray-stone ivied Episcopalian Church.

When Jock's face lighted up, I knew I had been right. But it would be alien country for me who'd never owned a prayer book. I knelt beside Jock as we went in, tried to pretend I wasn't shuffling the pages awkwardly. The young servers at the altar, the minister and surpliced choir sang incomprehensible chants but the words of the communion hymn, though the organ music was strange to my Methodist ears, was the old familiar cry of the lonely heart for sanctuary:

> Let thy Blood in mercy poured,
> Let thy gracious Body broken,
> Be to me, O gracious Lord,
> Of thy boundless love the token.
> Thou didst give thyself for me,
> Now I give myself to thee.

How was this different from the childhood hymn that had held me safe all my life? Except that it was, perhaps, more graciously phrased, a kind of King James version of "God will take care of you"? Beside me, Jock was kneeling, getting up, kneeling again, showing me eagerly the place in the little red prayer book. "Lord have mercy upon us," the minister intoned and the congregation answered, "Christ have mercy upon us."

"Once a Methodist, always a Methodist," Brother Wentworth used to insist passionately in prayer meeting. Could I really learn at this late date to pray printed prayers, to cry at the appointed time for mercy? *And mean it?*

The minister turned from the altar to face the kneeling congregation his voice rich, urgent as he invited:

"You who do truly and earnestly repent you of your sins and are in love and charity with your neighbors. . . ."

But I knew those words! They were exactly the same as my own communion service. *"and intend to lead a new life, following the commandments of God. . . ."*

How Beautiful upon the Mountain

I covered my face with my blind hands and seemed to kneel at another communion railing, to see walking back and forth again my Dad's worn black shoes he'd bought in the bargain basement so I could stay in college. I was back in prayer meeting with Teeta's red shoes stuck proudly into the aisle, and a dear familiar tenor voice was singing. How humble the shoe was didn't matter, Dad's, Teeta's or the Anglican minister's. "How beautiful upon the mountain are the feet of him who bringeth good tidings. . . ."

"What's wrong?" Jock whispered anxiously. "Do you want to go home?"

"No." I reached for the little red prayer book, held it tightly between us as I smiled up at him. *"Draw near by faith."* I whispered back, "I am at home."

Chapter Fifteen

THE DOOR OF THE TRUMPETS

I was ill in the hospital that next fall when Dad went, as he'd promised, "to stand up beside the Creator and fling out a few stars!" But I flew on from New Jersey to Boston to be with Mother and Ike.

As he had hoped, Dad's and Mother's last honeymoon had been in the little parish at Townsend where they had "retired" among the blue-hazed hills, but his "coronation service" was held in the big Tremont Street Church in Boston so that the hundreds who loved him could find seats. This was rather like Dad's friendly "Warm-Up-the-Heart" Sunday evenings, I whispered to Ike sitting there beside me in the front pew, with Mother on his other arm—all these parishioners from all over the state—Dad seemed actually closer than when I'd been in New Jersey and he in Townsend.

I had come straight from a hospital bed and would go back to one when this service was over, so when the church organ shouted the first triumphant notes of the "Hallelujah Chorus" and the great congregation of Dad's friends surged to their feet, I was so dizzy with fever I heard Dad's golden tenor, soaring above the rest. "Hallelujah! For the Lord God Omnipotent reigneth. . . ."

As I got up with the others, hung onto the pew in front of me, I closed my dizzy eyes, was back again on the Newagen veranda, staring up at the cloud that was filled with the glory of God. "Darling," I told Dad, "you know all the answers now!" But no word came back to me. Had Dad recognized Bildad, his son grown to a man in heaven? I wondered feverishly. Was Dad actually tall among the stars? "In this body" had he seen his Lord while the silver trumpets sounded?

"Hallelujah, Amen!"

As the organ shouted into silence I saw to my horror that the big platform, banked with flowers and black with church dignitaries, had begun to go round and round in dizzy pinwheels, while I still held onto the pew in front of me with desperate fingers.

"The car's here, dear, to drive you back to the Deaconess Hospital," Ike murmured, taking my elbow urgently. "Come along. You look exhausted. I still have to go with Mother out to Mt. Auburn; she wants me to say the committal service myself, as if it were family prayers. Then I'll take her back to Cleveland with me. Lillian and I will take care of her till you feel better."

I was glad, glad to climb back into the cool welcoming sheets of the bed at the hospital on whose board of managers Dad had been for so many years. As the nurse pulled down the shades, went quietly from the room, drums were thudding in my tired ears. No, it was the whirr of many wings Dad used to tell about. . . . Often when we children were small the parsonage telephone would ring at two in the morning, those hours when life is at its lowest ebb, calling Dad away into the chill darkness. At daybreak he'd come rattling back into the yard, bang old Jehu's door shut. As the front door opened, Mother, heavy-eyed with sleep, would come to the top of the stairs.

"You all right, dear?" she'd call. "What was the matter?"

My father's face, pale and drawn but filled with exaltation, would come up over the landing. "Old Mrs. Crane has been released at last. It was a glorious passing. You could almost hear the beat of wings about her head!"

Dear Dad, brushed by the wings of heaven as you kept last vigil with your people, the hem of your shining garment of belief had touched our childish minds with wonder. Heaven and hell, life and death, had marched in a grand pageant before our awe-filled eyes. "Faith is a lot like being in love," Dad used to chuckle. "When you're in love you don't need to be told about it, but when you're not, no words can tell you what it's like." I buried my face in the friendly hospital pillow and wept, not for Dad but for the dear lost childhood days when I'd prayed for an A in arithmetic, for the Lord to do a Lazarus miracle on poor Amelia's cracked doll head.

Mother, stunned with grief and loneliness, wandered like a pilgrim ghost for months between Ike's home and mine, after I recovered. When we had a decision to make, she always said firmly, "Your father thinks. . . . Your father says. . . ." refusing to admit even to herself that Dad was finally gone; he had just "gone apart for a little while." When she realized that she had to go back to the Townsend parsonage to pack up her things, I told Jock I couldn't let her go alone. Of course, I'd have to take Rick too, now a wild Indian three-year-old, never still an instant, to help Mother dig up her painful roots.

"Of course," Jock agreed. His job in New York would keep him busy daytimes though the house in New Jersey would be empty nights; but he knew what it would mean to Mother to go back to the place where she'd lived two honeymoons with Dad, without him there. Jock added, wistfully, "Wish it wasn't four hundred miles round trip. I'd drive up every weekend."

The new minister for the Townsend Church lived on a farm of his own nearby, so he let Mother and me use the empty parsonage for as long as we liked. It had a bathroom down-

The Door of the Trumpets

stairs but no furnace, so we were kept busy lugging fuel, fat chunks of wood for the iron stove in the front parlor (where Mother had her lonely bed set up so she could watch the busy street), heavy oil tanks for the dining room and kitchen heaters; but the upstairs on these chilly fall days was cold as yesterday's haddock.

Small Rick, however, was completely happy because here in the country he had acquired what city living would not permit—a pup of his own. Ha'penny (so-called because his mother's name had been Penny) was a brown fluffy ball, "Heinz pooch—57 varieties," I grumbled, but seldom had a dog been more a member of the family.

Rick was three, Mother nearing seventy, and Hape a roly-poly two months, but the three were inseparable cronies. Every sunny day they went for a walk together, usually in the nearby cemetery, parklike with its bright geraniums and clipped grass, Mother slow and sedate, Rick stopping to throw a stone at an impudent gray squirrel, and Hape barking happily, running ten cemetery blocks to their one.

"Stop barking, Hape!" Rick would order, "You'll wake up the sleepy people!"

For him death had no terror; he knew his Grandpa-up-in-heaven intimately because his Grammy talked about him all the time as if he were still pastor of the little Townsend church high upon its pine-clad hill. When Rick balked at being the littlest angel in the Sunday school pageant because the elastic on his cardboard halo hurt his forehead, Grammy said sternly, "But you're Grandpa-down-here! You have to go on with his job. Come here, young man, we'll learn the marching words together. 'Onward Christian soldiers. . . .' "

Mother couldn't seem to finish her packing. Everything she picked up was too precious to discard, though the attic was jammed with stuff—trunks, broken furniture Dad had planned to mend, twenty bags of old dyed rags and silk stockings Mother had hoped to hook into rugs. Certainly we couldn't afford to pay storage on all this junk—things, I amended quickly, seeing the horror on Mother's face. She said, "Why, your father and I picked up that old chest away up in the hills. The farmer let us have it for ten dollars because the top marble was cracked, but one of these days. . . ." If she let herself believe Dad wouldn't be back any day now to fix that crack, everything would be finished. Her eyes filled with tears. What could I do but kiss her, tell her we'd find a place for the old chest somewhere in our house in Jersey? Perhaps Ike could use some of the stuff too. But we couldn't possibly cram in a whole attic-full of past-parsonage mementos.

But old furniture was not the only heritage Dad had left for her children. One morning the phone rang and my world crashed down about my frightened ears. "There's been an accident. On Route Five," a strange voice said. "Your husband is here in the hospital in Hartford. Can you come at once?"

"Is he badly hurt?" I shivered. "What. . . ."

"It's his head, concussion."

I don't remember what Mother said. I didn't even answer young Rick yelling at me to take him and Ha'penny to ride, too. Frantic, hatless, I rushed out to my car in the back yard, jammed my foot onto the accelerator, roared out onto the state highway with a hundred-odd miles to go. When the state policeman's siren sounded behind me I was too upset to know it was I he was signaling until his dark-blue car forced me over to the side of the road. I had to get to the hospital now at once. My husband might be dying! I explained. The shock on my face, in my voice, must have convinced him.

"Follow me, lady," the state cop ordered.

With his siren blaring we rushed through red lights, traffic parting in frightened waves before us. When we came to the

The Door of the Trumpets

state line, a Connecticut police car was waiting and we roared on to the hospital, where I left my car door swinging heedlessly, to rush inside—to meet the bitterest moment of my life.

As I came into the hospital room, Jock's face, usually so loving, now dulled by pain and shock, stared at me with distrust. He looked at me with eyes of an utter stranger. "Go away!" he said. And turned his face to the wall.

But this was my darling! He must be out of his mind. Didn't he know me? After I'd rushed to him a hundred miles . . . it couldn't be true that my own husband didn't want me! But when I touched his hand, he drew it away. Stunned, bewildered, I tiptoed out into the hall where the doctor explained, "It isn't you he's rejecting; subconsciously, it's the pain and the fear."

Consciously, subconsciously—what did it matter? For the first time in the fifteen years we'd been married Jock didn't want me. I was falling down a deep well of loneliness, frightened as I had never been before. I asked the doctor, moistening my dry lips, "Is he going to die?"

"I don't know," the doctor said honestly. "We don't even know yet exactly what is wrong but we're making tests. Since he feels this way, I suggest that you go home, come back tomorrow."

Leave him when maybe I'd never see Jock alive again? Oh no! But already my husband was a thousand light miles away from me. Those hostile stranger's eyes. What could have happened to my love? The hospital walls swung around me dizzily as the nurse said, "Your mother phoned from Townsend to be sure you got here all right. She seemed upset about the little boy."

Rick? He and Mother needed me, anyway; I'd better do what the doctor advised. With the elaborate carefulness of one who is intoxicated with fear, I drove slowly out of the hospital yard, through the city, back onto the state highway. I could no longer see the road for my tears, so I braked by the roadside, leaned my hot forehead against the cool windshield. Great racking sobs shook my whole body and I knew then what it meant. *All thy waves and thy billows have gone over me.* For the significance of what the doctor had said had just come through to me. Now that Jock was too sick to cover up his naked subconscious thoughts, was I really learning the truth? *Had he stopped loving me a long time ago but been afraid to say so? Not wanting to hurt me?*

There is a bitter hill of sorrow which each man and woman must sometime climb alone. As I sat there in my car by the side of the road, too numb to drive on, a yellow leaf fell from a tree overhead onto the black hood of my car. The leaf grew larger and larger till it was the yellowed page of Dad's first sermon on "What Is Prayer?" But what could I pray when I didn't even know what was wrong with Jock? With us? I stared dully at the clock in the car dashboard. Two o'clock; I should go on; Mother would worry; Rick would need his supper. Should I pray for Jock's body to get well? Even if his mind were gone? Suddenly as if they had been printed on the car hood the vivid words came back to me:

Prayer is when what we want and what God wants are one and the same thing. Then only can we reach up. . . .

"O God! O God!" I didn't even bow my head or close my eyes but whispered deep down in my heart, "I don't know what to ask for. Thy will be done."

I came alive. The blood flowed back into my shocked body, and I could drive, dry-eyed, on toward home. I drove slowly, carefully, but I got back in time to give Rick his supper, tuck him into bed with Ha'penny on the rag rug in the corner, ready to scramble up onto the bed the moment I shut the door.

The Door of the Trumpets

Then I gathered together the tatters of my courage to call the hospital again to ask how Jock was.

"He's better, much better. About two this afternoon he rallied," the doctor told me, relieved but puzzled. "He asked for you. We told him you'd been here but had gone back to the little boy, that you'd see him tomorrow. He said that was fine; he guessed he'd go to sleep. His pulse has steadied and his fever is down. I think he'll make it now." "Thank you, doctor," I managed.

About two this afternoon, he rallied—he asked for you. The receiver dropped from my awed hand. *The exact time by the clock on the dashboard when I'd prayed.* It might never happen again, but for once in my life I had proved what my Dad had promised. I had reached up and touched the Hand of God.

It would be long months before Jock could safely go back to work, the doctor warned, so through the kindness of our minister friend we all stayed on at the Townsend parsonage. Rick and Mother grew closer together every day; she taught him the hymns she and Dad, Ike and I used to sing together, her soprano cracking at the high notes but still clear, with Rick's small-boy pipe shrill but true. I wondered sometimes uneasily if her calling him "Grandpa-down-here," identifying him with Dad, was good for young Rick. He might be a PK once removed living in a parsonage that housed no minister, but he mustn't be forced into copying even Dad.

The hurricane which couldn't happen to New England struck while Mother and Rick were alone in the Townsend parsonage. Jock and I had gone down to Newton to visit friends where we watched unbelieving while the lake in front of the house flung itself in a solid sheet of water against our friend's front door, while trees toppled, and the skylight blew off the roof. What could the storm be like in Townsend with all those tall elms shading the white parsonage? I worried. With only those two to cope, the old child and the young? With telephone and electric wires all down, it was impossible to find out.

Next morning, against all advice of police and friends, I started for Townsend in the car whose tank was fortunately full of gas, for none could be pumped electrically at the stations. The roads were such a tangle of fallen trees, fences, roofs, and wires that once I had to drive up over someone's concrete veranda, but I got by; in Groton I waited impatiently for several men to saw through the three-foot trunk of an ancient elm before I could inch through. But when I arrived at dusk at the Townsend Common where the great trees lay, bowled-over tenpins, I was scared to drive on into the parsonage yard. What would I find?

No one was in sight, but the house was still intact. Feeble candlelight shone from the kitchen and gay singing and pounding came out through the open cellar windows as I braked the car.

"Onward, Christian soldiers!" Mother's voice caroled. Bang, bang! "Now, Richard!"

"Marching as to war," his small voice piped obediently.

Bang, bang! "You still there? 'With the cross of Jesus. . . .'"

"Going on before!" came the shrill answer. Then as I walked into the kitchen, small Rick and his brown shadow, Hape, flung themselves into my arms. "Mommy, Mommy! The wind blowed. I knew you'd come!"

"Get *down*, Hape! What on earth were you doing, singing down cellar?" I gasped as Mother's curly gray head came up from down below.

"Oh, hello. Opening up the cellar windows so it'll dry out." Mother said calmly, brushing a cobweb out of her hair. She

The Door of the Trumpets

laid the hammer on the kitchen table. "I nailed them down when the wind was so bad last night. I was afraid the house would blow right off the foundation, like a Texas twister. Or the Wizard of Oz. I didn't want Rick to set the house afire with those candles so I kept him singing with me, so I'd be sure where he was." I stared at the two of them, April and December. If they could sing their way together through a hurricane unafraid, they couldn't do each other much psychological harm. Mother was merely passing on to young Rick his parsonage ticket; he would travel by his own route but he knew his destination.

Eventually Jock took a job in Boston; we moved to Sudbury where Rick went to Mary Lamb School at the Wayside Inn while Ike and his family were still rooted in Cleveland, Ohio. The years sliding by had separated Ike and me not only from the parsonage, shabby but burnished bright with love, where we had grown up, but from each other. His family and mine met infrequently summers but not too briefly to find out that more than eight hundred miles lay between us; different things interested us now. Ike had sold a fortune in life insurance; we barely squeaked by at the end of each month. He was an official of the huge Cleveland Methodist Church; we read from the Episcopal prayer book at St. Elizabeth's small neighborhood chapel built by Ralph Adams Cram from stones in his own back yard. Rick was now a server, his hair fair as his grandfather's shining gold above his red robe at the altar. Two world wars had numbed our generation into an uneasy tolerance far from the Puritan creed, prickly with inhibitions, of Ike's and my parsonage childhood. Underneath the successful businessman, the professional storyteller, were there buried still the Susie and Ike to whom heaven was as real a place as Boston or Chicago? I simply did not know.

I probably never would have written the book about Dad

if Ike hadn't convinced me that writing it was a debt I owed, rather like my testifying at prayer meeting, scared to death but not wanting to fail my Dad. When Ike flew on from Cleveland on urgent business, he came out to Sudbury to see me, to ask unexpectedly, "Susie, why don't you write about the 'patchwork quilt' the preacher and his family helped mend? About Dad and his red-hot rivet faith?"

"I tried to write a book once, not a formal biography, just Dad going on talking," I confessed. "But somehow—I don't know—it didn't jell. But I did jot down some of the stories he told me on the Snuggery veranda that summer before Rick was born. I may try again sometime."

"Why wait?" Ike said. When he ran his hands up over his thin face I noticed how deep the lines were around his mouth; very soon now, I realized, shocked, Ike and I would *be* "the older generation." "Dad was surprisingly modern," Ike went on. "He used to experiment with faith and prayer as a scientist does with his test tubes. Remember how he taught me to skate on our homemade ice rink out in the back yard in Dorchester? I was just pint-sized. Dad let me hang onto his coattails till I had the courage to let go. When I had faith, I could skate."

"All right, I'll get out my notes from Newagen sometime," I agreed. "They're down cellar somewhere."

"Not sometime. Now!" Ike urged as he left for Cleveland. Was he already sensing that there was not much time? And yet—how could Ike know? Perhaps some day we'll tune in on our subconscious as easily as we snap a button on the TV. Strangely, the following day when I was cleaning out an old trunk to send to the Goodwill Industries I found the letter Dad had written me some years ago, about the first draft of my parsonage notes which I had sent to him in Townsend for criticism. The envelope was tucked down inside the torn lin-

ing of the old trunk almost as if Dad had sent me the letter,
special delivery from heaven, when I needed it most:

> I'm ashamed to have waited so long to send back your
> notes, but I've had several weddings, a funeral, and I've
> been refereeing for the Epworth League Ball Games, be-
> sides preaching, making calls, and teaching a Sunday
> School Class. [This was what it meant to "retire" at sixty
> five in a country church! The only thing "retired" was his
> salary.] Some chapters of this are better than others, I
> think. The Briar Bush story about the blind woman's
> niece and her illegitimate baby whom the whole town
> adopted, is a gem. It has in it the whole anguish of human
> suffering, the triumph of an exalted faith. Make the other
> chapters like this and they will help people . . . which is
> success. . . .

But how was I to find the winged words to write down what
Dad knew? I, the housewife in my cellar cleaning out a trunk
and he up flinging out stars? But maybe he wasn't so far away,
after all. "He shall give his angels charge over thee, to keep
thee in all thy ways. . . ." What if my angel should be my own
Dad?

The weeks and months of writing fairly flew by. Dad's book
all but wrote itself, for after the strangeness of Jock's hospital
experience, I knew what Dad had meant, "You could almost
hear the beat of wings about her head!" I sent the manuscript
off to New York. Whether it would sell or not I did not greatly
care: I had done what I had to; I had paid my debt. I was
outside weeding my vegetable garden when one morning a
long-distance call came from New York to my white New England cottage, and the strange editor's voice said incredibly,
"I'm so enthusiastic about this book, I couldn't wait to write
you a letter!" I put down the receiver, chuckling to Dad,
"Well, you have a new parish! I must tell Ike."

I reached for the receiver again, then drew back my hand. Ike's birthday, the thirteenth of March, was next week. Why not wait to give him the good news as a birthday present? I must remember to wire flowers, too.

But time had already run out. Two days before his birthday Ike called me himself, long distance. We knew each other's voices too intimately to tell less than the whole truth. "I have cancer," Ike said, flatly, calmly. "The doctor just told me and I'm going to the hospital on my birthday for observation and tests. When they operate, they'll know if I have years to live or months, or—or what. I'm not worried, but I thought you ought to know."

Cancer. The dreaded word roared in my ears. *But he wasn't worried. Don't fuss, he means.* I couldn't speak. I could hear the miles of wire between us humming with disaster but all I could do was to stand there, the silent tears rolling salt onto my lips. "Ike!" I managed finally, "Oh, Ike!"

"I know," he said cheerfully. "If it isn't practicable to re-move—everything, I'm to have some radium pellets put in, instead. I told Lillian I'd get her a Geiger counter so she'd always know where I was!"

Ike could joke even now. Oh, my dear. Aloud I said, steadying my own voice, "Have Lillian let me know how things turn out. By the way, I wired you some flowers—Happy Birthday!" *Happy Birthday. Dear God. And yet what else could I say? If Ike and Lillian could take this standing up, surely I could.* "Good-by, Ike. Good luck, dear."

Foolish, stupid words. What did luck have to do with it? Whatever was already was settled. "Birth is the first door," Dad's voice said in my numbed mind. But this would be the twin door with the silver trumpets shouting, the door of. . . . No, no, I wouldn't even *think* the word; not yet. They could cure cancer these days, couldn't they? Some kinds, if they got

The Door of the Trumpets

it early enough. The doctor *had* to help Ike; he had to. *Dear Lord, please help this to be the kind of cancer they can cure.*

Ike's cheerful letter from the hospital thanked me for his birthday flowers, red gladiolas and white carnations; he'd worn a carnation in his buttonhole to the hospital, he reported. They were keeping him there nights only, for observation, but letting him go days to look after his affairs before they operated. He wanted to wind things up at his insurance office, to get everything in Lillian's name. Maybe they'd sell the big house they'd just bought; if there was enough left over from the mortgage, they could buy a small cottage outright; Lillian would have to pay only taxes.

So Ike knew. The letter dropped from my cold fingers into my lap. No matter what the doctor had said, Ike knew that for him the door was already opening on its hinges, the great door that swung only one way. Yet he wrote as matter-of-factly as when he'd announced that summer that all four of them were driving together up to Banff to see beautiful blue Lake Louise. Only, this trip Ike would have to make alone. Why couldn't whole families go together? It would save so much heartache. But the children had not yet really lived, Perry and Sue who were now Ike's immortality, the earth-born part, the part you could see, were sure of.

Ike's letter ended: "Don't worry, Susie. My job is to get this operation over, yours is to get the proof out on Dad's book. I want to read it. It may be some time before I know the score. Don't fuss, dear. Don't rush here till I need you. I'll let you know."

So I went on with my job of reading proof, and Ike with his of learning to face whatever he must. Dad's book would be on the news stands in May, but in a panic lest that be too late, I asked the editor to send page proofs, airmail, to Ike in the hospital. Ike was too weak from his second operation to hold a pen but Lillian wrote that reading all about us kids and Dad and Mother had done him as much good as medicine. Her letters were magnificent, never despairing, never giving Ike up, cherishing each new precious day they could be together. It is at once the tragedy and triumph of a long happy marriage that what happens to one happens to the other also; both live and die a little in each other. Mother and Dad had set the pattern; Ike and Lillian were following. For the first time I did not condone but I understood "suttee," the death within death the wives of ancient India had chosen. Could leaping onto a funeral pyre in Agra be any less agonizing than these long flaming weeks of shared pain in Cleveland? Ike's and Lillian's was indeed a blaze of courage.

Ike was still able to read when Dad's book finally was laid in his hands, but they were too weak to hold it. I wished he could read, too, the hundreds of letters filled with the old familiar parsonage shared laughter and bitter tears, that were pouring over my desk from Dad's new bigger parish. "My husband was a minister, too, only forty when he died a few weeks ago," one preacher's wife wrote me. "I couldn't accept it. How could he go so young, with so much of the Lord's work still to do? I couldn't even cry; my pent-up resentment made me sick. I was in the hospital when someone gave me your book about your dad's triumphant passing. As I read, the tight band of shock loosened and the healing tears came. And I was alive again." Perhaps I'd better read my own book, I advised myself ruefully. Maybe then I wouldn't wake up at night, sweating, listening for the telephone to ring from Cleveland. I mustn't go cold with panic whenever I thought of Ike; I must just wait till he needed me; and then I would go.

The call from Perry came a few weeks later. Ike wanted to talk to me while he still could; the doctor said it wouldn't be

The Door of the Trumpets

long now. I took the next plane but I saw nothing out the high windows, heard only dimly the roar of the engines, a baby crying across the aisle. My heart was thumping over and over, "Oh, Ike, how can I say, 'good-by'?" Once when we were both small, I'd been sent to bed supperless for being naughty. As evening fell, I was hungry, but even worse, I was scared to be alone in the dark room. Suddenly the door was pushed open to a bright crack of light, and Ike's hand slid through, full of squashed cake. "Eat it!" he whispered. "It's choc'lit!" Chocolate was his favorite but he'd saved it for me. And later he'd tried so hard to share with me his gaiety at Wilbraham, in college. If only I could have caught his lightness of heart, we might have stayed closer all these years. *Oh, my dear, it's growing dark in your room now, and what crack of light have I to give you?*

The house in Cleveland was bright with sun, flowers, and the tender love of his family but—how had I known?—Ike's bedroom alone was dark with the shades drawn because his eyes could no longer bear the bright sword of daylight. Could this really be my tall brother lying there, a dim, swollen mound of bedclothes? What had happened to his slender body which had danced so blithely with me and Chula? As I stood there, appalled that nature could be so cruel, Ike's hot hand crept across the bed to my icy one, drew me down to a chair by his bed with an effort that clearly cost him dear.

"If you hadn't made it, Susie, I'd have haunted you!" He gave the ghost of a chuckle. "Sit closer, dear, where I can see you."

Ike needed no crack of light from me, for he still carried his lantern of laughter toward the ultimate dark. In the warmth of his nearness, the misty years between us melted away; we were two preacher's kids again sitting there hand

253

in hand, seeing the pink-ruffled basinette our mother had sewed, singing, for little lost Bildad who lay there too still, but not frightening, just a baby asleep. We were back in the parsonage kitchen devouring "the last lick" of strawberry ice cream at midnight because Dad and Mother couldn't enjoy a treat without us kids. We were out skating that winter in our back yard, sharing my "single-runners" because we couldn't afford two pairs and not sorry for ourselves at all. Suddenly I couldn't bear to remember Ike any other way than with his round face red with winter wind, laughing. I hesitated. Would he understand?

"Ike?" I held his hand the more tightly. "I don't think I'll come back to Cleveland—later on."

"I've always hated funerals, too," he said calmly. "Don't come, Susie. I won't be here, either!"

The old boyish mischief twinkled in his heavy eyes. I wanted desperately to smile back at him but the best I could manage was to fight back my tears, for the beat of wings was louder now about my ears. When would I hear Ike's voice again except when young Rick spoke so like him from the next room? I heard no trumpets, only the sound of Ike's heavy breathing. How could I leave him lying there, swollen, helpless, whistling however bravely against the encroaching dark? My little brother whose name was laughter, flesh of my proud flesh.

Ike said quietly, his voice a mere thread of sound, "Why do you worry, Susie? I'll be all right. I'm not afraid. I'm still hanging onto my Dad's coattails!"

He was planning to skate into heaven on his single-runners! Of all Dad's myriad sons and daughters, Ike was the son most truly his, for his faith had already made him whole, here and now. And then at last I saw it—the bright crack in the dark door of death shining in Ike's steady eyes. *Who*

The Door of the Trumpets

knew there was nothing to be afraid of in this world or the next was already immortal, incorruptible.

I couldn't trust myself to speak but we smiled at each other with understanding as I kissed Ike and left him. And I didn't go back. Thus, I hold him, forever young, in my heart, this dear Isaac. Whenever I think of him, the trumpets sound, high and clear and silver, but underneath comes the tinkle and boom of our old upright piano, and my Dad's gay tenor. "The Lord is the strength of my life . . . Whom then shall I fear?" And, on my knees, I dare to claim my great heritage of the Kingdom, and the Power, and the Glory.